AWS Automation Cookbook

Continuous Integration and Continuous Deployment using
AWS services

Nikit Swaraj

BIRMINGHAM - MUMBAI

AWS Automation Cookbook

Copyright © 2017 Packt Publishing

First published: November 2017

Production reference: 1221117

Published by Packt Publishing Ltd.
Livery Place
35 Livery Street
Birmingham
B3 2PB, UK.
ISBN 978-1-78839-492-5

www.packtpub.com

Credits

Author
Nikit Swaraj

Reviewer
Gajanan Chandgadkar

Commissioning Editor
Vijin Boricha

Acquisition Editor
Meeta Rajani

Content Development Editor
Sharon Raj

Technical Editor
Mohit Hassija

Copy Editor
Charlotte Carneiro

Project Coordinator
Virginia Dias

Proofreader
Safis Editing

Indexer
Aishwarya Gangawane

Graphics
Kirk D'Penha

Production Coordinator
Shantanu Zagade

About the Author

Nikit Swaraj is an experienced professional DevOps/Solutions Architect. He understands the melding of development and operations to deliver efficient code. He has expertise in designing, developing, and delivering enterprise-wide solutions that meet business requirements and enhance operational efficiency. As an AWS solutions architect, he has vast experience in designing end-to-end IT solutions and leading and managing complete life cycle projects within optimal time and budget. He also contributes to Kubernetes (open source).

He has been associated with enterprises such as Red Hat and APNs (AWS Partner Network). He is a certified Red Hat/OpenStack architect, as well as being an AWS solutions architect. He also writes blogs on CI/CD with AWS Developer Tools, Docker, Kubernetes, Serverless, and much more.

Acknowledgments

I would like to express my gratitude to Packt Publishing who have given me the tremendous opportunity to write this book. I would like to thank Meeta Rajani (senior acquisition editor, *Packt*), who encouraged and enabled me to write this book.

I would like to show my appreciation and thanks to Sharon Raj, Mohit Hassija, and the team at Packt, who saw me through this book, provided support, talked things over, read, offered comments, reviewed, allowed me to quote their remarks, and assisted in the editing, proofreading, and design. This book would not have been completed without your help.

I would also like to thank some of my mentors, with whom I learned and implemented about AWS and DevOps, among which the first name is Tarun Prakash (senior DevOps engineer, MediaIQ Digital) who helped and guided me when I entered the world of DevOps and AWS. I would like to thank Rahul Natarajan (lead cloud architect and consultant, Accenture) who has given me guidance and enabled me to use Developer Tools and related services of AWS and DevOps tools and technologies. I would also like to thank Santosh Panicker (senior technical account manager, Amazon Web Services), under whom I have worked and learned a lot about infrastructure and client requirements. He made me understand which services can be used in the best way. My certifications are a different scenario, but this person had molded me into an actual solutions architect.

I would also like to thank my family and best friends Vijeta and Tanushree for encouraging me and providing me with the emotional support to complete this book.

About the Reviewer

Gajanan Chandgadkar has more than 12 years of IT experience. He has spent more than 6 years in the USA helping large enterprises in architecting, migrating, and deploying applications in AWS. He's been running production workloads on AWS for over 6 years. He is an AWS certified solutions architect professional and a certified DevOps professional with more than 7 certifications in trending technologies. Gajanan is also a technology enthusiast who has extended interest and experiences in different topics such as application development, container technology, and Continuous Delivery.

Currently, he is working with Happiest Minds Technologies as Associate DevOps Architect and has worked with Wipro Technologies Corporation in the past.

www.PacktPub.com

For support files and downloads related to your book, please visit www.PacktPub.com. Did you know that Packt offers eBook versions of every book published, with PDF and ePub files available? You can upgrade to the eBook version at www.PacktPub.com and as a print book customer, you are entitled to a discount on the eBook copy. Get in touch with us at service@packtpub.com for more details.

At www.PacktPub.com, you can also read a collection of free technical articles, sign up for a range of free newsletters and receive exclusive discounts and offers on Packt books and eBooks.

https://www.packtpub.com/mapt

Get the most in-demand software skills with Mapt. Mapt gives you full access to all Packt books and video courses, as well as industry-leading tools to help you plan your personal development and advance your career.

Why subscribe?

- Fully searchable across every book published by Packt
- Copy and paste, print, and bookmark content
- On demand and accessible via a web browser

Customer Feedback

Thanks for purchasing this Packt book. At Packt, quality is at the heart of our editorial process. To help us improve, please leave us an honest review on this book's Amazon page at `https://www.amazon.com/dp/1788394925`.

If you'd like to join our team of regular reviewers, you can email us at `customerreviews@packtpub.com`. We award our regular reviewers with free eBooks and videos in exchange for their valuable feedback. Help us be relentless in improving our products!

Table of Contents

Preface   1

Chapter 1: Using AWS CodeCommit   7

  Introduction   7
  Introducing VCS and Git   7
    What is VCS?   8
      Why VCS ?   8
      Types of VCS   8
    What is Git?   9
      Why Git over other VCSs?   9
      Features of Git   11
    How to do it...   12
      Installation of Git and its implementation using GitHub   12
  Introducing AWS CodeCommit - Amazon managed SaaS Git   16
    How to do it...   18
  Getting started with CodeCommit for HTTP users   19
    How to do it...   19
  Setting up CodeCommit for SSH users using AWS CLI   27
    Getting ready   27
    How to do it...   28
  Applying security and restrictions   31
    Getting ready   32
    How to do it...   32
  Migrating a Git repository to AWS CodeCommit   36
    How to do it...   36

Chapter 2: Building an Application using CodeBuild   41

  Introduction   41
  Introducing AWS CodeBuild   43
    How to do it...   44
    How it works...   44
      Pricing   45
  Building a Java application using Maven   46
    Getting ready   46
      Install Java and verify   46
      Install Apache Maven and verify   46
    How to do it...   47

Building a NodeJS application using yarn   51
  Getting ready   52
    Install NodeJS and verify   52
    Install Yarn and verify   52
  How to do it...   52
    Installing dependencies   54
  How it works...   56
Building a Maven application using AWS CodeBuild console   56
  Getting ready   56
  How it works...   57
Building a sample NodeJS application using AWS CodeBuild via Buildspec.yml   66
  Buildspec.yml   67
    Syntax   67
  Getting ready   69
  How to do it...   70

Chapter 3: Deploying Application using CodeDeploy & CodePipeline   79
  Introduction   79
  The Deployment strategy in AWS CodeDeploy   83
    In-place deployment   83
    Blue-green deployment   84
    How to do it...   84
  Writing an application-specific file   86
    How to do it...   86
  Deploying a static application in an EC2 instance from the S3 Bucket using AWS CodeDeploy   89
    Getting ready   89
    How to do it...   90
    How it works...   105
  Introducing AWS CodePipeline and its working   105
    How to do it...   105
    How it works...   107
  Continuous Deployment of static application to AWS S3 using AWS CodePipeline   107
    How to do it...   108

Chapter 4: Building Scalable and Fault-Tolerant CI/CD Pipeline   121
  Introduction   121
    Benefits of using the CI/CD pipeline   122
    How to achieve the benefits?   122

The scenario   122
The challenges   123
CI/CD pipeline workflow   123
Getting ready   124
How to do it...   124
Setting up AWS CodeCommit   127
Getting ready   128
How to do it...   128
Creating the S3 bucket and enabling versioning   131
Getting ready   131
How to do it...   131
Creating the launch configuration and Auto Scaling group   133
Getting ready   133
How to do it...   133
Creating AWS CodeDeploy application using the Auto Scaling group   140
Getting ready   141
How to do it...   141
Setting up the Jenkins Server and installing the required plugins   142
Getting ready   143
How to do it...   143
Integrating Jenkins with all of the AWS developers tools   145
Getting ready   145
How to do it...   146
Chapter 5: Understanding Microservices and ECS   161
Introduction   161
Understanding microservices and their deployment   162
Designing microservices   163
Deployment of microservices   164
Playing around with Docker containers   164
Containers   164
Docker   165
Images   165
Registry   165
Containers   165
Getting ready   166
Installation of Docker engine   166
Run Docker as a non-root user   167
How to do it...   167
Running a container   168
Starting the stopped container   169
Assigning a Name to a container   170

Creating daemonized containers 170
Exposing ports of a container 171
Managing persistent storage with Docker 172
Adding a data volume 172
Getting details of a container 172
Containerize your application using Dockerfile 173
Push the image to Dockerhub 175
Setting up AWS ECR and pushing an image into it 176
Getting ready 176
How to do it... 177
To authenticate Docker client with ECR 179
Tagging your Docker Image with the repository details 180
Pushing the image to ECR 181
Understanding ECS and writing task definitions and services 182
Getting ready 186
How to do it... 186
Verifying containers inside the Container instance 197

Chapter 6: Continuous Deployment to ECS Using Developer Tools and CloudFormation 201
Introduction 201
Understanding the architecture and workflow 202
How to do it... 202
How it works... 204
Setting up the infrastructure to host the application 205
Getting ready 206
How to do it... 206
Creating an ECS cluster 206
Creating a Load Balancer (Classic ELB) 209
Register Auto Scaling with Load Balancer 212
Creating an Amazon ECR 213
Setting Up CodeCommit for our application source 214
Getting ready 214
How to do it... 214
Creating a CodeBuild project for the build stage 216
Getting ready 217
How to do it... 217
Understanding the inside content of helper files (BuildSpec.yml, Dockerfile, and CF template) 219
How to do it... 219
Creating a CodePipeline using CodeCommit, CodeBuild, and CloudFormation 224

Getting ready 224
How to do it... 224
Chapter 7: IaC Using CloudFormation and Ansible 233
Introduction 233
AWS CloudFormation and writing the CloudFormation template 235
Terms and concepts related to AWS CloudFormation 236
For YAML 236
For JSON 237
How to do it... 238
Writing a CF template 238
Defining parameters 240
Using parameters 241
Creating stack using the CF template 245
Creating a production-ready web application infrastructure using CloudFormation 249
Getting ready 250
How to do it... 251
Automation with Ansible 254
Workflow 256
Installation 256
How to do it... 256
File structure and syntax 257
Deploying a web server using Ansible 258
Creating an AWS infrastructure using the Ansible EC2 dynamic inventory 259
Getting ready 260
How to do it... 261
Chapter 8: Automating AWS Resource Control Using AWS Lambda 265
Introduction 265
Creating an AMIs of the EC2 instance using AWS lambda and CloudWatch 266
Getting ready 266
How to do it... 267
Sending notifications through SNS using Config and Lambda 276
Getting ready 276
How to do it... 277
Configuring the AWS Config service for AWS resources 283
Creating a Lambda function 285
Creating a trigger 287

Streaming and visualizing AWS CloudTrail logs in real time using Lambda with Kibana   290
  - Workflow   291
  - Getting ready   292
  - How to do it...   292
    - Enabling CloudTrail logs   292
    - Configuring CloudWatch   294
    - Creating Elasticsearch   295
    - Enabling the streaming of CloudWatch logs in Elasticsearch   300
    - Configuring Kibana to visualize your data   304

Chapter 9: Microservice Applications in Kubernetes Using Jenkins Pipeline 2.0   309
  - **Introduction**   310
    - K8s architecture   310
      - Master components   311
      - Node components   312
  - **Deploying multinode clusters on AWS using the Ansible playbook**   312
    - Getting ready   313
    - How to do it...   314
  - **Deploying a multinode production-ready cluster on AWS using Kops**   316
    - Getting ready   317
    - How to do it...   318
      - Creating bucket   318
      - DNS configuration   318
      - Creating a cluster   319
      - Kubernetes dashboard (UI)   321
      - Clean up   322
  - **Deploying a sample application on Kubernetes**   323
    - Getting ready   323
    - How to do it...   323
      - Configuration file   326
        - Deployment configuration file   326
        - Service configuration file   327
  - **Working with Kubernetes on AWS using AWS resources**   328
    - Getting ready   330
    - How to do it...   330
      - Creating a persistent volume claim   330
      - Deployment configuration file (includes ECR image and PVC)   332
      - Service configuration file (type Loadbalancer)   334
  - **Jenkins pipeline 2.0 (Pipeline as Code) using Jenkinsfile**   336
    - How to do it...   339
      - Declarative pipeline   340

Sections	341
Application deployment using Jenkinsfile	342
Getting ready	342
How to do it...	343
Create a pipeline in the BlueOcean	343
Clean Up	351
Creating a Pipeline using existing Jenkinsfile	352
Deploying microservices applications in Kubernetes using Jenkinsfile	353
Getting ready	354
How to do it...	355
Workflow	355
Chapter 10: Best Practices and Troubleshooting Tips	361
Best practices with AWS CodeCommit	361
Troubleshooting with CodeCommit	362
Troubleshooting with CodeBuild	364
Index	365

Preface

AWS provides a set of powerful services that help companies to increase or improve rapid build and reliable build processes to deliver products using AWS and DevOps practices. These services help to simplify the provision and management of infrastructures, the building of applications, and deploying application code in an environment. DevOps is basically a combination of practices, culture, and tools that increase an organization's productivity. It helps to increase the ability to deliver applications and services efficiently. This helps organizations to serve their customers in a better way and to compete more effectively in the market.

You can leverage AWS services for DevOps, meaning you can use AWS services to increase an organization's productivity by automating CI/CD to deliver products quickly. The Developer Tools of AWS include CodeCommit, which uses Git for VCS; CodeBuild, which helps to build the code; CodeDeploy, which helps to deploy application code to servers; and CodePipeline, which helps to integrate all of the previous services to create an automated pipeline. So, this book covers how to use the AWS Developer Tools and how to integrate them with each other. Further, this book covers enterprise-grade scenarios and creates CI/CD pipelines for application deployment. Since this book covers the details of how to use the core services, you can also create your CI/CD pipeline based on your use cases.

This book also covers how to set up production-ready infrastructures using CloudFormation and Ansible. Since many enterprises are migrating their applications to microservices and the best enterprise-grade container orchestration tool is Kubernetes, I will cover how you can deploy Kubernetes on AWS using KOPS, and how you can automate application deployment in Kubernetes using Jenkins Pipeline, which is Pipeline as Code. This book covers the automation of daily jobs and security compliance using AWS Lambda and some other services of AWS services, such as SNS, Config, and Elasticsearch.

What this book covers

Chapter 1, *Using AWS CodeCommit*, covers the basic concepts of VCS. Here, you will learn how to create a repository in GitHub and upload local files to the remote repository. Then, you will learn CodeCommit in detail and also play with some operations, such as cloning using SSH or HTTPS and migrating from GitHub to CodeCommit.

Chapter 2, *Building an Application Using AWS CodeBuild*, introduces how to build two different applications developed in Java and NodeJS using CodeBuild. This chapter will also show you how you can use a build specification file.

Chapter 3, *Deploying an Application Using AWS CodeDeploy and AWS CodePipeline*, covers the basics of the deployment strategy used by CodeDeploy. Then, post that you will learn how to write an application specification file that helps CodeDeploy to deploy an application to the servers. You will also learn how CodePipeline is used to integrate the Developer Tools.

Chapter 4, *Building a Highly Scalable and Fault-Tolerant CI/CD Pipeline*, includes recipes which include the steps to create a highly scalable and fault-tolerant pipeline. The recipes include setting up CodeCommit, S3 buckets, Auto Scaling, CodeDeploy projects, and more.

Chapter 5, *Understanding Microservices and AWS ECS*, covers microservices and its deployment. You will also learn to play around with Docker containers. Then, you will learn about ECS and its components, and also how to deploy a containerized application in ECS.

Chapter 6, *Continous Deployment to AWS ECS Using CodeCommit, CodeBuild, CloudFormation, and CodePipeline*, contains recipes to build a pipeline for the continuous deployment of a containerized application to AWS ECS using other AWS services.

Chapter 7, *IaC Using CloudFormation and Ansible*, contains the syntax and structure that helps you write a CloudFormation template to spin-up AWS resources. It also includes a CloudFormation template that will help with setting up production-ready infrastructures. The same thing is also mentioned regarding Ansible.

Chapter 8, *Automating AWS Resource Control Using AWS Lambda*, contains recipes that are related to audit compliance and automation with AWS resources, such as creating an AMI of the EC2 instance using AWS Lambda and CloudWatch, sending notifications through SNS using Config and Lambda, and streaming and visualizing AWS CloudTrail logs in real time using Lambda with Kibana.

Chapter 9, *Deploying Microservice Application in Kubernetes using Jenkins Pipeline 2.0*, contains recipes covering the deployment of Kubernetes on AWS using KOPS and custom Ansible playbooks. You will also learn to use Jenkinsfile and using Jenkinsfile, deploy a containerized application in Kubernetes.

Chapter 10, *Best Practices and Troubleshooting Tips*, includes some best practices with CodeCommit and CodeBuild and also covers troubleshooting tips.

What you need for this book

The following are the basic requirements to get the most out of this book:

- A Linux system (preferably CentOS/Red Hat) with a browser and a good editor
- An AWS account

Who this book is for

This book targets developers and system administrators who are responsible for hosting an application and managing instances in AWS. DevOps engineers looking at providing continuous integration and deployment and delivery will also find this book useful. A basic understanding of AWS, Jenkins, and some scripting knowledge will be needed.

Sections

In this book, you will find several headings that appear frequently (*Getting ready, How to do it..., How it works..., There's more...,* and *See also*). To give clear instructions on how to complete a recipe, we use these sections as follows:

Getting ready

This section tells you what to expect in the recipe, and describes how to set up any software or any preliminary settings required for the recipe.

How to do it...

This section contains the steps required to follow the recipe.

How it works...

This section usually consists of a detailed explanation of what happened in the previous section.

There's more...

This section consists of additional information about the recipe in order to make the reader more knowledgeable about the recipe.

See also

This section provides helpful links to other useful information for the recipe.

Conventions

In this book, you will find a number of text styles that distinguish between different kinds of information. Here are some examples of these styles and an explanation of their meaning. Code words in text, database table names, folder names, filenames, file extensions, pathnames, dummy URLs, user input, and Twitter handles are shown as follows: "The reason for this is we have given access to only two operations or actions: `git push` and `git clone`."

A block of code is set as follows:

```
{
  "Version": "2012-10-17",
  "Statement": [
  {
    "Effect": "Allow",
    "Action": [
      "codecommit:GitPull",
      "codecommit:GitPush"
    ],
    "Resource": "arn:aws:codecommit:us-east-1:x60xxxxxxx39:HelloWorld"
  }
  ]
}
```

Any command-line input or output is written as follows:

```
# git config --global user.name "awsstar"
```

New terms and **important words** are shown in bold. Words that you see on the screen, for example, in menus or dialog boxes, appear in the text like this: "Click on **Create Policy;** then we will have our own custom policy."

Warnings or important notes appear like this.

 Tips and tricks appear like this.

Reader feedback

Feedback from our readers is always welcome. Let us know what you think about this book-what you liked or disliked. Reader feedback is important for us as it helps us develop titles that you will really get the most out of. To send us general feedback, simply email feedback@packtpub.com, and mention the book's title in the subject of your message. If there is a topic that you have expertise in and you are interested in either writing or contributing to a book, see our author guide at www.packtpub.com/authors.

Customer support

Now that you are the proud owner of a Packt book, we have a number of things to help you to get the most from your purchase.

Errata

Although we have taken every care to ensure the accuracy of our content, mistakes do happen. If you find a mistake in one of our books-maybe a mistake in the text or the code- we would be grateful if you could report this to us. By doing so, you can save other readers from frustration and help us improve subsequent versions of this book. If you find any errata, please report them by visiting http://www.packtpub.com/submit-errata, selecting your book, clicking on the **Errata Submission Form** link, and entering the details of your errata. Once your errata are verified, your submission will be accepted and the errata will be uploaded to our website or added to any list of existing errata under the Errata section of that title. To view the previously submitted errata, go to https://www.packtpub.com/books/content/support and enter the name of the book in the search field. The required information will appear in the **Errata** section.

Piracy

Piracy of copyrighted material on the internet is an ongoing problem across all media. At Packt, we take the protection of our copyright and licenses very seriously. If you come across any illegal copies of our works in any form on the internet, please provide us with the location address or website name immediately so that we can pursue a remedy. Please contact us at copyright@packtpub.com with a link to the suspected pirated material. We appreciate your help in protecting our authors and our ability to bring you valuable content.

Questions

If you have a problem with any aspect of this book, you can contact us at questions@packtpub.com, and we will do our best to address the problem.

1
Using AWS CodeCommit

The following recipes will be covered in this chapter:

- Introducing VCS and Git
- Introducing AWS CodeCommit - Amazon managed SAAS Git
- Getting started with CodeCommit for HTTP users
- Setting up CodeCommit for SSH users using AWS CLI
- Applying security and restrictions
- Migrating a Git repository to AWS CodeCommit

Introduction

In this chapter, we will be working with Git and will mostly play around with AWS CodeCommit. We will set up a repository in AWS CodeCommit using the console, as well as CLI, and enforce a security policy on top of it. We will also migrate the basic Git-based repository to AWS CodeCommit, and will cover some best practices and troubleshooting while dealing with issues on AWS CodeCommit.

Introducing VCS and Git

VCS comes under the category of software development, which helps a software team manage changes to source code over time. A VCS keeps track of each and every modification to the code in a database. If a mistake is made, the developer can compare earlier versions of the code and fix the mistake while minimizing disturbance to the rest of the team members.

The most widely used VCS in the world is Git. It's a mature and actively maintained open source project developed by Linus Torvalds in 2005.

What is VCS?

A **version control system** (**VCS**) is the system where the changes to a file (or a set of files) usually get recorded so that we can recall it whenever we want. In this book, we mostly play around with the source code of software or applications, but that does not mean that we can track the version changes to only the source code. If you are a graphic designer or infrastructure automation worker and want to keep every version of image layout or configuration file change, then VCS is the best thing to use.

Why VCS ?

There are lots of benefits to using VCS for a project. A few of them are mentioned here:

- **Collaboration**: Anyone or everyone in the team can work on any file of the project at any time. There would be no question where the latest version of a file or the whole project is. It's in a common, central place, your version control system.
- **Storing versions properly**: Saving a version of a file or an entire project after making changes is an essential habit, but without using a VCS, it will become very tough, tedious, and error-prone. With a VCS, we can save the entire project and mention the name of the versions as well. We can also mention the details of the projects, and what all changes have been done in the current version as compared to the previous version in a README file.
- **Restoring previous versions**: If you mess up with your present code, you can simply undo the changes in a few minutes.

There are many more features of using VCS while implementing or developing a project.

Types of VCS

The types of VCS are mentioned as follows:

- **Local version control system**: In a local VCS, all the changes to a file are kept in the local machine, which has a database that has all the changes to a file under revision control, for example, **Revision control system** (**RCS**).

- **Centralized version control system**: In a centralized VCS, we can collaborate with other developers on different machines. So in these VCS, we need a single server that contains all the versioned files and the number of clients can check out files from that single server, for example, **Subversion** (**SVN**).
- **Distributed version control system**: In a distributed VCS, the client not only checks out the latest version of the file but also mirrors the whole repository. Thus if any server dies, and these systems were collaborating via it, any of the client repositories can be copied back to the server to restore it. An example of this is Git.

What is Git?

Git is a distributed VCS, and it came into the picture when there was some maintenance needed in the Linux Kernel. The Linux Kernel development community was using a proprietary **Distributed version control system** (**DVCS**) called **BitKeeper**. But after some time, the relationship between the Linux community developers and the proprietary software BitKeeper broke down, which led to Linux community developers (in particular Linux creator Linus Torvalds) developing their own DVCS tool called Git. They took a radical approach that makes it different from other VCSs such as CVS and SVN.

Why Git over other VCSs?

It wouldn't be appropriate to say Git is better than SVN or any other VCS. It depends on the scenario and the requirements of the project. But nowadays, most enterprises have chosen Git as their VCS for the following reasons:

- **Distributed nature**: Git has been designed as a distributed VCS, which means every user can have a complete copy of the repository data stored locally, so they can access the file history extremely fast. It also allows full functionality when the user is not connected to the network, whereas in a centralized VCS, such as SVN, only the central repository has the complete history. This means the user needs to connect with the network to access the history from the central repository.

- **Branch handling**: This is one of the major differences. Git has built-in support for branches and strongly encourages developers to use them, whereas SVN can also have branches, but its practice and workflow does not have the inside command. In Git, we can have multiple branches of a repository, and in each repository, you can carry out development, test it, and then merge, and it's in a tree fashion. In SVN, everything is linear; whenever you add, delete, or modify any file, the revision will just increment by one. Even if you roll back some changes in SVN, it will be considered a new revision:

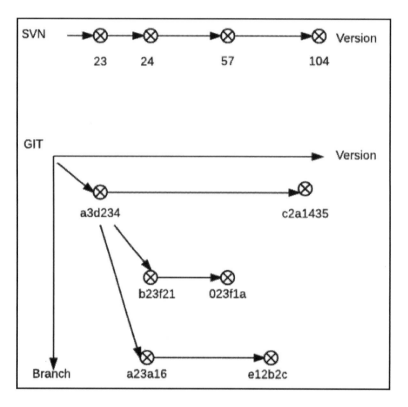

- **Smaller space requirements**: Git repositories and working directory sizes are very small in comparison with SVN.

Features of Git

The following are some of the features of Git:

- **Captures snapshots, not entire files**: Git and other VCSs had this major difference; VCS keeps the record of revisions in the form of a file. This means it keeps a set of files for every revision. Git, however, has another way of accounting for changes. Every time you commit or save the state of your project in Git, it basically takes a snapshot of what your files look like at that very moment and stores a reference to that snapshot. If files have not been changed, Git does not store the file again; it stores a link to the previous identical file it has already stored.

- **Data integrity**: Before storing any data in a Git repository, it is first checksummed, and is then referred to by that checksum. That means, if you carry out any other modification in the file, then Git will have every record of every modification. The mechanism used by Git for checksumming is known as SHA-1 hash.
  SHA-1 hash looks something like this:

  - `b52af1db10a8c915cfbb9c1a6c9679dc47052e34`

- **States and areas**: Git has three main states and views all files in three different states:

  - **Modified**: This is the modification that has been done in the file, but not yet written or committed in the database.
  - **Committed**: This ensures that the source code and related data are safely stored in your local database or machine
  - **Staged**: This ensures that the modified file is added in its current version and is ready for the next commitment.

How to do it...

Here are the steps and commands that will guide you through installing and setting up Git and creating a repository in a very famous self-hosted Git, GitHub.

Installation of Git and its implementation using GitHub

1. If you want to use Git, we have to install the Git package on our system:
   - For Fedora distributions (RHEL/CentOS):

   ```
   # yum install git
   ```

- For Debian distributions (Debian/Ubuntu):

   ```
   # apt-get install git
   ```

2. Configure your identity with Git because every Git commit uses this information, for example, the following commit has been done by User `awsstar` and email is `awsstar@foo.com`:

   ```
   # git config --global user.name "awsstar"
   # git config --global user.email "awsstar@foo.com"
   ```

3. Check your settings. You will find the above username and email-id:

   ```
   # git config --list
   ```

4. Now, let's try to create a repository on GitHub:
   - Hit `www.github.com` in your web browser and log in with your credentials
   - Click on create **New Repository**

Then, we will get something like the following screenshot. We have to mention the **Repository name** and a **Description** of the repository. After that, we need to select **Public** or **Private** based on our requirements. When we opt for **Public**, then anyone can see your repository, but you pick who can commit; when you opt for **Private**, then you pick who can see and who can commit, meaning by default it won't be visible to anyone. After that, we have to initialize the README, where we can give a detailed description of the project and click on **Create Repository**:

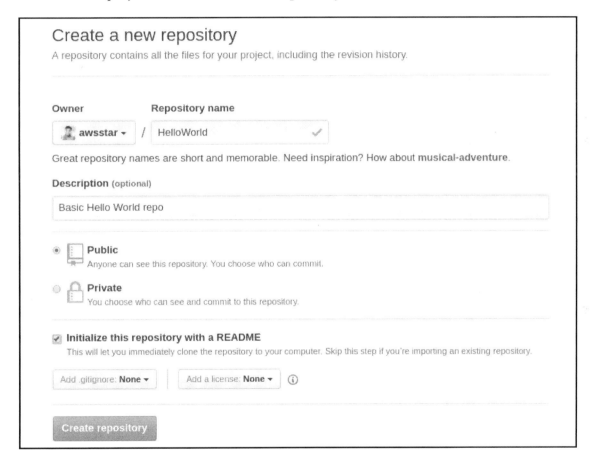

5. Once we have a repository, **HelloWorld**, then let's try to clone it to our local machine and some program files. Cloning a repository means creating a local copy of the repository and it can be done as follows:

  - Fetch the Git URL by clicking on **Clone or Download** (`https://github.com/awsstar/HelloWorld.git`):

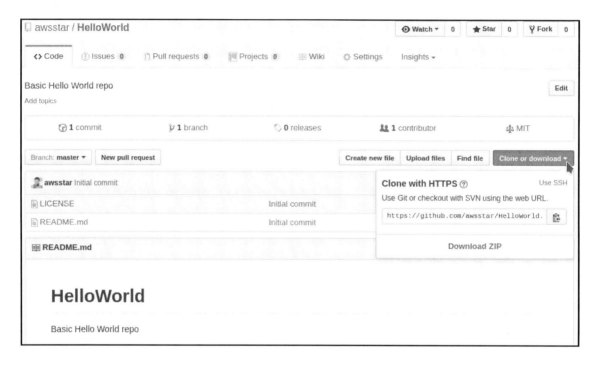

  - Now, clone the URL:

```
root@awsstar:~# git clone https://github.com/awsstar/HelloWorld.git
Cloning into 'HelloWorld'...
remote: Counting objects: 4, done.
remote: Compressing objects: 100% (3/3), done.
remote: Total 4 (delta 0), reused 0 (delta 0), pack-reused 0
Unpacking objects: 100% (4/4), done.
Checking connectivity... done.
root@abae81a80866:~# ls
HelloWorld
root@awsstar:~# cd HelloWorld
root@awsstar:~/HelloWorld# ls
LICENSE README.md
root@awsstar:~/HelloWorld#
```

6. We have the `HelloWorld` repository on our local machine. So, let's add `index.html` and push it back to the repository. Create a file, `index.html`, and write `HelloWorld` inside it:

```
root@awsstar:~/HelloWorld# echo '<h1> HelloWorld </h1>' > index.html
```

7. The `git status` command checks the current status and reports whether there is anything left to commit or not:

```
root@awsstar:~/HelloWorld# git status
On branch masterYour branch is up-to-date with
'origin/master'.Untracked files: (use "git add <file>..." to include      in
what will be committed)
    index.html
    nothing added to commit but untracked files present (use "git add"
to track)
```

8. Now to add the changes to the repository, we have to enter this command:

```
root@awsstar:~/HelloWorld# git add .
```

9. To store the current contents of the index in a new commit, along with a log message from the user describing the changes, we need to enter this command:

```
root@awsstar:~/HelloWorld# git commit -m "index.html added"
[master 7be5f57] index.html added 1 file changed, 1 insertion(+)
create mode 100644 index.html
```

10. Push your local changes to the remote repository:

```
root@awsstar:~/HelloWorld# git push origin master
Username for 'https://github.com': awsstar
Password for 'https://awsstar@github.com':
Counting objects: 3, done.
Delta compression using up to 4 threads.
Compressing objects: 100% (2/2), done.
Writing objects: 100% (3/3), 327 bytes | 0 bytes/s, done.
Total 3 (delta 0), reused 0 (delta 0)
To https://github.com/awsstar/HelloWorld.git
a0a82b2..7be5f57 master -> master
```

Here, we can see that `index.html` is now in our GitHub repository:

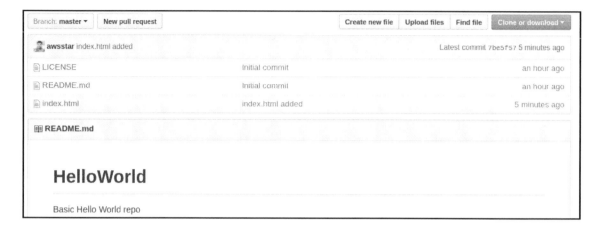

You can set up Git on your own server. Refer to this for more info:
`https://git-scm.com/book/en/v2/Git-on-the-Server-Setting-Up-the-Server`

Introducing AWS CodeCommit - Amazon managed SaaS Git

AWS CodeCommit is a version control system, which is managed by Amazon Web Services, where we can privately store and manage assets in the Cloud and integrate with AWS. It is a highly scalable and secure VCS that hosts private Git repositories and supports the standard functionality of Git, so it works very well with your existing Git-based tools.

The following are the benefits of CodeCommit:

- **Managed service**: CodeCommit is fully managed, distributed, fault tolerant, and carries no administrative overhead. It is elastic (able to adapt to a high workload) and, as mentioned, integrated with other AWS services.
- **No limit to storage and file type**: We can store as many files as we want, because CodeCommit does not have space limitations. We can store not only source code but also documents and binary files.
- **Data and access security**: CodeCommit repositories are encrypted while they are in AWS CodeCommit or when getting cloned somewhere. It is also integrated with IAM for user-level or specific API-level security.
- **HA (high availability)**: Whatever data we push into the repository, it will replicate across AZs (Availability Zones).
- **Easy migration of Git-based repository**: We can easily migrate a remote Git-based repository to AWS CodeCommit.

These are some limitations or drawbacks of self-hosted VCS (BitBucket/GitHub/GitLab), which you won't find in AWS CodeCommit:

- We may have to pay a license fee on a per-developer basis
- We may end up with high hardware maintenance costs and high support staffing costs
- Limitation on the amount and types of files that can be stored and managed
- Limitation on the number of branches, the amount of version history, and other related metadata that can be stored

How to do it...

AWS CodeCommit is configured just like other Git-based repositories, such as GitHub. The following diagram shows how we use a development machine, AWS CLI/AWS Console, and CodeCommit to create and manage a repository:

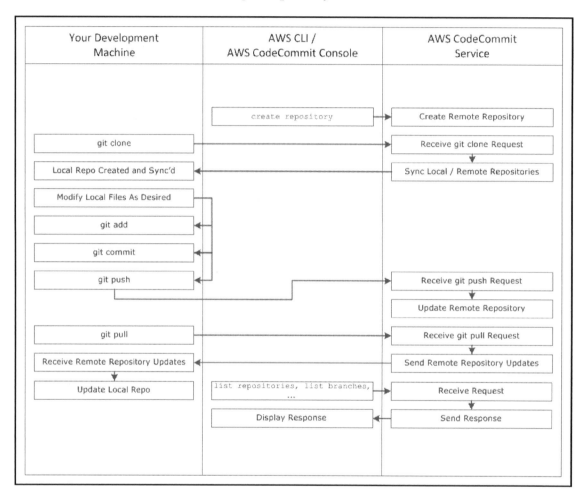

(Reference: AWS CodeCommit Docs)

The basic workflow is described as follows:

1. Using AWS CLI or CodeCommit Console, we can create a CodeCommit repository.

2. Post that, use `git clone` in the CodeCommit repository URL on your local development machine.

3. Once the repository gets cloned into the development machine, make the changes in the repository by adding to or editing the files. After that, enter the `git add` command and put it into the staging area, `commit` by giving a change message, and then `push` it back to the repository.

4. After that, we can carry out `git pull` to synchronize the code in the AWS CodeCommit repository with our local repository. At this point in time, you will be working with the latest changes and the versions of the files.

Getting started with CodeCommit for HTTP users

AWS provides both Console and CLI access to create a repository in AWS CodeCommit. Let's get started and create a repository, then clone it in development using HTTPS credentials.

How to do it...

1. Open the AWS CodeCommit console at `https://console.aws.amazon.com/codecommit`.

2. On the welcome page, choose **Get Started Now** (if a dashboard page appears instead of the welcome page, choose **Create repository**):

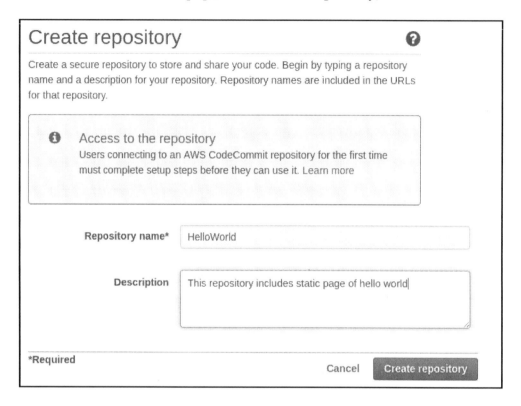

3. Then, we will get a box, **Connect to your Repository**, which will provide further instructions on ways of connecting to CodeCommit via HTTPS or SSH. We can close that and move further, but it's advisable to read every message or information prompt from AWS.

4. Now, we will clone the repository, but before that, we need HTTPS Git credentials. We will get the HTTPS Git credentials of an IAM user, which is attached with the policy of CodeCommit access through IAM console. So let's try to create a user first, assign the CodeCommit policy, and get the HTTPS Git credentials for that user.

5. Open the AWS IAM console by hitting `https://console.aws.amazon.com/iam` in a new tab.

6. Click on **Add User**.

7. Give IAM user a username as `awsccuser` and check both the **Access type** boxes (**Programmatic access /AWS Management Console access**), set a **Custom password**, and click on **Next:Permission:**

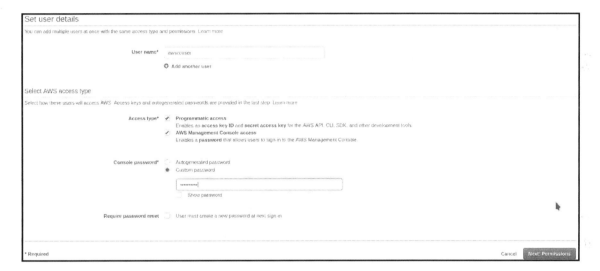

8. We then get the set permission on the username page. On this page, first click on **Attach existing Policies directly** after which we search `CodeCommit` in the search box of **Policy type**:

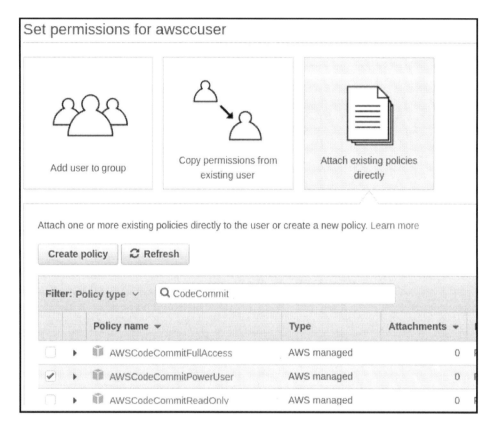

9. Click on the **AWSCodeCommitPowerUser** policy and click on **Next.**
10. Post review, click on **Create User.**
11. Download **credentials** provided by the AWS IAM user; these credentials are basically **secret and access key**.
12. After that, we need to click on the **User** section. Then, click on **Security credentials**.

13. Scroll down and we will see a section called **HTTPS Git credentials for AWS CodeCommit**; after that, click on **Generate**:

14. Once we click on **Generate**, we will get a **username and password**; then, click on **Download credentials**.
15. Again, let's go to the CodeCommit console and click on **Clone URL** and then **HTTPS**.
16. Copy the link and enter the following command on the development machine:

```
# git clone https://git-codecommit.us-east-
1.amazonaws.com/v1/repos/HelloWorld
```

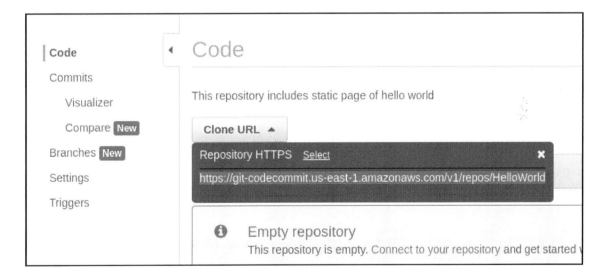

```
root@awsstar:~# git clone https://git-codecommit.us-east-
1.amazonaws.com/v1/repos/HelloWorld
    Cloning into 'HelloWorld'...
    Username for 'https://git-codecommit.us-east-1.amazonaws.com':
awsccuser-at-160384169139
    Password for 'https://awsccuser-at-160384169139@git-    codecommit.us-
east-1.amazonaws.com':
    warning: You appear to have cloned an empty repository.
    Checking connectivity... done.
    root@awsstar:~# ls
    HelloWorld
    root@awsstar:~#
```

17. We just cloned an empty repository; now, it's time to put a sample index.html
    file in the CodeCommit HelloWorld repository. We will now create a file
    named index.html and put some content in it. Add content and commit it,
    before pushing it to the repository:

```
root@awsstar:~# cd HelloWorld/
root@awsstar:~/HelloWorld# echo '<h1> Hello World </h1>' >
index.html
root@awsstar:~/HelloWorld# git add .
root@awsstar:~/HelloWorld# git commit -m " index.html push "
[master (root-commit) bc76f76] index.html push
1 file changed, 1 insertion(+)
create mode 100644 index.html
root@awsstar:~/HelloWorld# git push origin master
Username for 'https://git-codecommit.us-east-1.amazonaws.com':
awsccuser-at-160384169139
    Password for 'https://awsccuser-at-160384169139@git-
codecommit.us-    east-1.amazonaws.com':
    Counting objects: 3, done.
    Writing objects: 100% (3/3), 233 bytes | 0 bytes/s, done.
    Total 3 (delta 0), reused 0 (delta 0)
    To https://git-codecommit.us-east-
1.amazonaws.com/v1/repos/HelloWorld
    * [new branch]      master -> master
```

18. Now, we pushed a file to our newly created repository in AWS CodeCommit. To
    verify this, let's see the AWS CodeCommit console, and see whether the checked-
    in file is there or not (refresh the CodeCommit console, if you were there from the
    start):

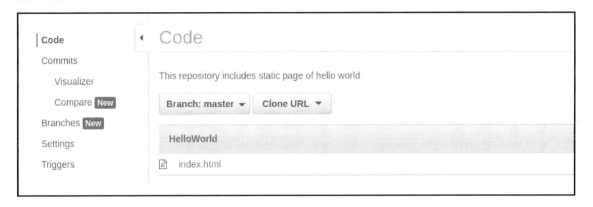

19. To see more details, click on **Commits,** and see which user has committed and which files have changed:

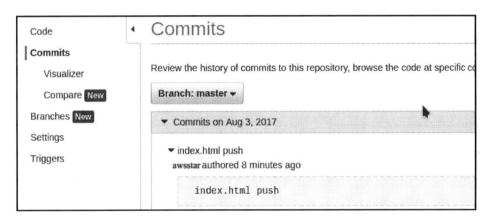

20. This shows information such as when `index.html` got pushed, on what date, and by whom.

21. Now, to wrap up or to delete the repository, click on the **Settings** section and on the **Delete Repository**; then a prompt box will pop up, where we put the repository name and click on **Delete**:

22. After clicking on **Delete**, your repository will get deleted:

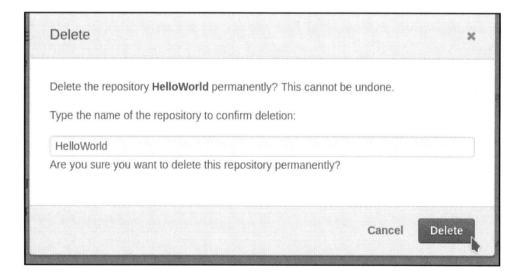

Setting up CodeCommit for SSH users using AWS CLI

In the previous recipe, we saw how we can access the repository using the username and password. In this section, we will use SSH private and public keys to access the repository. We will be accessing the repository using SSH connections.

This topic assumes that you already have, or know how to create, a pair of public/private keys. You should be familiar with SSH and its configuration files.

Getting ready

Before setting up CodeCommit for SSH users, we need the AWS CLI installed and configured with the respective AWS account. To install the AWS CLI on our development machine, we need to perform these steps:

1. We need to install python-pip and AWS CLI tools. Usually, in CentOS/RHEL, python-pip comes with EPEL (Extra Package for Enterprise Linux):

```
# yum install epel-release python-pip
# pip install awscli
```

2. Once we have the awscli command installed in our system, we have to configure it using the access and secret Key, as well as the region we will use the AWS account in. If you remember, we had created a user while generating the https git credentials, but at that moment, we also downloaded another type of credentials, the secret and access key. So, we need that over here.

3. Now, let's configure AWS CLI:

```
awsstar@awsstar:~$ aws configure
 AWS Access Key ID [None]: AKIxxxxxxxxxxxxxxDDA
 AWS Secret Access Key [None]: b+GEuc2u3xxxxxxxxxxxxxxx+av/5eK
 Default region name [None]: us-east-1
 Default output format [None]:
```

4. Once the configuration is done, let's try to list the repository:

```
awsstar@awsstar:~$ aws codecommit list-repositories
 {
 "repositories": [
 {
 "repositoryName": "NixSrj",
```

```
"repositoryId": "73caf1e3-65a9-44bf-8c6a-a3bd3e0260b0"
},
{
"repositoryName": "ECS-POC",
"repositoryId": "62063220-b0fc-4519-9d54-896be46a7521"
},
{
"repositoryName": "terraform-Openshift",
"repositoryId": "20f88492-81bb-4068-8867-5d17a1d3ec5b"
}
]
}
```

5. So it's showing the repository, which means the credentials are working fine and we are good to go to create a repository now.

How to do it...

1. Create a repository, `HelloWorld`:

```
awsstar@awsstar:~$ aws codecommit create-repository --repository-
name HelloWorld --repository-description "This repository includes
static page of HelloWorld"
    {
    "repositoryMetadata": {
    "repositoryName": "HelloWorld",
    "cloneUrlSsh": "ssh://git-codecommit.us-east-
1.amazonaws.com/v1/repos/HelloWorld",
 "lastModifiedDate": 1501778613.664,
 "repositoryDescription": "This repository includes static page of
HelloWorld",
 "cloneUrlHttp": "https://git-codecommit.us-east-
1.amazonaws.com/v1/repos/HelloWorld",
 "creationDate": 1501778613.664,
 "repositoryId": "53866a81-8576-4e79-ab5a-36882c33b717",
"Arn": "arn:aws:codecommit:us-east-1:160384169139:HelloWorld",
"accountId": "160384169139"
}
}
```

2. Now, check it using the following command:

```
awsstar@awsstar:~$ aws codecommit list-repositories
 {
 "repositories": [
```

```
    {
    "repositoryName": "HelloWorld",
    "repositoryId": "53866a81-8576-4e79-ab5a-36882c33b717"
    }
    ]
}
```

3. Let's try to clone the `HelloWorld` repository from CodeCommit to our development machine; but before that, we have to establish SSH authentication. To do that, we have to perform the following operations to generate the SSH keys:

```
awsstar@awsstar:~$ ssh-keygen
  Generating public/private rsa key pair.
  Enter file in which to save the key (/home/awsstar/.ssh/id_rsa):
  Created directory '/home/awsstar/.ssh'.
  Enter passphrase (empty for no passphrase):
  Enter same passphrase again:
  Your identification has been saved in /home/awsstar/.ssh/id_rsa.
  Your public key has been saved in /home/awsstar/.ssh/id_rsa.pub.
  The key fingerprint is:
  SHA256:NMUiRSDRD9SxrSIcYm9A4BYau2TOaeEfk5TgRmy3i4o
root@aa21529d724f
  The key's randomart image is:
  +---[RSA 2048]----+
  |+=. o+o=+o. |
  |=*o...+ o+. |
  |+O=oo ++.. |
  |Oo+*.. ..o |
  |.*.+* . S |
  |...oo. . |
  |o . |
  |E |
  | |
  +----[SHA256]-----+
```

4. The preceding command will create two keys; one is the public key (`id_rsa.pub`) and the other one is the private key (`id_rsa`).

5. Now, we have to upload the public key to the user of AWS we created:

```
awsstar@awsstar:~$ cd .ssh
awsstar@awsstar:~/.ssh$ aws iam upload-ssh-public-key --user-name
awsccuser --ssh-public-key-body "ssh-rsa
AAAAB3NzaC1yc2EAAAADAQABAAABAQCk437p8/JmhGOdM9oYNK/r1xpOnuA2cQNfYys7lnE9gXJ
dTEjniHNFcJZMkIVmtYQGAqEh37BWGfX14s5iw/NSfkDuZf8zegAgyPryROKTTUG2f/rrtyLtlA
PlSXjtCmHakZzhwIoRJtzkDbSpKoUOD8fNnS3kKIwk7Dp3+gGLLgo9eoZdud9h/E5+NpORog7wg
7xaTgg3mwa9StaPHKMxJNwNc71dIuUyAh2S6bDbHB3QWLNfrJABYqPq5HGFh3KLogH9GHBMajsh
```

```
LEOS4Ygk3uC8FzB+eP4oneuWd2n68N3qg5RmX0U5lAL8s3+ppuhmjlbSvDOdBUJdpgEL/AQZ
awsstar@awsstar"
```

6. We need to make a note of some details, such as the SSHPublicKeyId provided as output in thew JSON format, while uploading the SSH public key.

7. We have to bring about some modification in the `config` file lying in `$HOME/.ssh/config`:

```
awsstar@awsstar:~$ vi .ssh/config
Host git-codecommit.us-east-1.amazonaws.com
User APKAIGJDPRJL3INHSJ6Q
IdentityFile ~/.ssh/id_rsa
```

8. Once we are done saving the `config` file, let's see the connectivity between the development machine and AWS CodeCommit:

```
awsstar@awsstar:~$ ssh git-codecommit.us-east-1.amazonaws.com
    The authenticity of host 'git-codecommit.us-east-1.amazonaws.com
(54.239.20.155)' can't be established.
    RSA key fingerprint is
SHA256:eLMY1j0DKA4uvDZcl/KgtIayZANwX6t8+8isPtotBoY.
    Are you sure you want to continue connecting (yes/no)? yes
    Warning: Permanently added 'git-codecommit.us-east-
1.amazonaws.com,54.239.20.155' (RSA) to the list of known hosts.
    You have successfully authenticated over SSH. You can use Git to
interact with AWS CodeCommit. Interactive shells are not
supported.Connection to git-codecommit.us-east-1.amazonaws.com closed
by remote host.
    Connection to git-codecommit.us-east-1.amazonaws.com closed.
```

9. We get the output that says `Successfully authenticated over SSH`, so now we are ready to clone the repository. We can clone the SSH URL of the repository, which we obtain from the JSON output while creating the repository:

```
awsstar@awsstar:~$ git clone ssh://git-codecommit.us-east-
1.amazonaws.com/v1/repos/HelloWorld
    Cloning into 'HelloWorld'...
    warning: You appear to have cloned an empty repository.
    checking connectivity... done
awsstar@awsstar:~$ ls
HelloWorld
awsstar@awsstar:~$
```

10. So, we cloned an empty repository; now it's time to put a sample `index.html` file in the CodeCommit `HelloWorld` repository:

```
awsstar@awsstar:~/HelloWorld$ echo '<h1> Hello World </h1>' >
index.html
awsstar@awsstar:~/HelloWorld$ git add .
awsstar@awsstar:~/HelloWorld$ git commit -m " index.html push "
[master (root-commit) bc76f76] index.html push
1 file changed, 1 insertion(+)
create mode 100644 index.html
root@awsstar:~/HelloWorld# git push origin master
Counting objects: 3, done.
Writing objects: 100% (3/3), 233 bytes | 0 bytes/s, done.
Total 3 (delta 0), reused 0 (delta 0)
To ssh://git-codecommit.us-east-
1.amazonaws.com/v1/repos/HelloWorld
 * [new branch] master -> master
```

11. In this stage, we successfully pushed our local file into the AWS CodeCommit `HelloWorld` repository.

Applying security and restrictions

In an enterprise where a product is being developed, we find lots of developers on different teams working with different repositories but in the same Git-based VCS.

Here in CodeCommit, if we give a user CodeCommitPowerUser access, then the user will have full control over all the repositories, except the deletion of repositories. So, a Power User will be able to see the source code of all other repositories, that is, there won't be any privacy. This is the kind of permission you should avoid giving another user.

In some companies, they have different use cases, for example, they only require a few of their developers to have access to all Git-based commands and on the specific repository. We dive into how to implement this type of scenario.

Getting ready

To implement this scenario, we use AWS IAM services, where we will create a user and attach it to a CodeCommit custom policy, and that policy will have access to only a specific repository with specific Git commands.

How to do it...

Let's get started with that, and perform the following operations:

1. First of all, let's create a custom policy where we will give the restriction definition.
2. Go to IAM Console and click on the **Policies** section. Then, click on **Create Policy:**

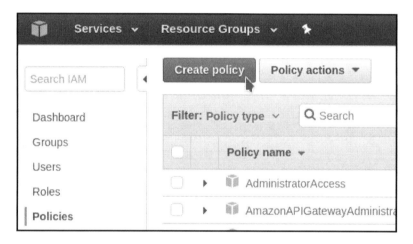

3. Click on **Create Your Own Policy:**

4. You will be redirected to another page where you have to fill in the **Policy Name**, a description of the policy, and a policy document. The policy document will be the definition, where we will mention the resources and actions:

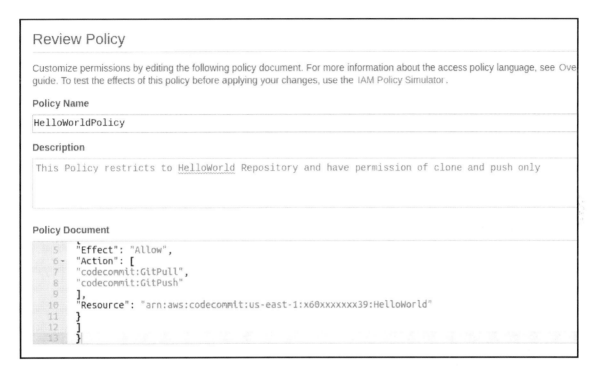

5. Insert the following policy definition (x60xxxxxxx39 will be basically your account ID):

```
{
  "Version": "2012-10-17",
  "Statement": [
  {
  "Effect": "Allow",
  "Action": [
  "codecommit:GitPull",
  "codecommit:GitPush"
  ],
  "Resource": "arn:aws:codecommit:us-east-1:x60xxxxxxx39:HelloWorld"
  }
  ]
  }
```

6. Click on **Create Policy;** then we will have our own custom policy:

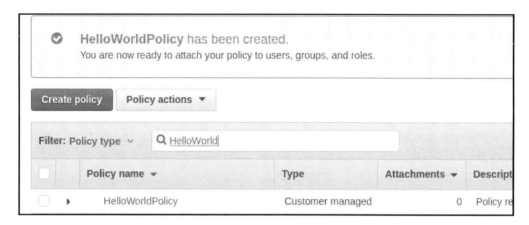

7. Now, let's remove the AWSCodeCommitPowerUser access from the IAM user that we created to clone the repository by clicking on x:

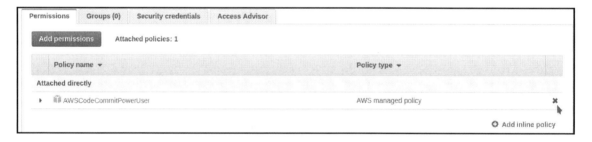

8. Click on **Add permissions,** after that click on **Attach Existing Policies Directly** and search for **Policy name** in filter, check that, and save it:

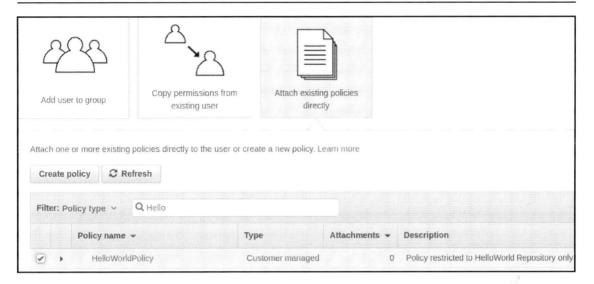

9. We will have a user with only our custom policy, which means the user will only have access to the `HelloWorld` repository and only two actions, `git push` and `git clone`:

```
awsstar@awsstar:~$ aws codecommit list-repositories
    An error occurred (AccessDeniedException) when calling the
ListRepositories operation: User:
arn:aws:iam::16xxxxxx139:user/awsccuser is not authorized to perform:
codecommit:ListRepositories
```

The preceding command output shows `AccessDeniedException`, that is, `awsccuser` is not authorized to perform `codecommit:ListRepositories`. The reason for this is we have given access to only two operations or actions: `git push` and `git clone`.

Migrating a Git repository to AWS CodeCommit

As a developer, it's highly possible that we have our code in a GitHub account. So, we will see the migration of a GitHub repository to AWS CodeCommit. Customers often need to replicate commits from one repository to another to support disaster recovery or cross-region CI/CD pipelines. AWS CodeCommit has lots of flexibility when it comes to AWS developer services, such as CodeBuild, CodeDeploy, and CodeStar. Most companies nowadays will think to migrate from those repositories to AWS CodeCommit:

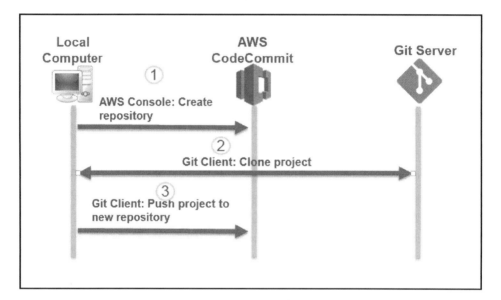

How to do it...

The following are the steps for migrating a project or repository hosted on another Git repository to AWS CodeCommit:

1. Firstly, we have to create a CodeCommit repository named HelloWorld (refer to the previous CodeCommit repository either using HTTPS or SSH).

2. After creating a CodeCommit repository, clone it to the local machine. Since we are cloning the repository using an HTTPS connection, then we need to give the HTTPS credentials of username and password (you can refer to the previous recipe):

```
root@awsstar:~# git clone https://git-codecommit.us-east-
1.amazonaws.com/v1/repos/HelloWorld
    Cloning into 'HelloWorld'...
    Username for 'https://git-codecommit.us-east-1.amazonaws.com':
awsccuser-at-1xxxxxxxx39
    Password for 'https://awsccuser-at-16xxxxxxx39@git-codecommit.us-
east-1.amazonaws.com':
    warning: You appear to have cloned an empty repository.
    Checking connectivity... done.
```

3. Now, clone a GitHub repository using `--mirror` into another new folder. Here we have a GitHub repository whose name is **Docker-Compose-CI-CD**, which will be cloned into a pre-existing empty folder `precommit`:

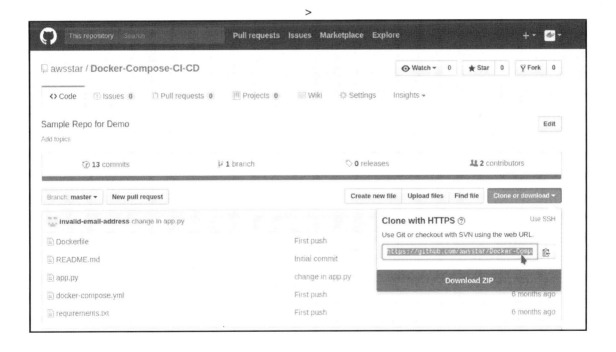

```
    root@awsstar:~# mkdir precommit
    root@awsstar:~# git clone --mirror
https://github.com/awsstar/Docker-Compose-CI-CD.git precommit
    Cloning into bare repository 'precommit'...
    remote: Counting objects: 36, done.
    remote: Total 36 (delta 0), reused 0 (delta 0), pack-reused 36
    Unpacking objects: 100% (36/36), done.
    Checking connectivity... done.
```

4. Go to the directory where you made the clone:

```
    root@awsstar:~# cd precommit/
```

5. Run the `git push` command, specifying the URL and name of the destination AWS CodeCommit repository and the `--all` option:

```
    root@awsstar:~/precommit# git push https://git-codecommit.us-east-
1.amazonaws.com/v1/repos/HelloWorld --all
    Username for 'https://git-codecommit.us-east-1.amazonaws.com':
awsccuser-at-160384169139
    Password for 'https://awsccuser-at-160384169139@git-    codecommit.us-
east-1.amazonaws.com':
 Counting objects: 36, done.
    Delta compression using up to 4 threads.
    Compressing objects: 100% (33/33), done.
    Writing objects: 100% (36/36), 3.73 KiB | 0 bytes/s, done.
    Total 36 (delta 17), reused 0 (delta 0)
    To https://git-codecommit.us-east-
1.amazonaws.com/v1/repos/HelloWorld
    * [new branch] master -> master
```

6. Now, let's view the migrated files in AWS CodeCommit:

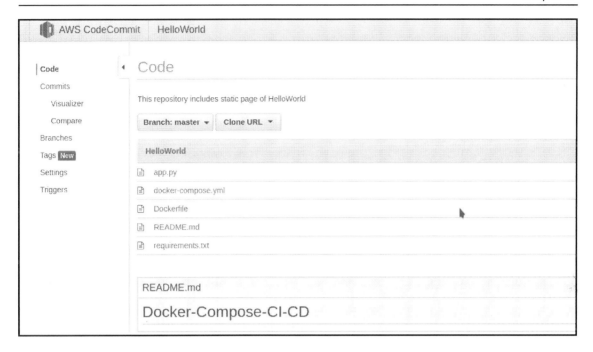

Here, we can see how easily we have migrated the project from GitHub to AWS CodeCommit.

2

Building an Application using CodeBuild

In this chapter, the following recipes will be covered:

- Introducing AWS CodeBuild
- Building a Java application using Maven
- Building a NodeJS application using yarn
- Building a Maven application using AWS CodeBuild console
- Building a sample NodeJS application using AWS CodeBuild via Buildspec.yml

Introduction

People working as Developer, DevOps, or SysOps hear a lot about the build of an application, screams that the build failed, and requests to not break the build all the time. So, what do they mean about the build? The developers write code and push it to a version control system such as GitHub, SVN, or CodeCommit. This source code needs to be analyzed and processed further so that it can be deployed to the production server or platform.

The processing step can be any of the following:

1. Source code usually consists of classes, objects, methods, and functions. So, we have to compile and link them to make it in an installable or binary format.
2. Running test cases or quality analysis on source code means that the source code will pass through the seven axes of code quality--duplication, code coverage, complexity, comments, bugs, unit test, and architecture and design.
3. Minimizing the image assets and JavaScript to decrease its downloadable size.

In layman terms, it is packaged and compiled, which makes the code ready for deployment on Production. Different programming languages are built in a different manner and using different tools and utilities. For example, Ruby and ROR uses *rake*, C and C++ use *make*, Java project uses M*aven*, NodeJS uses *yarn*, and Python uses *PyBuilder*.

Many enterprises use tools to automate these steps in order to obtain a reproducible and easily executable output. Some teams in an enterprise run the build tools or commands manually once the changes to the source code are done, and some team uses Continuous build tool such as CircleCI, Jenkins, and AWS CodeBuild, which automatically detects the changes made to the source code and act accordingly. When your teammate says *don't break the build*, they meant don't make changes in the source code in such a manner that let build fail. If the build fails, then it will stop all the developers from building the latest versions of code, until the previous code is fixed.

When we build an application, sometimes it creates another folder and adds all the binaries or packaged source code into the new folder. Later, those binaries or packaged source codes are directly deployed into the production. So, the preceding things differ based on the application stack. The build output that we usually obtain with Java-related applications may differ with the output that we will get with the NodeJS application.

In this chapter, we will cover two different applications both in different languages, that is, Java and NodeJS. We will understand why exactly we need to build the application. We will build Maven- and NodeJS-related applications on a local machine. Later on, we will see how CodeBuild works and how we can build both the Maven- and NodeJS-related applications in CodeBuild. So, specifically we will be covering the following topics:

- Understanding of the Maven-based application and building it
- Understanding of the NodeJS-based application and building it using yarn
- Features and advantages of AWS Codebuild and the workflow of it
- Building sample Maven-based web application using a CodeBuild console
- Building a NodeJS application using the Build Specification file

Introducing AWS CodeBuild

When it comes to cloud-hosted and fully managed build services, which compiles our source code, runs unit tests, and produces artifacts that are ready to deploy, then AWS CodeBuild comes into the picture.

Instead of using Jenkins or Bamboo, we can use AWS CodeBuild, and then skip the following issues:

- Setting up a Jenkins on a server and maintaining it
- Maintaining the cluster security
- Upgrading the Jenkins software over time
- Monitoring and recovering from Jenkins downtime
- Capacity planning so the cluster can handle all our build volume

If you setup the build server of your own, then you have to pay a big bill to the engineers to keep the cluster scaled up 24/7 and maintain the Jenkins cluster. If the build server will have any issues, then the team won't be able to ship the latest code, until the build server is fixed.

AWS CodeBuild is elastic, scalable, and easy to use. It has a couple of inbuilt build environments for popular programming languages and build tools such as Gradle, Maven, and more. You can modify the build environments in AWS CodeBuild accordingly, to use your own build tools.

With AWS CodeBuild operations are negligible and costs are reduced to on-demand usage. So, your team is now only focused on pushing code, and lets CodeBuild build all the artifacts.

Let's take a look at the necessary components of AWS CodeBuild:

- Source repository: This is the location of your source code
- Build spec: This builds commands
- Build environment: This is your runtime environment
- Compute type: This is the amount of memory and compute power required
- IAM role: This grants CodeBuild the permission to access specific AWS services and resources

How to do it...

1. Run AWS CodeBuild using the AWS CodeBuild or AWS CodePipeline (Chapter 3, *Deploying an application using AWS CodeDeploy and AWS CodePipeline*) console.

2. Automate the running of AWS CodeBuild using AWS CLI or AWS SDKs.

3. Start the build manually using the AWS CodeBuild console, but if you want that it should get triggered automatically then you need to integrate it with AWS CodePipeline.

How it works...

Let's first see how it works while starting the build manually. The following diagram is the reference of explanation:

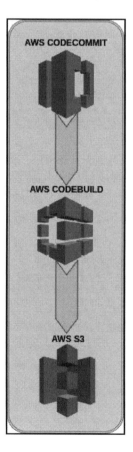

Firstly, we need a source repository; it can be either CodeCommit, GitHub, or s3. BitBucket is also supported now. Post that, we have to set up the environment where the build will take place. The environment will be Docker image. Now, here, we have two types of images-one is managed by AWS, which will runtime as Linux platform and have the necessary package of Java, Android, Python, Go, Ruby, and so on, and the other image will be given by us, which will be the custom image. For the custom image, we have to pass the registry detail as well, that is, from where they will pull the Docker image.

In the environment setup, you will find one parameter called **Build Specification**, where you can enter your build command or specify the `buildspec.yml` file (build step file). After that, you have to set up the artifacts location, mostly AWS S3, where you can put the build files.

When you insert the updated source code in CodeCommit and trigger CodeBuild to build the project, it will pull the latest code from the repository and launch a container with the platform and prepackaged application, which means that the image of Java with Maven will run. In this environment, the application code will be built, using the Buildspecific file or Build commands mentioned in the Build Specification. Once the build happens, then it will put the artifacts to the S3 bucket.

Pricing

Pricing of AWS CodeBuild depends on compute resources based on the duration it takes for your build to execute. The per-minute rate depends on the selected compute instance type. **Build duration** is calculated in minutes, from the time you submit your build until your build is terminated, rounded up to the nearest minute. AWS CodeBuild, as of August 2017, offers three compute instance types with different amounts of memory and CPU. Charges vary by the compute instance type that you choose for your build:

Compute instance type	Memory (GB)	vCPU	Price per build minute ($)
build.general1.small	3	2	0.005
build.general1.medium	7	4	0.010
build.general1.large	15	8	0.020

Building a Java application using Maven

Maven provides benefits for our build process by employing standard conventions and practices to accelerate our software development cycle and help us to achieve a higher rate of success. We will now see the build of a Maven application.

Getting ready

To play around with the Java application and build it using Maven, we need JDK7/8 and Maven to be installed on our local machine.

Install Java and verify

In this section, we will be installing Java-8 and verify it:

```
[root@awsstar ~]# yum install java-1.8.0-openjdk -y
[root@awsstar ~]# java -version
openjdk version "1.8.0_141"
OpenJDK Runtime Environment (build 1.8.0_141-b16)
OpenJDK 64-Bit Server VM (build 25.141-b16, mixed mode)
```

Install Apache Maven and verify

In this section, we will be installing Maven 3.3.9 and after that, we will set the environment path:

```
[root@awsstar ~]# wget
http://www-eu.apache.org/dist/maven/maven-3/3.3.9/binaries/apache-maven-3.3
.9-bin.tar.gz
[root@awsstar ~]# tar -xf apache-maven-3.3.9-bin.tar.gz
[root@awsstar ~]# mv apache-maven-3.3.9 /opt
[root@awsstar ~]# vi /etc/bashrc

Add
export PATH=/opt/apache-maven-3.3.9/bin:$PATH
:wq (save and quit)

[root@awsstar ~]# source /etc/bashrc
[root@awsstar ~]# mvn -version
Apache Maven 3.3.9 (bb52d8502b132ec0a5a3f4c09453c07478323dc5;
2015-11-10T16:41:47+00:00)
Maven home: /opt/apache-maven-3.3.9
Java version: 1.8.0_141, vendor: Oracle Corporation
```

```
Java home: /usr/lib/jvm/java-1.8.0-openjdk-1.8.0.141-2.b16.el6_9.x86_64/jre
Default locale: en_US, platform encoding: ANSI_X3.4-1968
OS name: "linux", version: "4.10.0-28-generic", arch: "amd64", family:
"unix"
```

How to do it...

Now, we have both the JDK and Maven installed on our local machine. Let's create or initialize a web project in Java using Maven project template toolkit Archetype.

 The Archetype plugin will create the necessary folder structure that is required by the developers to quickly start their development.

```
[root@awsstar ~]# mvn archetype:generate -DgroupId=com.awsstar -
DartifactId=javawebapp -DarchetypeArtifactId=maven-archetype-webapp -
DinteractiveMode=false
```

The preceding command will take some time if you are running it for the first time.

The preceding executed command will give the output in the `javawebapp` folder, because if you take a look at the parameter passed, `-D artifactID` is `javawebapp`.

If we go in the `webapp` folder and try to view the directory and file structure, then it will be as follows:

```
[root@awsstar ~]# cd javawebapp/
[root@awsstar javawebapp]# tree
.
|-- pom.xml
`-- src
    `-- main
        |-- resources
        `-- webapp
            |-- WEB-INF
            |   `-- web.xml
            `-- index.jsp

5 directories, 3 files
```

TIP

If the `tree` command is not present in your system, then install it by typing the command, `# yum install tree`. Basically, this commands shows the directory and file structure.

Maven uses a standard directory format. With the help of the output of the preceding command, we can understand following key concepts:

Folder Structure	Description
`javawebapp`	This contains the `src` folder and `pom.xml`
`src/main/webapp`	This contains the `index.jsp` and `WEB-INF` folder
`src/main/webapp/WEB-INF`	This contains `web.xml`
`src/main/resources`	This contains images or properties files

Apart from the source code, we need `pom.xml` to get built by a Maven tool. **Project Object Model (POM)** is a necessary part of work in Maven. It is basically an XML file. This file resides in the root directory of the project. It contains various configuration details and information about the project which will be used by Maven to build the project.

When Maven executes, it will look for the `pom.xml` file in the present working directory. If it finds the `pom.xml` file, then Maven will read the file and get all the necessary configuration mentioned in it and executes it.

Some configurations that can be specified in `pom.xml` are mentioned as follows:

- Developers
- Build profiles
- Project dependencies
- Mailing list
- Project version
- Plugins
- Goals

Before jumping to create a `pom.xml` file, we should first decide the project group (`groupid`), name (`artifactid`), and its version because these attributes will help in identifying the project. So, we can see that the command that we used to initialize in the Java Maven project contains both the project group (`groupId`) and name (`artifactId`). If we don't mention the version, then by default it takes 1.0-SNAPSHOT. The following is the snippet of our `pom.xml`:

```
[root@awsstar javawebapp]# cat pom.xml
<project xmlns="http://maven.apache.org/POM/4.0.0"
xmlns:xsi="http://www.w3.org/2001/XMLSchema-instance"
   xsi:schemaLocation="http://maven.apache.org/POM/4.0.0
http://maven.apache.org/maven-v4_0_0.xsd">
  <modelVersion>4.0.0</modelVersion>
  <groupId>com.awsstar</groupId>                       -----> groupId
  <artifactId>javawebapp</artifactId>                  -----> artifactId
  <packaging>war</packaging>
  <version>1.0-SNAPSHOT</version>                      -----> version
  <name>javawebapp Maven Webapp</name>
  <url>http://maven.apache.org</url>
  <dependencies>
    <dependency>
      <groupId>junit</groupId>
      <artifactId>junit</artifactId>
      <version>3.8.1</version>
      <scope>test</scope>
    </dependency>
  </dependencies>
  <build>
    <finalName>javawebapp</finalName>
  </build>
</project>
```

Let's try to play with the source code. By default, we have an automatic generated `Hello World` application in `index.jsp`. We need to modify and rebuild the application, and then we will try to look at the output:

```
[root@awsstar javawebapp]# cat src/main/webapp/index.jsp
<html>
<body>
<h2>Hello World!</h2>
</body>
</html>
```

Now, edit the file and put the new source code:

```
[root@awsstar javawebapp]# vi src/main/webapp/index.jsp
```

Replace the new code. Once we have the new code or feature with us, let's try to build the application:

```
[root@awsstar javawebapp]# mvn install
[INFO] Scanning for projects...
[INFO]
[INFO] ------------------------------------------------------------------
----
[INFO] Building javawebapp Maven Webapp 1.0-SNAPSHOT
[INFO] ------------------------------------------------------------------
----
[INFO]
[INFO] --- maven-resources-plugin:2.6:resources (default-resources) @
javawebapp ---
[WARNING] Using platform encoding (ANSI_X3.4-1968 actually) to copy
filtered resources, i.e. build is platform dependent!
[INFO] Copying 0 resource
[INFO]
[INFO] --- maven-compiler-plugin:3.1:compile (default-compile) @ javawebapp
---
[INFO] No sources to compile
[INFO]
-------
CONTENTS SKIPPED
-------
[INFO] Webapp assembled in [18 msecs]
[INFO] Building war: /root/javawebapp/target/javawebapp.war    ---> Build
[INFO] Installing /root/javawebapp/target/javawebapp.war to
/root/.m2/repository/com/awsstar/javawebapp/1.0-SNAPSHOT/javawebapp-1.0-
SNAPSHOT.war
[INFO] Installing /root/javawebapp/pom.xml to
/root/.m2/repository/com/awsstar/javawebapp/1.0-SNAPSHOT/javawebapp-1.0-
SNAPSHOT.pom
[INFO] ------------------------------------------------------------------
----
[INFO] BUILD SUCCESS
[INFO] ------------------------------------------------------------------
----
[INFO] Total time: 9.651 s
[INFO] Finished at: 2017-08-14T17:47:15+00:00
[INFO] Final Memory: 15M/295M
[INFO] ------------------------------------------------------------------
----
```

We can see the output such as Build Success and we also get the path of the Build `.war` file. So the application was a web application, as mentioned in `pom.xml` to generate the `.war` file; it did the same and created a .war file in new `target` folder:

```
[root@awsstar javawebapp]# ls
pom.xml src target                            ------> New target folder
[root@awsstar javawebapp]# cd target/
[root@awsstar target]# ls
classes javawebapp javawebapp.war maven-archiver
```

Now, copy `javawebapp.war` created in a target folder to your webserver webapp directory and restart the webserver. Post that, try to access it:

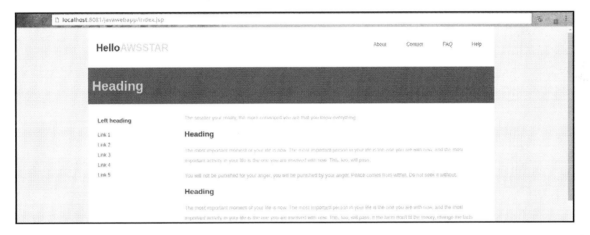

So, basically, a Java web application initialized with Maven generally have a pom.xml for build specification and it generates a war (web archive file) in a target folder after the build happened with the `mvn` command.

Building a NodeJS application using yarn

NodeJS, built on Google Chrome's JavaScript engine, is a server-side platform developed by Ryan Dahl in 2009. It is widely used by lots of big enterprises due to its features. So, we will see how we can build the NodeJS application using yarn.

Getting ready

To play around with the NodeJS application and build it using yarn, we need to install NodeJS and a yarn package on our development machine.

Install NodeJS and verify

```
[root@awsstar ~]# curl --silent --location
https://rpm.nodesource.com/setup_6.x | sudo bash -
[root@awsstar ~]# yum install -y nodejs gcc-c++ make
[root@awsstar ~]# node --version
v6.11.2
```

Install Yarn and verify

```
[root@awsstar ~]# wget https://dl.yarnpkg.com/rpm/yarn.repo -O
/etc/yum.repos.d/yarn.repo
[root@awsstar ~]# yum install yarn
[root@awsstar ~]# yarn --version
0.27.5
```

Now, we have both the package NodeJS and yarn installed on our development machine; so let's create a project using yarn, where we can start our application development.

How to do it...

We can initiate the project by hitting yarn init:

```
[root@awsstar ~]# mkdir example-node-server
[root@awsstar ~]# cd example-node-server
[root@awsstar ~]# yarn init
yarn init v0.27.5
question name (example-node-server): example-node-server
question version (1.0.0):
question description: sample nodejs webapp
question entry point (index.js): lib/index.js
question repository url:
question author: Nikit Swaraj
question license (MIT): MIT
success Saved package.json
Done in 53.06s.
```

In the preceding output of execution of the `yarn init` command, we get some parameter where we have to fill some input from our end. After initiating the project, we will get a file called `package.json`.

`package.json` is a file where we can fill the dependency's name and build step or set some script to get executed. At this moment, we will see the parameter values, which we entered while initiating the project:

```
[root@awsstar example-node-server]# ls
package.json
[root@awsstar example-node-server]# cat package.json
{
 "name": "example-node-server",
 "version": "1.0.0",
 "description": "sample nodejs webapp",
 "main": "lib/index.js",
 "author": "Nikit Swaraj",
 "license": "MIT"
}
```

Let's write some basic code:

```
[root@awsstar example-node-server]# mkdir lib && cd lib
[root@awsstar example-node-server]# vi index.js

import http from 'http';
http.createServer((req, res) => {
 res.writeHead(200, {'Content-Type': 'text/plain'});
 res.end('Hello AWSSTAR\n');
}).listen(1337, '127.0.0.1');
console.log('Server running at http://127.0.0.1:1337/');

:wq (save and quite)
```

Write one small test case, which will check `200 status OK`:

```
[root@awsstar example-node-server]# mkdir test && cd test
[root@awsstar example-node-server]# vi index.js

import http from 'http';
import assert from 'assert';
import '../lib/index.js';
describe('Example Node Server', () => {
 it('should return 200', done => {
 http.get('http://127.0.0.1:1337', res => {
 assert.equal(200, res.statusCode);
 done();
```

```
});
});
});

:wq (save and quit)
```

We will use some commands to build the application, which are dependencies. So, we have to tweak the `package.json` file by mentioning the dependencies and required scripts:

```
[root@awsstar example-node-server]# vi package.json
{
  "name": "example-node-server",
  "version": "1.0.0",
  "description": "sample nodejs webapp",
  "main": "lib/index.js",
  "scripts": {
  "start": "nodemon lib/index.js --exec babel-node --presets
es2015,stage-2",
  "build": "babel lib -d dist",
  "serve": "node dist/index.js",
  "test": "mocha --compilers js:babel-register"
  },
  "author": "Nikit Swaraj",
  "license": "MIT",
  "devDependencies": {
  "babel-cli": "^6.24.1",
  "babel-preset-es2015": "^6.24.1",
  "babel-preset-stage-2": "^6.24.1",
  "babel-register": "^6.11.6",
  "mocha": "^3.0.1",
  "nodemon": "^1.11.0"
  }
}
```

Once we fill all the dependencies and necessary scripts, its time to install the dependencies, build the application, run it, and test it.

Installing dependencies

```
[root@awsstar example-node-server]# yarn install
yarn install v0.27.5
info No lockfile found.
[1/4] Resolving packages...
[2/4] Fetching packages...
warning fsevents@1.1.2: The platform "linux" is incompatible with this
module.
info "fsevents@1.1.2" is an optional dependency and failed compatibility
```

```
check. Excluding it from installation.
[3/4] Linking dependencies...
[4/4] Building fresh packages...
success Saved lockfile.
Done in 8.18s.
```

Build the application by hitting `yarn run build`, once the build happens, we get the `dist` folder:

```
[root@awsstar example-node-server]# yarn run build
yarn run v0.27.5
$ babel lib -d dist
lib/index.js -> dist/index.js
Done in 0.43s.
[root@awsstar example-node-server]# ls
dist lib node_modules package.json test yarn.lock
[root@awsstar example-node-server]# ls dist
index.js
```

It's time to run the server and access the application:

```
[root@awsstar example-node-server]# yarn serve
yarn serve v0.27.5
$ node dist/index.js
Server running at http://127.0.0.1:1337/
```

Check the test case by hitting `yarn test`:

```
[root@awsstar example-node-server]# yarn test
Server running at http://127.0.0.1:1337/
Example Node Server
  ✓ should return 200
1 passing (43ms)
```

We can also use npm instead of yarn for building the NodeJS application. In the next example, I have used npm to build the NodeJS application using CodeBuild.

How it works...

We saw that we can build the application manually, and we need an environment compatible for the build to take place, we also get the artifact. Here, the artifact is the .war file, in case of the Maven project, and the dist folder, in case of the NodeJS application. Later, we have to deploy that .war file or dist folder in the production environment and restart the servers to access the application.

We have a lot of tools that provide the build environment, such as Jenkins, CircleCI, and AWS CodeBuild.

Building a Maven application using AWS CodeBuild console

In the previous section, we saw the brief steps of flow of work in CodeBuild. Now, let's try to build some real application with CodeBuild.

Getting ready

Before proceeding, make sure you clone the application from GitHub (https://github.com/awsstar/CB-Maven-App-UI.git) and create a new CodeCommit repository in your account and migrate the GitHub code to your CodeCommit repository.

The following are the details that we will be going to use in CodeBuild:

- Source repository: AWS CodeCommit
    - Repository name: CB-MAVEN-Book
- Build environment: AWS CodeBuild
    - Environment image: Image managed by AWS CodeBuild
    - OS: Ubuntu (only OS provided by CodeBuild)
    - Runtime: Java

- Version: aws/codebuild/java:openjdk-8
- Build specification: Insert build commands
- Build command: `mvn install`
- Artifacts: AWS S3
    - Artifacts type: **Amazon S3**
    - Artifacts name: `Books`
    - BucketName: `awsstar-s3`
    - Output files: `books.war`

How it works...

1. Open the AWS console and go to the AWS CodeBuild service. You will get the CodeBuild console. Click on **Get started**:

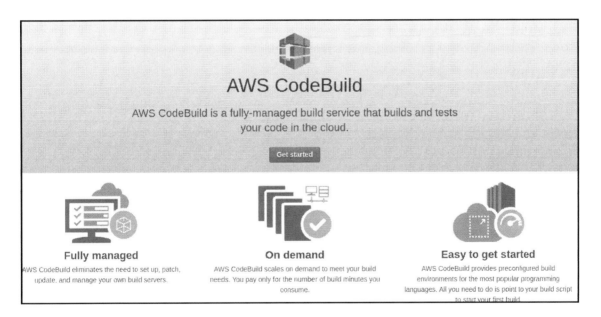

2. You will get a page where you have to fill all the details that I mentioned earlier. The page will look as follows:

3. We will mention the Project name as CB-Build-Book in the **Configure your project** section:

4. In the **Source** section, choose **AWS CodeCommit** as **Source provider** and select the **Repository** name where you have migrated the book application. In my case, the AWS CodeCommit repository name, where the book application code resides, is **CB-MAVEN-Book**:

5. In the **Environment** section, **Environment image** will be **Use an image managed by AWS CodeBuild**. The **Operating System** will be **Ubuntu**, **Runtime** will be **Java**, **Version** will be **aws/codebuild/java:openjdk8**, **Build specification** will be **Insert build commands** and **Build command** will be mvn install:

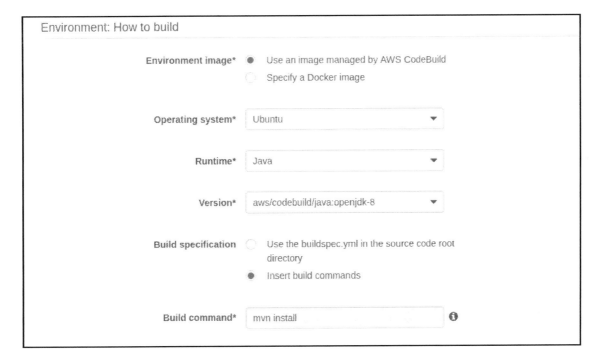

6. Now in the **Artifacts** section, we have to use AWS S3 to store the build output. So, **Artifact type** will be **Amazon S3**. The **Artifacts name** will be **book, Bucket name** where you want to put the artifact; in my case, its **awsstar-s3** and the **Output files** field will contain the file name which will be the build output, in my case, it's **target/books.war** (you should know in what way the build output will come):

7. Now, **Service role** is the most important section over here, which allows AWS Codebuild to access another AWS resources such as CodeCommit and S3. In the initial stage, you can create a new service role. Else, you can create a new IAM Role, which will have the following policy document:

```
{
"Version": "2012-10-17",
"Statement": [
{
"Sid": "CloudWatchLogsPolicy",
"Effect": "Allow",
"Action": [
"logs:CreateLogGroup",
"logs:CreateLogStream",
"logs:PutLogEvents"
],
"Resource": [
"*"
]
},
{
"Sid": "CodeCommitPolicy",
"Effect": "Allow",
"Action": [
```

```
"codecommit:GitPull"
],
"Resource": [
"*"
]
},
{
"Sid": "S3GetObjectPolicy",
"Effect": "Allow",
"Action": [
"s3:GetObject",
"s3:GetObjectVersion"
],
"Resource": [
"*"
]
},
{
"Sid": "S3PutObjectPolicy",
"Effect": "Allow",
"Action": [
"s3:PutObject"
],
"Resource": [
"*"
]
}
]
}
```

8. Once we create the policy, we need to create the IAM role, in which AWS Service role will be AWS CodeBuild and we will attach the newly created policy with the IAM role. Post that, we have to select a service role in the AWS CodeBuild **Service Role** section:

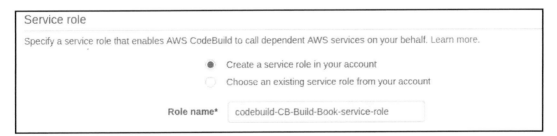

9. In the **Advanced** section, we can tweak the compute settings and pass the environment variables, but at this moment, it is not required.
10. Finally, we click on **Continue** and review the configuration:

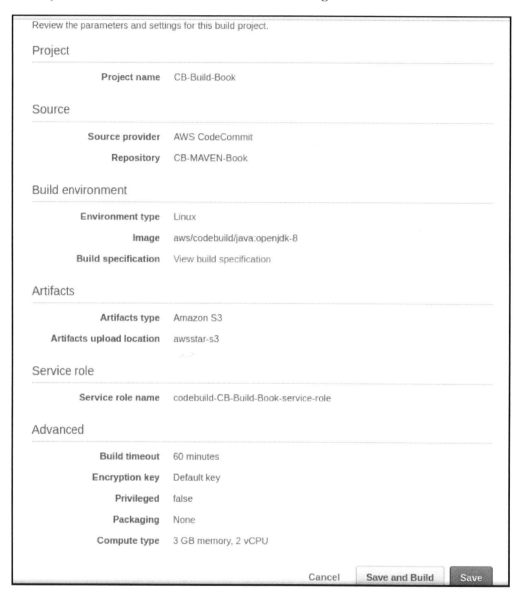

Review the parameters and settings for this build project.

Project

Project name	CB-Build-Book

Source

Source provider	AWS CodeCommit
Repository	CB-MAVEN-Book

Build environment

Environment type	Linux
Image	aws/codebuild/java:openjdk-8
Build specification	View build specification

Artifacts

Artifacts type	Amazon S3
Artifacts upload location	awsstar-s3

Service role

Service role name	codebuild-CB-Build-Book-service-role

Advanced

Build timeout	60 minutes
Encryption key	Default key
Privileged	false
Packaging	None
Compute type	3 GB memory, 2 vCPU

Cancel   Save and Build   Save

11. Once you are done reviewing, then click on **Save and Build**. We will be asked which branch we want to build:

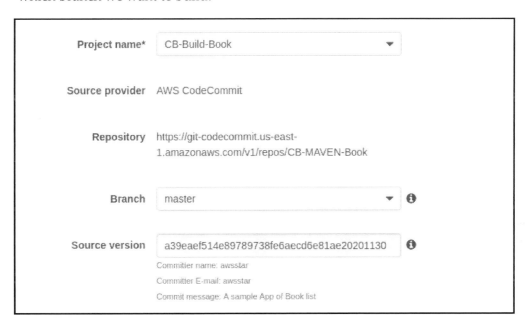

12. Once you select the **master**, the source version will show up automatically. Then, click on **>Start Build.** We will see that the build process will start:

13. We will see different phases of Build as well:

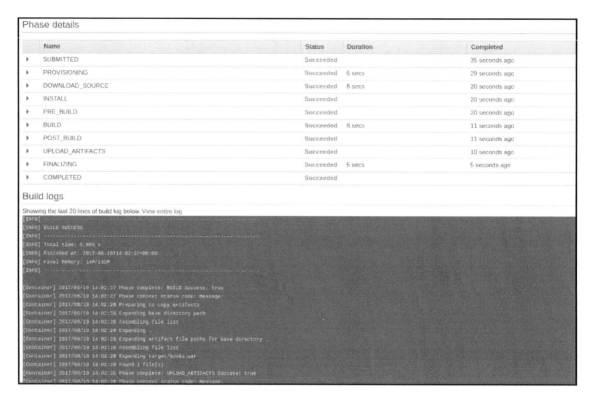

14. In **Build details** section, we can see **Output artifacts.** When we click on the **Build artifacts**, we will be redirected to the S3 bucket, where our artifact will reside after the successful build:

15. The following diagram shows the artifact in the S3 bucket:

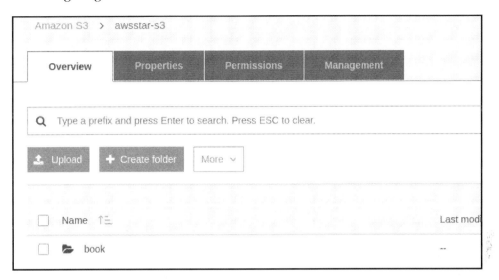

16. When you click on **book**, you will get a folder called `target`. Click on the `target` folder to get the `books.war` file:

17. Now, we can download `books.war` into the server or machine, and copy `books.war` to your webserver `webapp` directory and restart the webserver and access it from the web browser:

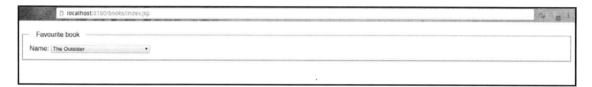

Building a sample NodeJS application using AWS CodeBuild via Buildspec.yml

In the previous recipe, we saw how to build the application using AWS CodeBuild. However, in that case, we used the build commands (`mvn install`) in the console only, as shown in the following image:

When it comes to the complex scenario, it means we need more than one build commands and need to perform some additional operations in the build environment. For this, we use the `buildspec.yml` file.

Buildspec.yml

A **build spec** is a collection of build commands and related settings; in the YAML format, AWS CodeBuild is used to run a build. This file needs to be checked in with the `root` folder of the application code. This file will possess Build steps as well as other things. So, let's see the syntax of `buildspec.yml` file.

Syntax

Build specs must be expressed in the YAML format:

```yaml
version: 0.2
env:
    variables:
        key: "value"
        key: "value"

phases:
    install:
        commands:
                - command
                - command
    pre_build:
        commands:
                - command
                - command
    build:
        commands:
                - command
                - command
    post_build:
        commands:
                - command
                - command
artifacts:
    files:
        - location
        - location
    discard-paths: yes
    base-directory: location
```

Now, let's see what each term means to CodeBuild.

- `version`: This represents the build spec version. AWS recommends the usage of `0.2`.
- `env` *:* This represents the information of custom variables that we can assign.
  - `variables`*:* This represents the mapping of key and value, where it represents a custom environment variable, for example:

    ```
    env:
        variables:
            JAVA_HOME: "/opt/java-7-openjdk-amd64"
    ```

- `phases`: It contains commands that AWS CodeBuild will run during each phase of the build.
  - `install`: This represents the commands that AWS CodeBuild will run during installation. It is recommended to use the install phase only for installing packages in the build environment, for example:

    ```
    phases:
        install:
            commands:
                    - apt-get update -y
                    - apt-get install -y maven
    ```

  - `pre_build`: This represents the commands that AWS CodeBuild will run before the build.
  - `build`: This contains the commands that AWS CodeBuild will run during the build. For example:

    ```
    build:
        commands:
                - echo Build started on `date`
                - mvn install
    ```

  - `post_build`: This contains the commands that AWS CodeBuild will run after the build. For example, you might use Maven to package the build artifacts into a JAR or WAR file.

- `artifacts`: This represents the information about where AWS CodeBuild can find the build output and how AWS CodeBuild will prepare it so that it can be uploaded to the Amazon S3 output bucket.

That was all about how we can write the buildspec.yml file according to our need. Now, let's write a buildspec.yml file for our NodeJS application. This time, we are using the npm tool to build the application.

 Before proceeding, make sure you clone the code from GitHub (`https://github.com/awsstar/CB-NodeJS-BS.git`) and create a new repository in CodeCommit and migrate the GitHub code to the newly created CodeCommit repository.

Let's take a look at the `BuildSpec.yml` file that we will be checking in with the application code:

```
version: 0.2
phases:
  pre_build:
    commands:
       - npm install
  build:
    commands:
       - npm run build
  post_build:
    commands:
       - echo Build completed on `date`
artifacts:
  files:
     - '**/*'
```

Getting ready

Now, we will use these details to set up the CodeBuild configuration:

- Source repository: AWS CodeCommit
  - Repository name: CB-NODEJS-Site
- Build Environment: AWS CodeBuild
  - Environment image: Image Managed by AWS CodeBuild
  - OS: Ubuntu
  - Runtime: NodeJS
  - version: aws/codebuild/nodejs:4.3.2
  - Build specification: Use the buildspec.yml in the source code root directory

- Artifacts: AWS S3
    - Artifacts type: Amazon S3
    - Artifacts Name: CB-Nodejs-BS
    - BucketName: awsstar-s3
    - Output files: **/* (means all the files and folder after the build will be considered as the build output)

How to do it...

1. Go to the AWS Console and click on the AWS CodeBuild Service. After that, click on **Create project.**
2. We will get a page where we have to fill all the details that I have mentioned in the *Getting ready* section in this recipe. The page will look like as follows:

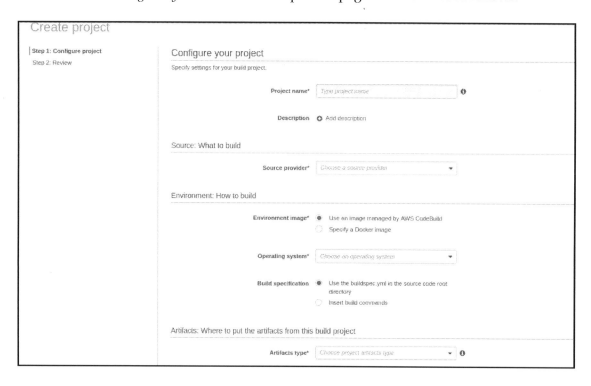

3. We will mention the **Project name** as **CB-NodeJS-BS** in the **Configure your project** section:

4. In the **Source** section, choose **AWS CodeCommit** as **Source provider**. Select the repository name where you migrated the book application. In my case, the AWS CodeCommit repository name where the book application code resides is **CB-NODEJS-Site**:

5. In the **Environment** section, **Environment image** will be **Image managed by AWS CodeBuild**. The OS will be **Ubuntu**, **Runtime** will be **Node.js**, **Version** will be **aws/codebuild/nodejs:4.3.2**, **Build specification** will be **Use the buildspec.yml in the source code root directory**:

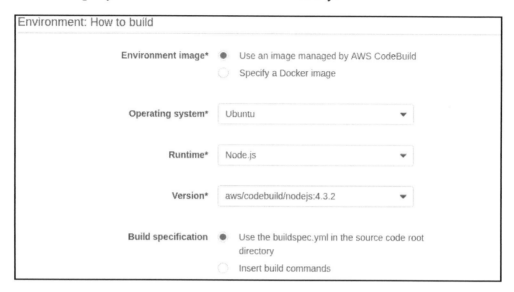

6. Now in the **Artifact** section, we use AWS S3 to store the build output. So, **Artifact type** will be **Amazon S3**. The **Artifacts name** will be Nodejs-bs; **Bucket name** is where you put the artifact. In my case, its **awsstar-s3**:

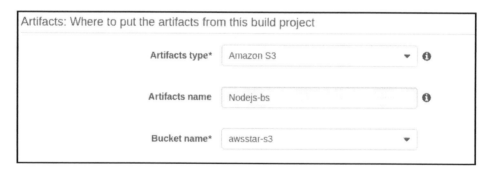

7. Now choose any existing service role, which will allow AWS CodeBuild to access any other AWS resources:

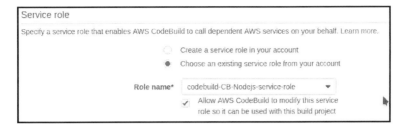

8. In advance, we can tweak the compute settings and pass the environment variables; but at this moment, it is not required.

9. Finally, we click on **Continue** and review the configuration:

10. Once you are done reviewing, then click on **Save and Build**. We will be asked which branch we want to build. In the advanced options, we will be asked regarding the Artifact Package, which we will put as zip. Then, click on **start build:**

11. We will see that the build process has been started and succeeded in a minute:

Build	
Build ARN	arn:aws:codebuild:us-east-1:160384169139:build/CB-NodeJS-BS:0452e204-957c-47bb-b1e0-eb 125ddab515
Build project	CB-NodeJS-BS
Source provider	AWS CodeCommit
Repository	https://git-codecommit.us-east-1.amazonaws.com/v1/repos/CB-NODEJS-Site
Start time	1 minute ago
End time	3 seconds ago
Status	Succeeded

12. We will see different phases of the build as well:

	Name	Status	Duration	Completed
▶	SUBMITTED	Succeeded		1 minute ago
▶	PROVISIONING	Succeeded	32 secs	38 seconds ago
▶	DOWNLOAD_SOURCE	Succeeded	10 secs	27 seconds ago
▶	INSTALL	Succeeded		27 seconds ago
▶	PRE_BUILD	Succeeded	15 secs	12 seconds ago
▶	BUILD	Succeeded	1 sec	10 seconds ago
▶	POST_BUILD	Succeeded		10 seconds ago
▶	UPLOAD_ARTIFACTS	Succeeded	1 sec	9 seconds ago
▶	FINALIZING	Succeeded	5 secs	3 seconds ago
▶	COMPLETED	Succeeded		

Build logs

Showing the last 20 lines of build log below. View entire log

```
[90mcompiled[0m static/css/index.css

[Container] 2017/08/19 21:50:59 Phase complete: BUILD Success: true
[Container] 2017/08/19 21:50:59 Phase context status code: Message:
[Container] 2017/08/19 21:50:59 Entering phase POST_BUILD
[Container] 2017/08/19 21:50:59 Running command echo Build completed on `date`
Build completed on Sat Aug 19 21:50:59 UTC 2017

[Container] 2017/08/19 21:50:59 Phase complete: POST_BUILD Success: true
[Container] 2017/08/19 21:50:59 Phase context status code: Message:
[Container] 2017/08/19 21:50:59 Preparing to copy artifacts
[Container] 2017/08/19 21:50:59 Expanding base directory path
[Container] 2017/08/19 21:50:59 Assembling file list
[Container] 2017/08/19 21:50:59 Expanding .
[Container] 2017/08/19 21:50:59 Expanding artifact file paths for base directory .
[Container] 2017/08/19 21:50:59 Assembling file list
[Container] 2017/08/19 21:50:59 Expanding **/*
[Container] 2017/08/19 21:50:59 Found 2466 file(s)
[Container] 2017/08/19 21:51:00 Phase complete: UPLOAD_ARTIFACTS Success: true
```

13. In the **Build details** section, we can see the output artifact; when we click on **Build artifacts**, we will be redirected to the S3 bucket where our artifact will reside after the successful build:

14. The following screenshot shows the artifact in the S3 bucket:

15. Now, download the zip file and unzip it to your production machine and place it on the proper path where webserver can read it. After that, restart the webserver and try to access the page:

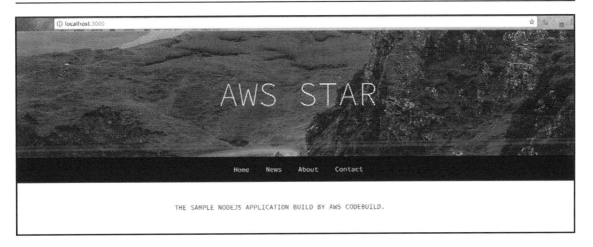

In both the preceding examples, we saw how we can work with AWS CodeBuild either using build commands in the console or using the buildspec.yml file.

3

Deploying Application using CodeDeploy & CodePipeline

In this chapter, the following recipes will be covered:

- The deployment strategy in AWS CodeDeploy
- Writing an application-specific file
- Deploying a static application in an EC2 instance from the S3 bucket using AWS CodeDeploy
- Introducing AWS CodePipeline and its working
- Continuous deployment of static application to AWS S3 using AWS CodePipeline

Introduction

Deployment is the activity that will make your software available, that is, ready for end customer or market. So basically when we have tested the code, the post building process, we will have the build artifacts, which we need to deploy to the production machine so that the latest feature should be available for the end users to use.

Deployment can be done manually as well as automatically. Sometimes, some enterprises keep this process manual, but most of the companies are automating it. Let's list out the benefits of automated deployment:

- **Less error prone and more repeatable**: Manual deployments are error-prone because it involves human interference. It's obvious that sometime deployment engineers forget to perform important steps in a release accidentally, which leads to incorrect versions of software, or broken software will get deployed, which of course is not wanted. When it comes to automated deployment, it doesn't suffer from variability; once the configuration and process is set, it will be the same in every deployment.

- **Anyone can deploy:** In a manual or partial-automated deployment, specific expertise of build and release are required. The deployment will be the responsibility of specific people in an organization. But when it comes to the automated deployment process, the knowledge of releasing software is captured in the system, not in an individual's brain.

- **Deploying to another environment is not a problem anymore:** Automated deployments are configurable and give lots of flexibility (depending on the tool). Although the base release process is permanent, the target environments and machines can be changed easily, so the overhead of deploying to that additional target is negligible.

There are a couple of very famous tools around the world, which help the enterprise to automate their deployments process. For example, Jenkins, AWS CodeDeploy, CircleCi, and so on. In this chapter, we will be looking at AWS CodeDeploy.

AWS CodeDeploy is the deployment service provided by AWS that automates the deployment of the application to Amazon EC2 instance, Elastic Beanstalk, and on-premise instances. It provides the facility to deploy unlimited variants of application content such as code, configuration, scripts, executables, multimedia, and much more. CodeDeploy can deploy application files stored in Amazon S3 buckets, GitHub repositories, or BitBucket repositories.

AWS CodeDeploy makes it easier to rapidly release new features and helps in avoiding downtime during application deployment. It also handles the complexity of updating applications, without many of the risks associated, which can occur due to manual deployment.

Benefits of AWS CodeDeploy

AWS CodeDeploy provides lots of benefits. Some of them are listed as follows:

- **Automated deployments**: AWS CodeDeploy automates the deployment of your application across all environments, such as development, test, and production. It scales your infrastructure in such a way that you can deploy to one instance or hundreds of instances.
- **Decrease downtime**: AWS CodeDeploy increases application availability. It has all the inbuilt configuration that needs to be carried out during the deployment phase. For example, during the blue-green deployment, once the deployment is done, traffic rerouting to the instances will be taken by AWS CodeDeploy only.
- **Stop and roll back**: You can stop and rollback deployments if there are any errors.

Components of AWS CodeDeploy

Before deep diving with CodeDeploy, first let's see the terminologies that are used in the reference of CodeDeploy.

- **Application:** It represent the application name that needs to get deployed. This name also ensures the correct combination of the deployment group, configuration, and revision.
- **Deployment configuration**: It consists of a set of deployment rules and some condition of deployment success and failure used by CodeDeploy at the time of deployment.
- **Deployment group**: It represents the individual tagged instances or an instance in auto scaling groups where the deployment needs to be done.
- **Deployment type**: The deployment strategy used to make the latest application available on instances or auto scaling after the deployment. AWS CodeDeploy provides two different deployment types:
  - In-place deployment
  - Blue-green deployment

The deployment type is discussed in details in the next section of this chapter.

- **IAM instance profile**: IAM instance profile is basically an IAM role that needs to get attached with Amazon EC2 instances. This role should have the permission to access the S3 bucket or GitHub, where the latest revision of the application is stored.

- **Revision**: It is basically an archive file, which contains source code, deployment scripts, and the `AppSpec.yml` file. It is stored in the S3 bucket or GitHub repository.
- **Service role**: It's an IAM role, which provides permission to an AWS service to access AWS resources. The details of which AWS resources needs to get accessed by the AWS service should be mentioned in policy that is attached. In case of AWS CodeDeploy, a service role generally has the following permissions:
  - Reading the tags of instances and auto scaling groups to identify the instances in which an application can get deployed.
  - Performing operations on instances, auto scaling groups, and ELB.
  - Accessing SNS for publishing information and CloudWatch for alarm monitoring.
- **Target revision:** This is basically the latest application code, which is tagged for the next deployment. It is stored in either the S3 or GitHub repository.

 Make sure to install the AWS CodeDeploy agent on every instance of the deployment group that will be used by AWS CodeDeploy for the deployment purpose.

In this chapter, we will be seeing the deployment of build artifact in to the production server using AWS CodeDeploy. We will discuss some deployment strategies that will help in deploying the build artifacts without hurdles and with less or no downtime. The application specification file is also discussed. Post that, we will see how AWS CodePipeline will help in automating the pipeline with AWS resources such as AWS S3 and AWS CodeDeploy. Specifically, we will see the following points:

- Working with the AWS CodeDeploy deployment types
- Using CodeDeploy deployment types and writing AppSpec.yml
- Deploying one static application in an EC2 instance from the S3 bucket
- Configuring CodePipeline with CodeDeploy
- Creating a CI/CD pipeline with AWS CodeDeploy

The Deployment strategy in AWS CodeDeploy

AWS CodeDeploy provides two deployment types, which are discussed in the following sections.

In-place deployment

In this deployment type, the running application on each instance in the deployment group needs to stop. Post that, the latest application gets installed on the instances and then start the application. Once the application get started, it need to get validated. ELB can be used to deregistered each instance during its deployment and then restored to service after the deployment is complete.

The following is the diagram and workflow of a typical AWS CodeDeploy in-place deployment type:

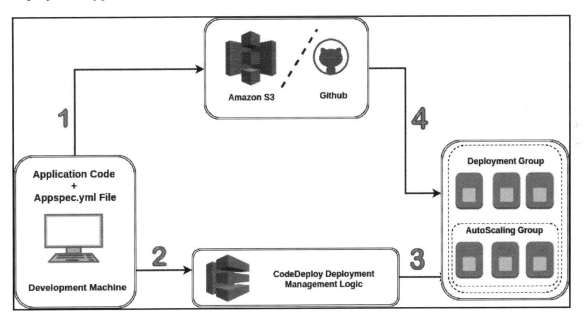

Blue-green deployment

Blue-green deployment is the deployment strategy or a pattern where we can reduce the downtime by having two production environments. It provides near zero-downtime rollback capabilities. The basic idea of blue-green deployment is to shift the traffic from the current environment to another environment. Both the environments will be identical and run same application, but of different versions.

How to do it...

Here's the workflow for in-place deployment:

1. First of all, your application code should be ready with the `AppSpec.yml` file inside the root directory of the application. Then, bundle the application code and `AppSpec.yml` file into an archive file and push it to the AWS S3 bucket or GitHub. This file is known as revision.

2. Second, we have to provide information on deployment-related components in AWS CodeDeploy such as from which s3 bucket or GitHub repository, revisions should get pulled and in which set of instance or auto scaling group those revision should get deployed.

3. Now, at this stage, the AWS CodeDeploy agent is installed on each instance polls AWS CodeDeploy to check what and when to pull from the AWS S3 bucket or GitHub repo.

4. Once the revision from the S3 bucket of GitHub gets pulled by the instances, using the `AppSpec.yml` file, the content will get deployed or installed into the correct location. If there will be a requirement of restarting the server, then also it will be done, but we have to mention that in the `AppSpec.yml` file.

Here's the workflow for blue-green deployment:

1. The **blue environment** is the one, which runs the current application version and serves production traffic; the **green environment** is the one which runs the same application with the latest version. Once the latest application of green environment is ready and tested, then the production traffic will be switched from blue to green.

2. This is the replacement process while deployment with near zero downtime. If any issue is found in the live environment, we can roll back by reverting traffic to the previous environment.

3. So in case of CodeDeploy, let's say there is already one application running live in an Autoscaling group, then CodeDeploy will automatically provision similar Auto Scaling group and deploy the latest version of the application on that Auto Scaling environment. Select the load balancer that is currently routing traffic to your original environment. After a blue-green deployment is complete, the load balancer you select will route all traffic to the replacement environment.

The following is the diagram that gives a detailed understanding of the blue-green deployment:

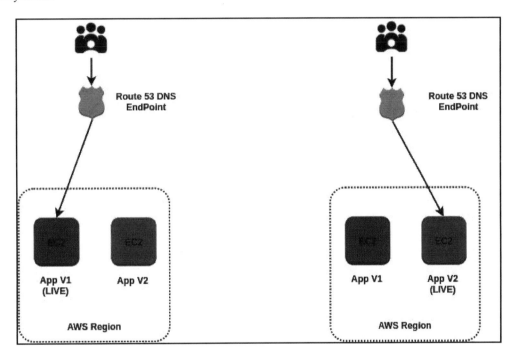

In the preceding diagram, we can see that initially, the live application was running in the blue environment, which has App v1; later, it got switched to green, which is running the latest version of the application App v2.

With AWS CodeDeploy, we will have a couple of additional benefits while implementing blue-green.

1. While creating the helper or parallel environment, we can start with a low-value resource that means low instance type. Once it is ready for production purpose, we can increase the instance type to handle the production traffic.
2. Traffic switching will be very easy using either Route 53 or ELB.
3. The best part is that you can automate the setting up on-demand infrastructure using AWS resources and use it efficiently.

Writing an application-specific file

The application file is a YAML, which eliminated the manual intervention of human, after deploying the artifact to the production machine. The AppSpec file will only work with AWS CodeDeploy. Let's try to understand what kind of manual operation done by human is eliminated by the `AppSpec.yml` file.

Let's say we have a `build` folder ready to deploy to the production server. While deploying this package or archive, let's say some modification is required in the production server such as relocation of some file, restarting some services, and running some scripts. These things are mentioned in the `AppSpec.yml` file. That's why the `AppSpec.yml` file is checked in within the root directory of the application, so once it gets deployed to production server along with the application code, AWS CodeDeploy will start running the `AppSpec.yml` file. The deployment steps are mentioned in the `AppSpec.yml` file, such as copying some file from one location to another or restarting some services.

How to do it...

The high-level structure of the `AppSpec.yml` file is as follows:

```
version: 0.0
os: operating-system-name
files:
  source-destination-files-mappings
permissions:
  permissions-specifications
hooks:
  deployment-lifecycle-event-mappings
```

Let's look into all the directives in detail:

- `version`: This directive specifies the version of the AppSpec file, which is currently 0.0. This value is not supposed to change by any means because it is reserved by CodeDeploy for future use.
- `os`: By the name itself, we can understand that it refers to the OS of the instance where it will get deployed. It has two possible values: Linux (Amazon Linux, Ubuntu Server, or RHEL) or Windows Server.
- `files`: This directive is basically for the files, which need to copy from the source code directory and are placed somewhere on the instance. So, by default, it has two parameters, that is, `source` and `destination`, for example:

```
files:
 - source: configuration/config.txt
   destination: /var/Config
```

In this example, the following operation will be performed during the `install` event:

- `configuration/config.txt` : This is placed in the source code directory and will be copied to the `/var/Config/config.txt` path on the instance.
- `permissions`: This directive gives permission to the file which get copied to the instance. The following is an example of giving permission to an object:

```
- object: /tmp/webapp/src
  group: wheel
  mode: 564
  type:
    - directory
```

For the folder `/tmp/webapp/src`, group = wheel and mode = 564 (dr-xrw-r--), so the permission of that folder will be:

```
dr-xrw-r-- root wheel src
```

- `hooks`: This directive contains the mapping of the deployment life cycle event with respective scripts. If any event hook is not present, that means there is no script or operation for execution for that event. This section is used only when you need to run any script on the instances. The following is the list of life cycle event hooks:

  - `ApplicationStop`: An AppSpec file does not exist on an instance before you deploy to it. For this reason, the `ApplicationStop` hook will not run the first time you deploy to the instance. You can use the `ApplicationStop` hook the second time you deploy to an instance.

 DownloadBundle is the second lifecycle event in which the AWS CodeDeploy agent pulls the application revision to the temporary location (`/opt/codedeploy-agent/deployment-root/deployment-group-id/deployment-id/`). This event can't be mapped with any script, because it is reserved for the AWS CodeDeploy.

- `BeforeInstall`: This deployment life cycle event can be used for preinstalling tasks, such as decrypting files and creating a backup of the current version.
- `Install`: During this life cycle event, the CodeDeploy agent copies the revision files from the temporary location to the final destination folder. This event can't be used to run scripts.
- `AfterInstall`: This life cycle event can be mapped to a script, which will perform tasks such as configuring your application or changing file permissions.
- `ApplicationStart`: This life cycle event is used to restart services that were stopped during `ApplicationStop`.
- `ValidateService`: This life cycle event is used to verify that the deployment was completed successfully.

By seeing the preceding syntax, we can write one sample `AppSpec.yml` as follows:

```
version: 0.0
os: linux
files:
  - source: /
    destination: /srv/mynodeapp
hooks:
  ApplicationStop:
    - location: scripts/stopnode.sh
      timeout: 300
      runas: root
  ApplicationStart:
```

```
    - location: scripts/start_nodeserver.sh
      timeout: 300
      runas: root
  ValidateService:
    - location: scripts/MonitorService.sh
      timeout: 3600
      runas: root
```

Deploying a static application in an EC2 instance from the S3 Bucket using AWS CodeDeploy

We saw a lot of theoretical stuff related to AWS CodeDeploy. Now with the help of those theories and concepts, we will try to deploy a sample NodeJS application on an EC2 machine using AWS CodeDeploy. The revision means source code build with AppSpec.yml file will be zipped and placed in the S3 bucket.

Getting ready

Before moving forward, one should know the following things first:

1. Creating an IAM role and attaching permission to that role.
2. Creating an EC2 instance in a public subnet and attaching the role in it.
3. Creating the S3 bucket and uploading the file in that.

If you know these things, then you can continue.

 Refer to this link to know more about the IAM role, http://docs.aws. amazon.com/IAM/latest/UserGuide/id_roles.html.

How to do it...

1. First of all, we have to create an IAM role for the EC2 instance and attach AWS CodeDeploy and AWS S3 access. We have named the role **CodeDeploy-Instance-Profile:**

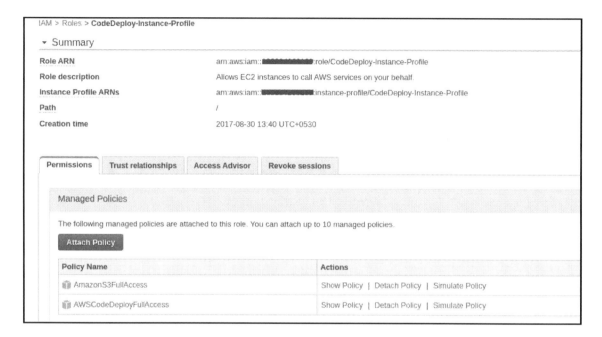

2. Once the role gets created, we have to launch an EC2 instance in the public subnet with the IAM role. So, we named the EC2 instance **AWS-CodeDeploy-Instance:**

3. Now, we have to install the CodeDeploy agent on the servers and dependencies of the application that is NodeJS:

```
# yum update
# yum install ruby
# yum install wget
# wget https://BUCKET-NAME.s3.amazonaws.com/latest/install
# chmod +x install
# ./install auto
# service codedeploy-agent start
# yum install nodejs
```

Now here BUCKET-NAME needs to replaced according to the following table:

Region name	BUCKET-NAME replacement	Region identifier
US East (Ohio)	aws-codedeploy-us-east-2	us-east-2
US East (N. Virginia)	aws-codedeploy-us-east-1	us-east-1
US West (N. California)	aws-codedeploy-us-west-1	us-west-1
US West (Oregon)	aws-codedeploy-us-west-2	us-west-2
Canada (Central)	aws-codedeploy-ca-central-1	ca-central-1
EU (Ireland)	aws-codedeploy-eu-west-1	eu-west-1
EU (London)	aws-codedeploy-eu-west-2	eu-west-2
EU (Frankfurt)	aws-codedeploy-eu-central-1	eu-central-1
Asia Pacific (Tokyo)	aws-codedeploy-ap-northeast-1	ap-northeast-1
Asia Pacific (Seoul)	aws-codedeploy-ap-northeast-2	ap-northeast-2
Asia Pacific (Singapore)	aws-codedeploy-ap-southeast-1	ap-southeast-1
Asia Pacific (Sydney)	aws-codedeploy-ap-southeast-2	ap-southeast-2

Asia Pacific (Mumbai)	`aws-codedeploy-ap-south-1`	`ap-south-1`
South America (São Paulo)	`aws-codedeploy-sa-east-1`	`sa-east-1`

For example, if your instance is running in Singapore, you have to hit the following command to install the CodeDeploy agent:

```
wget https://aws-codedeploy-ap-southeast-1.s3.amazonaws.com/latest/install
```

4. There are few prerequisites for configuring AWS CodeDeploy; we have to first create the CodeDeploy service role. To do that, we have to create an IAM role for AWS CodeDeploy and select S3, EC2, SNS, Lambda, and whatever service you want CodeDeploy to access, so create a Service Profile named **CodeDeploy-service-profile:**

5. Let's configure the AWS CodeDeploy, so go to the AWS console and then AWS CodeDeploy. You will get the following page (if you haven't configured CodeDeploy in that region):

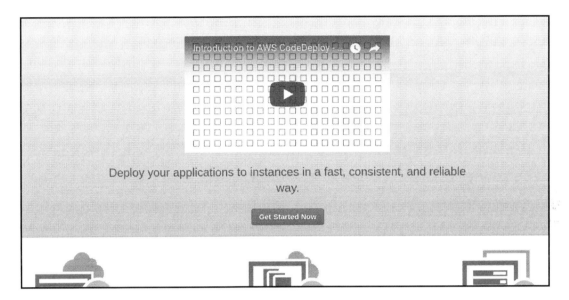

6. Click on **Get Started Now** and go ahead.

7. We will get the following screen, with two options. **Sample deployment,** which is recommended for new AWS CodeDeploy users. This option will let you deploy the sample application provided by AWS. In this option, the EC2 instance will also get created. Another option is **Custom deployment**, in which the user needs to provide their own data such as information of resources such as s3 bucket and EC2 instance. Here, we will click on **Custom deployment** and then **Skip Walkthrough:**

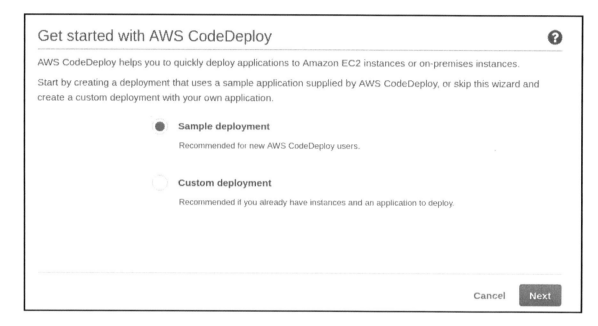

8. We will get another screen where we have to fill the details of AWS CodeDeploy. The first section will be related to **Create Application,** where we have to fill the **Application Name** and **Deployment Group Name**. The **Application name** over here is given as **AWS-CodeDeploy-AN** and the **Deployment Group Name** is **AWS-CodeDeploy-GN**. Also, the **Deployment type** selected by default is **in-place deployment**:

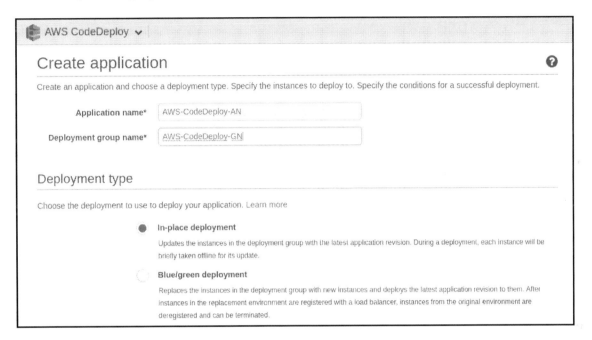

9. Now in the **Environment configuration** section, we will find three tabs: **Auto Scaling Groups**, **Amazon EC2 Instances,** and **On-premises Instance**. Here, we are looking for single Amazon EC2 instances, so click on Amazon EC2 instances. Then, fill the **key tag** as **Name** and **value** will be the name of the instance **AWS-CodeDeploy-Instance,** where you want to deploy the application. For now, we will ignore the load balancing option. We will look that in the later chapter:

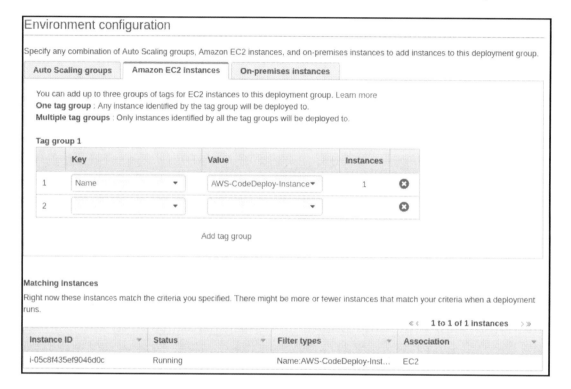

10. The next section is related to **Deployment configuration**. These are rules that determine how smooth and fast an application will be deployed. It also tells the success or failure conditions for a deployment. AWS CodeDeploy provides three type of deployment configuration:

    - **CodeDeployDefault.OneAtATime**: Deploys to one instance at a time. Succeeds if all instances or all but the last instance succeeds. Fails after any instance, except the last instance fails. Allows the deployment to succeed in some instances, even if the overall deployment fails.
    - **CodeDeployDefault.AllAtOnce**: Deploys to up to all instances at once. Succeeds if at least one instance succeeds. Fails after all instances fail
    - **CodeDeployDefault.HalfAtATime**: Deploys to up to half of the instances at a time. Succeeds if at least half of the instances succeed; fails otherwise. Allows the deployment to succeed in some instances, even if the overall deployment fails.

11. Right now, we are moving ahead with **CodeDeployDefault.OneAtATime** as follows:

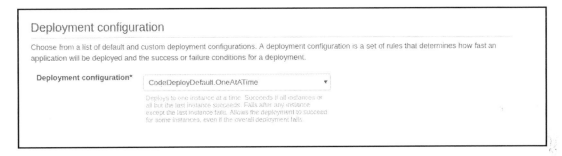

12. In the **Service Role** section, we have to select the service profile ARN that we created **COdeDeploy-service-profile** before configuring AWS CodeDeploy:

13. Now, Click on **Save**.

14. Then, we will get a deployment group called **AWS-CodeDeploy-GN**:

15. Our deployment group is ready. Now, let's see the application that we will be going to deploy.

16. We will be deploying the same NodeJS application that we did in AWS CodeBuild but additionally, it will have `appspec.yml`.

17. To clone the Git URL (`https://github.com/awsstar/CD-Node.JS-AS.git`), you will have a zip file named as `NodeApp.zip`. Let's check out all the files it contains after unzipping `NodeApp.zip`:

```
root@awsstar:~/CD-Node.JS-AS# ll
total 4236
drwxr-xr-x 7 root root 4096 Sep 2 23:57 ./
drwx------ 44 root root 102400 Sep 2 23:50 ../
-rw-r--r-- 1 root root 383 Aug 30 15:01 appspec.yml
-rw-r--r-- 1 root root 214 Aug 20 02:23 buildspec.yml
drwxr-xr-x 8 root root 4096 Sep 2 23:56 .git/
-rw-r--r-- 1 root root 3614970 Sep 2 23:51 NodeApp.zip
drwxr-xr-x 219 root root 12288 Aug 30 14:58 node_modules/
-rw-r--r-- 1 root root 723 Aug 20 01:55 package.json
-rw-r--r-- 1 root root 566855 Aug 20 01:55 screenshot.png
drwxr-xr-x 2 root root 4096 Aug 30 15:59 scripts/
-rw-r--r-- 1 root root 524 Aug 20 01:55 server.js
drwxr-xr-x 4 root root 4096 Aug 20 01:55 source/
drwxr-xr-x 3 root root 4096 Aug 30 14:58 static/
```

Here, we can see a file `BuildSpec.yml`, which is basically used to build the project. Another one is `AppSpec.yml`, which will be used by AWS CodeDeploy to deploy the application in such a manner, which is defined under this file. Let's see the `AppSpec.yml` file:

```
root@awsstar:~/CD-Node.JS-AS# cat appspec.yml
version: 0.0
os: linux
files:
  - source: /
    destination: /srv/mynodeapp
hooks:
  ApplicationStop:
    - location: scripts/stopnode.sh
      timeout: 300
      runas: root
  ApplicationStart:
    - location: scripts/start_nodeserver.sh
      timeout: 300
      runas: root
  ValidateService:
    - location: scripts/MonitorService.sh
      timeout: 3600
      runas: root
```

18. Let's try to understand the content of the file one by one:
    - First, the `files` directive, in which all the files will be copied to the /srv/mynodeapp *instance* path.
    - In the hooks section, I defined three events. In `ApplicationStop` event, one script will be triggered at the second run of the deployment. The name of the script is `stopnode.sh`, which reside in the `scripts` folder. Small script written inside `stopnode.sh` is given as follows:

```
root@awsstar:~/CD-Node.JS-AS# cat scripts/stopnode.sh
#!/bin/bash
forever stop /srv/mynodeapp/server.js
```

- In the `ApplicationStart` event, another script will be triggered and that resides in scripts folder. The name of the script is `start_nodeserver.sh` and the inside content of it is given as follows:

```
root@awsstar:~/CD-Node.JS-AS# cat scripts/start_nodeserver.sh
#!/bin/bash
forever start /srv/mynodeapp/server.js
```

- The last event `ValidateService`, mentioned in the `AppSpec.yml` file, is to validate whether the application is running or not. To check it another script is getting triggered called `MonitorService.sh`. It also resides in `scripts` folder and the inside content is given as follows:

```
root@awsstar:~/CD-Node.JS-AS# cat scripts/MonitorService.sh
#!/bin/bash
curl -Is http://localhost:3000 | head -n 1 | grep 200
STATUS=$(echo $?)
if [ "$STATUS" == 0 ]
then
 echo " Application is Running Successfully "
else
 echo " Application is not running "
fi
```

- These were the files and folders zipped under `NodeApp.zip`.

19. Now, upload the `NodeApp.zip` file in the S3 bucket. I created a bucket named `nodeapp-s3` and uploaded the `NodeApp.zip` file:

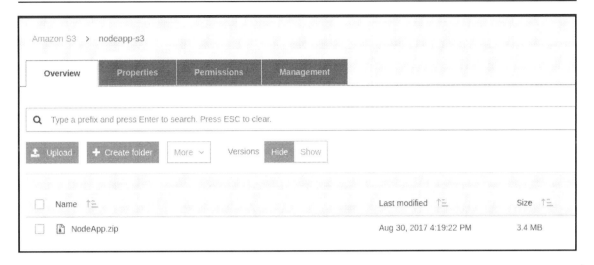

20. Coming back to the AWS CodeDeploy console, we had a deployment group in the CodeDeploy application. We have to select the radio button and click on **Actions** and select **Deploy new revision**:

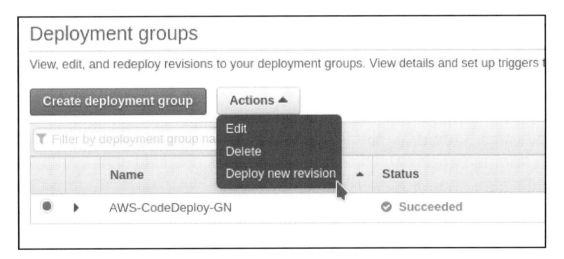

21. We get another page where we have to fill the details, such
    as **Application (AWS-CodeDeploy-AN)**, **Deployment group (AWS-
    CodeDeploy-GN)**, **Repository type** (location where the application with
    `AppSpec.yml` resides. It will be either S3 or GitHub. In our case the application is
    in S3 bucket), **Revision location** (path of s3 bucket , **s3://nodeapp-
    s3/NodeApp.zip**), **File type** (.zip) and **Deployment configuration**
    (**CodeDeployDefault.OneAtATime**). The rest can be left as it is by default, and
    click on **Deploy**:

22. Once we will click on **Deploy**, deployment will start and we will get the deployment ID. Click on the deployment ID to see the event details:

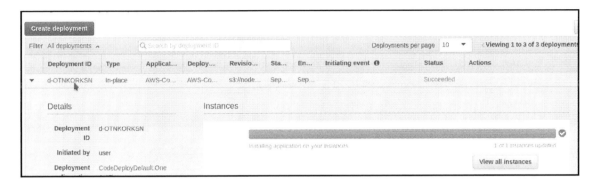

23. Once we will click on the **Deployment Id,** we will be redirected to a page, where we can see which application event is running on the EC2 instance. Click on **View events** to see a detailed event phase:

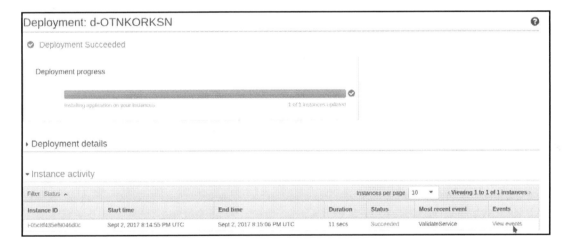

24. Once we click on **View** events, we will get details of phases that run on the instance and its status:

25. So, we can see every event status is succeeded, so we can hit the Pub IP to check whether our application got deployed or not:

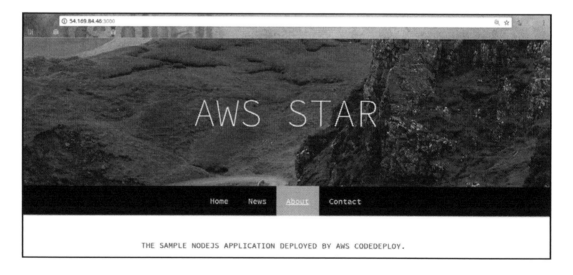

How it works...

We successfully deployed an application using AWS CodeDeploy, but we did put the application zip file manually in the S3 bucket and triggered the deployment manually. Now, if we want the application to get build and automatically get uploaded to S3, and from S3 the application should automatically get deployed to the EC2 instance, then we need to implement Pipeline, which senses the event and triggers automatically. To implement pipeline in AWS, we will be using AWS CodePipeline, which we are going to look in next topic.

Introducing AWS CodePipeline and its working

AWS CodePipeline comes into the picture, when you want to automate all the software release process. AWS CodePipeline is a continuous delivery and release automation service that helps in smoothen deployment. You can quickly configure the different stages of a software release process. AWS CodePipeline automates the steps required to release software changes continuously.

With AWS CodePipeline, we can achieve the following:

- Automate the release process
- Establish consistent and stable release process
- Improve and speed up the delivery quality
- Integration with other developers tools of AWS, and other software, such as Jenkins, CircleCI, and many more
- View pipeline history and detail logging

Before diving deep in AWS CodePipeline, let's see how it works.

How to do it...

AWS CodePipeline helps to create and manage software release process workflow with pipelines. A pipeline is a workflow construct that describes how software changes go through a release process. AWS CodePipeline divides the workflow into multiple stages, for example, **Source** commit, build application, **Staging,** and then deployment to production. Each stage contains at least one action which refers to some kind of task. Every action has some type, and based on the type, it will have input artifact and output artifact.

The following is the simple Pipeline created with AWS CodePipeline:

Now in the preceding diagram, we can conclude the following:

1. The entire software release process is broken into three stages. The first stage has the action related to S3, means whenever there is a change in version of S3 bucket content, the pipeline will get triggered. The name of the stage is Source, means it is referring to the source code that is stored in the S3 bucket and maintained as a version.
2. The second stage name is **Staging**, which refers to that source code that is deployed into the staging environment and is in the testing phase.
3. The third stage name is production, which will get triggered when there is a successful status from the preceding stage.

How it works...

We can make the pipeline in different manners and different way. We can add a different stage in the middle of the existing pipeline, where we can define action such as running the AWS lambda function and many more. We will see one sample application deployment to the S3 bucket using AWS CodePipeline.

Continuous Deployment of static application to AWS S3 using AWS CodePipeline

Before continuing, one should know the following things:

- *Creating an S3 bucket*
- *Setting up CodeCommit* (refer Chapter 1)
- *Setting up CodeBuild* (refer Chapter 2)

If you are comfortable in implementing the preceding, then you are good to go.

The workflow of the pipeline is as follows:

- The sample application code will reside in the CodeCommit repository
- Once there will be a change in the code, the CodeBuild will pull and upload the latest revision in S3
- The S3 bucket will be enabled to serve as website hosting

How to do it...

1. Create a CodeCommit repository **CP-StaticApp** and put the source code file in the repository:

2. Create an S3 bucket **cp-statapp** in the same region where you created the CodeCommit repository. We have to enable **Versioning** and **Static website hosting**:

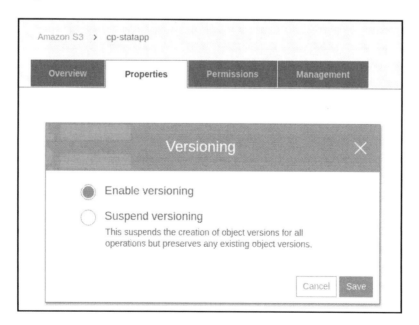

3. The static website can be enabled by going to the **Properties**:

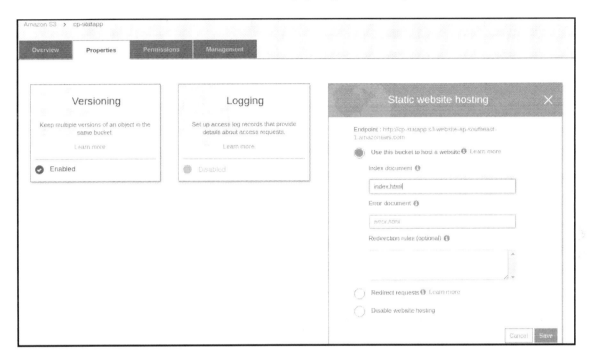

4. Post that, we need to apply bucket policy by going to the **Permission** section of the bucket and click on **bucket policy** and paste the following content:

```
{
    "Version": "2012-10-17",
    "Statement": [
        {
            "Sid": "PublicReadGetObject",
            "Effect": "Allow",
            "Principal": "*",
            "Action": "s3:GetObject",
            "Resource": "arn:aws:s3:::cp-statapp/*"
        }
    ]
}
```

5. Now, create a CodeBuild project **CP-CB-StatApp** with the details given as follows in the image. In the **build command,** we only have to mention the following command:

```
aws s3 cp index.html s3://cp-statapp
```

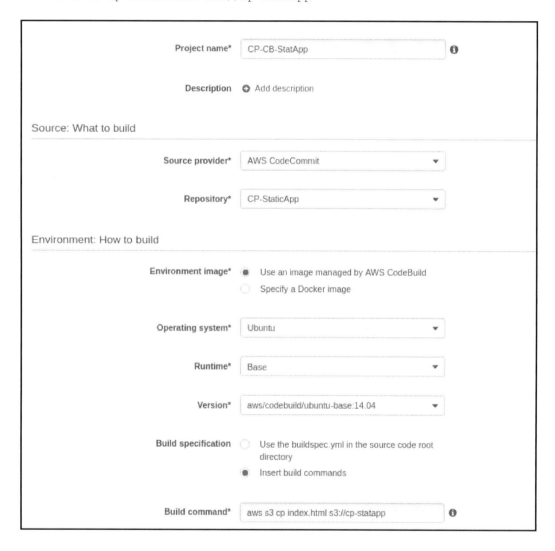

6. We have to configure AWS CodePipeline. So, go to AWS CodePipeline, it will look like the following image if you have not configured AWS CodePipeline before in the region. Click on **Get started** to continue:

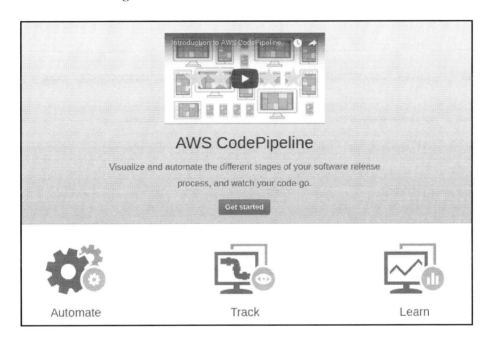

7. We have to name the CodePipeline project **CP-STATICAPPLICATION** and click on **Next step** and continue:

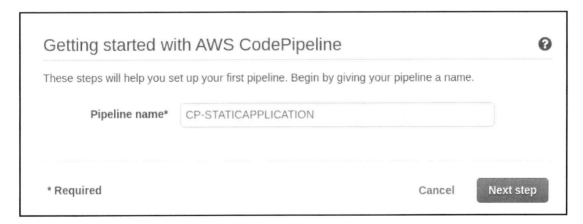

8. We will get **Source location** section where we will enter CodeCommit details. In the **Advanced** section, we will get pipeline execution method. which will ask when to run the pipeline. So we had selected to run the pipeline whenever there is a change in source code. To continue click on **Next step**:

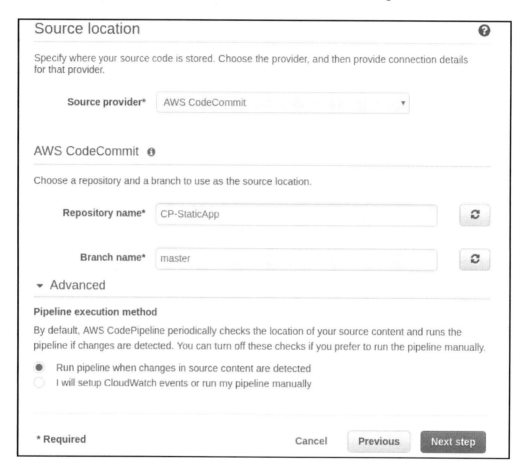

9. We will get to the **Build** section, where we have to enter the CodeBuild project name. Click on **Next step** to go ahead:

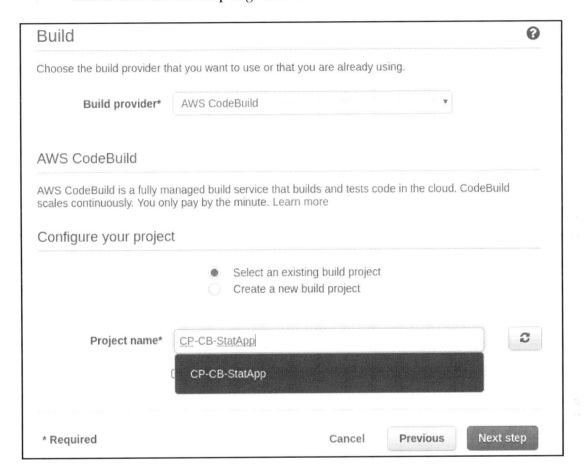

10. We will get to the deployment section, but we have to select **No Deployment,** because we are not deploying the source code in any EC2 or ElasticBeanStalk. The code will automatically get uploaded to the S3 bucket within the build command only. Now, click on **Next step**:

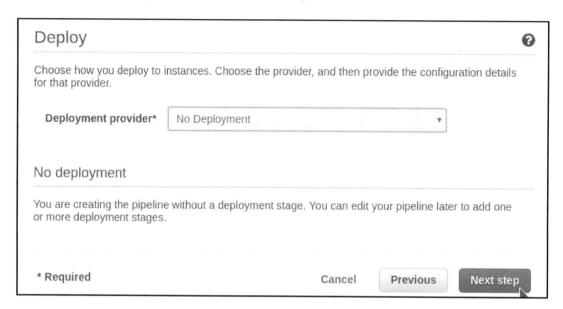

11. We have to create the AWS Service role for AWS CodePipeline by clicking on **Create role**:

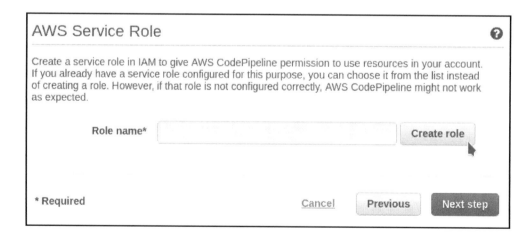

12. It will automatically create the role with the name **AWS-CodePipeline-Service**. We need to click on **Allow**:

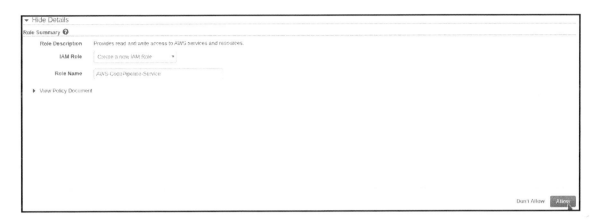

13. When we will click on Allow, the **Service role** field will automatically get filled. Then, click on **Next step**:

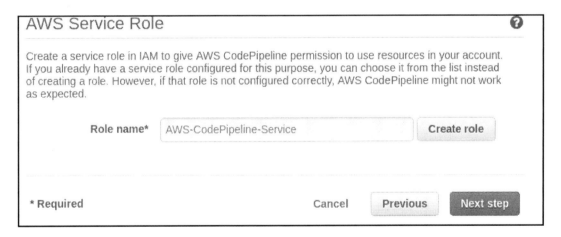

14. We will get a page to review the configuration. Post reviewing, we need to click on **Create pipeline**:

15. After clicking on **Create pipeline**, we will get the following image:

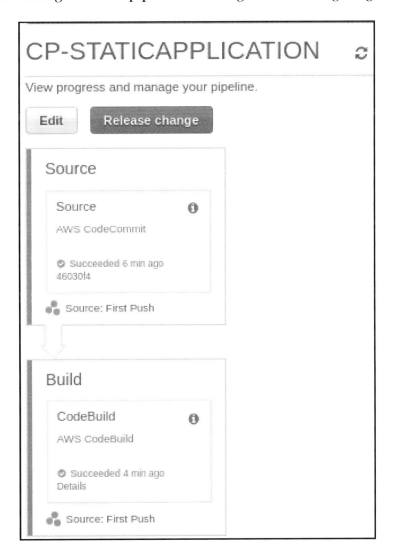

16. In the preceding image, we can see both the stages got success; now, let's hit the endpoint of the S3 bucket. The **endpoint of S3** bucket can be retrieved by the following image:

17. By hitting the endpoint, we will get the following webpage:

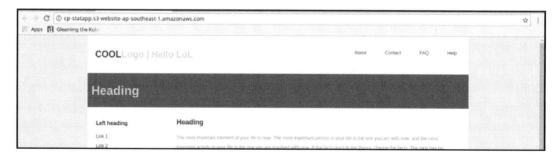

Now, let's change the source code. I will simply replace COOL with AWSome, and once I will commit the code in CodeCommit, the pipeline will get triggered.

18. In the following image, we can see the commit message is the latest one **change in index.html**:

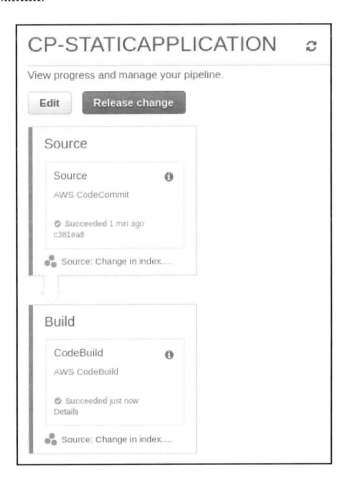

19. We can refresh the s3 endpoint again, and we will see the change in the webpage (AWSome).

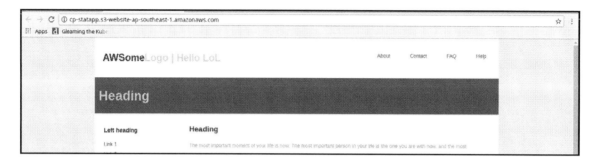

In this way, CodePipeline works. AWS Developer tools are very flexible and can integrate with one another.

4
Building Scalable and Fault-Tolerant CI/CD Pipeline

In this chapter, the following recipes will be covered. Each recipe is basically a different stage of an aggregated highly scalable CI/CD pipeline:

- CI/CD pipeline workflow
- Setting up AWS CodeCommit
- Creating the S3 bucket and enabling versioning
- Creating the launch configuration and Auto Scaling group
- Creating AWS CodeDeploy application using the Auto Scaling group
- Setting up the Jenkins Server and installing the required plugins
- Integrating Jenkins with all of the AWS developers tools

Introduction

In software engineering or in the IT industry, CI/CD basically refers to continuous integration and delivery or deployment.

- Continuous integration: It is a software development practice where continuous changes and updates in code base are integrated and verified by an automated build script using various tools.
- Continuous deployment: It is also a software development practice. Its role is to automatically deploy the code to the application folder on the specified server.

Basically, in this chapter, we will be building a fully automated and highly scalable CI/CD pipeline using Jenkins and AWS tools.

Benefits of using the CI/CD pipeline

A `2016 State of DevOps Report` indicates that high-performing organizations deploy 200 times more frequently, with 2,555 times faster lead times, recover 24 times faster, and have 3 times lower change failure rates. Irrespective of whether your app is greenfield, brownfield, or legacy, high performance is possible due to lean management, Continuous Integration (CI), and Continuous Delivery (CD) practices that create the conditions for delivering the value faster and sustainably.

How to achieve the benefits?

With `AWS Auto Scaling`, you can maintain application availability and scale your Amazon EC2 capacity up or down automatically according to the conditions you define. Moreover, Auto Scaling allows you to run your desired number of healthy Amazon EC2 instances across multiple availability zones (AZs).

Additionally, Auto Scaling can also automatically increase the number of Amazon EC2 instances during demand spikes (increase of CPU utilization or high load) to maintain performance and decrease the instance during less busy periods (Less CPU utilization) to optimize costs.

We can also use AWS Elastic Load Balancer (ELB) for distributing incoming application traffic across designated Amazon Elastic Compute Cloud (Amazon EC2) instances. Whenever there is traffic, based on the load of EC2 servers, it distributes the traffic; the server which has less load will serve the request. This is also known as the least outstanding requests routing algorithm for HTTP and HTTPS listeners, and for TCP listeners ELB uses the Round Robin routing algorithm.

The scenario

We have a NodeJS application of `www.awsstar.com`. The web servers are set up on Amazon Web Services (AWS). As a part of the architecture, our servers are featured with the AWS Auto Scaling service, which is used to help scale our servers, depending on the metrics and policies that we specified. Every time a new feature is developed, we have to manually run the test cases before the code gets integrated and deployed. There are lots of manual tasks that need to be done, and there are several challenges while doing it manually.

This means here we have the assumption that when the latest and tested code will merge with the master branch, it becomes production ready post that. We need to pull the latest code to all the environment servers manually. Instead of doing it manually and slowing down your productivity, you can automate it by implementing the CI/CD pipeline.

The challenges

The challenges of manually running the test cases before the code gets integrated and deployed are as follows:

- Pulling and pushing code for the deployment from a centralized repository.
- Working manually to run test cases and pull the latest code on all the servers.
- Deploying code on a new instance that is configured in AWS Auto Scaling.
- Pulling the latest code on a server, taking the image of that server, reconfiguring it with AWS Auto Scaling, since the servers were auto scaled.
- Deploying build automatically on instances in a timely manner.
- Reverting back to the previous build.

The preceding challenges require lots of time and human resources. So, we have to find a technique that can save time and make our life easy while automating all the process from CI to CD.

Here's a complete guide on how to automate app deployment using AWS S3, CodeDeploy, Jenkins, and Code Commit.

CI/CD pipeline workflow

This recipe will cover all the prerequisites and workflow of the pipeline that we will be implementing.

Getting ready

To that end, we're going to use:

- AWS CodeCommit as application Git repository to automate the code push process
- AWS S3 as an artifact storage tool
- AWS Auto Scaling
- AWS CodeDeploy as the CD tool
- Jenkins as the CI tool

How to do it...

Now, let's walk through the flow, how it's going to work, and what the advantages are before we implement it all. When a new code is pushed to a particular GIT repository/AWS CodeCommit branch, then following steps will take place:

1. Jenkins will first build and then run the test cases (Jenkins listening to a particular branch through Git webhooks).
2. If the test cases fail, it will notify us and stop the further after-build actions.
3. If the test cases are successful, it will go to post-build action.

 In our case, the application is ready to be deployed and is merged with the master branch of the application. So, Jenkins will pull the latest revision and build it.

4. Later on, Jenkins will push the latest code in the zip file format to AWS S3 on the account we specify.
5. AWS CodeDeploy will pull the zip file in all the Auto Scaled servers that have been mentioned.
6. For the Auto Scaling server, we can choose the AMI that has the default AWS CodeDeploy agent running on it. This agent helps AMIs to launch faster and pulls the latest revision automatically.
7. Once the latest code is copied to the application folder, it will once again run the test cases.
8. If the test cases fail, it will roll back the deployment to the previous successful revision.

9. If it is successful, it will run post-deployment build commands on the server and ensure that the latest deployment does not fail.

10. If we want to go back to the previous revision, then we can roll back easily.

This way of automation using CI and CD strategies makes the deployment of the application smooth, error tolerant, and faster.

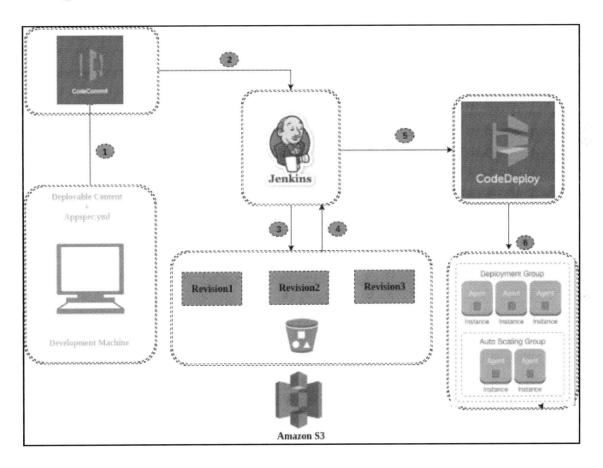

Here's the workflow steps of the preceding architecture:

1. The application code with the `AppSpec.yml` file will be pushed to the AWS CodeCommit. The `AppSpec.yml` file includes the necessary scripts path and command, which will help the AWS CodeDeploy run the application successfully.

2. As the application and `AppSpec.yml` file will get committed in the AWS CodeCommit, Jenkins will automatically get triggered by the poll SCM function.

3. Now, Jenkins will pull the code from AWS CodeCommit into its workspace (path in Jenkins where all the artifacts are placed), build it, and archive it. This can be considered as Job 1.

4. Later in Job2 of Jenkins, the build artifact will get uploaded to the S3 Bucket.

5. Post the success of Job2, the AWS CodeDeploy plugin of Jenkins will get triggered, which will deploy the latest revision present in the S3 bucket. So, this job can be considered as Job3.

Building pipeline means breaking the big Job into small individual jobs, relying on which, if first job fails, it will trigger the email to the admin and stop the building process at that step only and will not move to the second job.

To achieve the pipeline, one should need to install the pipeline plugin in Jenkins.

According to the previous scenario, the Jobs will be broken into three individual jobs:

- **Job 1**: When the code commit runs, Job 1 will run and it will pull the latest code from the CodeCommit repository; it will archive the artifact and email the status of Job 1, whether it is successfully built or failed altogether with the console output. If Job 1 gets built successfully, then it will trigger Job 2.

- **Job 2**: This Job will run only when Job 1 is stable and runs successfully. In Job 2, the artifacts from Job 1 will be copied to workspace 2 and will be pushed to the AWS S3 bucket. Post that, if the artifacts is sent to the S3 bucket, an email will be sent to the admin. Then, it will trigger Job 3.

- **Job 3**: This Job is responsible to invoke the AWS CodeDeploy and pulls the code from S3 and pushes it either to run the EC2 instance or AWS Auto Scaling instances. When all the job will be finished, then it will look like the following screenshot.

The following screenshot shows the structure of the pipeline:

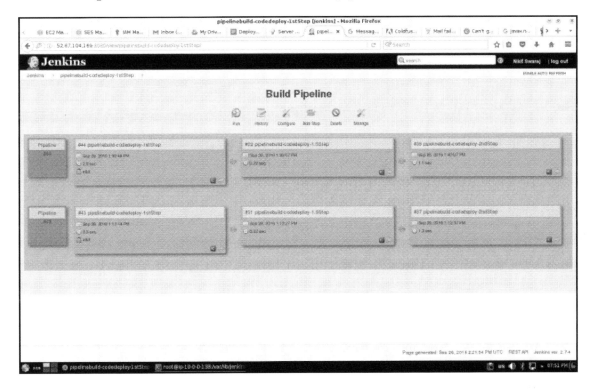

Setting up AWS CodeCommit

In this section, we will be setting up the AWS CodeCommit repository to store the application source code along with the AppSpec.yml file. You can refer to Chapter 1, *Using AWS CodeCommit,* to create the AWS CodeCommit repository and migrate a GitHub repository to AWS CodeCommit.

Getting ready

To set up a CodeCommit repository for our pipeline, we first need to carry out the following steps:

1. Create an IAM user and attach the CodeCommit PowerUserAccess Policy.
2. Retrieve the HTTP-based Git username and password for pushing or pulling the code from the CodeCommit repository.
3. Clone the sample application from GitHub (`https://github.com/awsstar/GIT-AWSSTAR-APP.git`)
4. Create a CodeCommit repository and migrate the sample application from the GitHub to CodeCommit repository.

How to do it...

To set up a CodeCommit repository, one should have access to the AWS CodeCommit service.

1. First of all, we need to follow the steps mentioned in the *Getting started with CodeCommit for HTTP users* recipe in `Chapter 1`, *using AWS CodeCommit*), to create an IAM user and retrieve the username and password.
2. Now, we need to create a CodeCommit repository, for which we need to perform the following steps:
    1. Open the AWS CodeCommit console at `https://console.aws.amazon.com/codecommit`.
    2. On the welcome page, choose **Get Started** (If a **Dashboard** page appears instead of the welcome page, choose **Create new repository**).

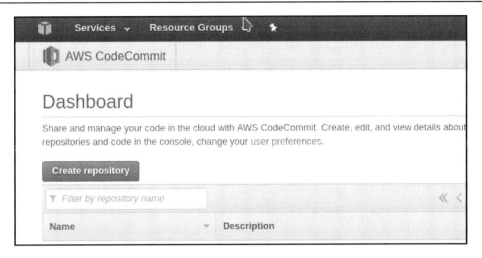

3. On the **Create repository** page, in the repository name box, type CC-AWSSTAR-APP.

4. In the **Description** box, type application repository of CC-AWSSTAR-APP.

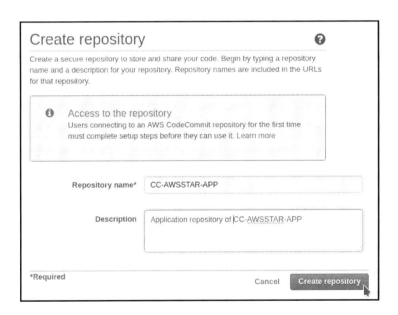

5. Choose **Create repository** to create an empty AWS CodeCommit repository named **CC-AWSSTAR-APP**

6. Now, migrate a Git repository (`https://github.com/awsstar/GIT-AWSSTAR-APP.git`) to the AWS CodeCommit repository, that is, CC-AWSSTAR-APP. You can refer to the *Migrating a Git Repository to AWS CodeCommit* recipe in `Chapter 1`, *Using AWS CodeCommit*, to do that.

7. Once we are done with the migration, we will have the source code of the application along with the `AppSpec.yml` file in the **CC-AWSSTAR-APP** repository:

3. Clone this repository to your development environment using the Git HTTP username and password of the IAM user.

 The Application Code that we migrated to CC-AWSSTAR-APP is the same NodeJs Application that we had deployed in the previous chapter. The appspec.yml file is also the same, so the deployment steps will be the same as earlier.

4. We will create the S3 bucket in the next section.

Creating the S3 bucket and enabling versioning

Once we are done with creating the CodeCommit repository, we have to create two S3 buckets, one for storing versions of application and the other for deploying content that will be used by AWS CodeDeploy.

Getting ready

We need to create two S3 buckets in the same region where the CodeCommit repository CC-AWSSTAR-APP lies. We also need to enable versioning in a bucket which will have different versions of the application.

How to do it...

We have to follow the steps to create an S3 bucket and enable versioning:

1. Go to the AWS console and click on the S3 service in the **Storage** section; then we will get the S3 console page.
2. Click on **Create bucket** and enter the name of the first bucket where revisions of the application will be stored, **awsstar-s3-code,** and apply proper permission:

3. Once you create the S3 bucket, click on that bucket and go to the **Properties** section of that; click on **versioning** and the select radio button of **Enable Versioning:**

4. In the same manner, create another bucket named **awsstar-s3-bucket,** which will contain the zip format of the artifact that will be used by AWS CodeDeploy to deploy it into **Deployment group** with EC2 instances in Auto Scaling groups.

Once we are done with creating S3 buckets, we will move ahead to create a Launch Configuration which will be used by Auto Scaling group to launch instances.

Creating the launch configuration and Auto Scaling group

Auto Scaling is an AWS Service, which allows us to scale up (adding EC2 instance) or scale down (destroying EC instance) infrastructure automatically in a horizontal manner. Scaling up or scaling down of EC2 instance depends on some policy metrics such as CPU Utilization, health status checks.

AWS Auto Scaling service launches the EC2 instance with the help of the launch configuration. It basically includes the template in which we will mention which AMI, instance type, network configuration, user-data script, and many more, will be used to launch the instance.

Getting ready

To create a launch configuration, we need to create a custom AMI, which should have an application-dependent package such as NodeJS and npm preinstalled on the server. Once we will have the custom AMI, we can create a launch configuration.

Once our launch configuration will be created with the custom AMI, we need to set the desired--minimum and maximum--number of instance. We also need to set the scaling policy.

How to do it...

Since the application lies in our `CC-AWSSTAR-APP`, the CodeCommit repository is a NodeJS application, so we need to install NodeJS and npm packages in the instance. To do that, we need to perform the following steps:

1. Launch an EC2 instance preferably CentOS/Red Hat/Amazon Linux in the same region and install the necessary packages by running the following commands:

```
# yum update -y
# yum install epel-release curl wget gcc make g++ bind-utils -y
# yum install nodejs -y
# npm install -g forever
```

2. Once we are done installing the application-dependent package, we have to install the AWS CodeDeploy agent tool. To install the agent, refer *How to do it...* section of *Deploy a static application in an EC2 instance from S3 Bucket using AWS CodeDeploy* recipe in Chapter 3 *Deploying an application using AWS CodeDeploy and AWS CodePipeline.*

3. Once the CodeDeploy agent is installed on the server and its service is running, we have to take the AMI of that EC2 instance. To do that, select that instance where you have installed the application-dependent package, then select **Action,** go to **Image**, and click on **Create Image**:

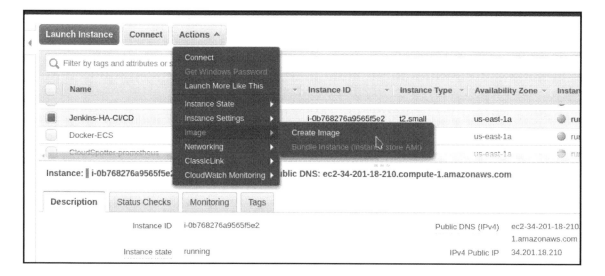

4. Enter the **Image name** and **Image description** and click on **Create Image**:

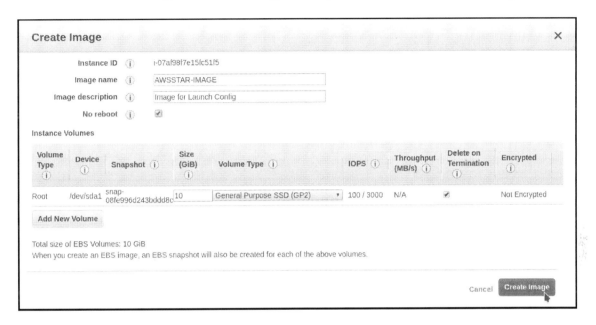

5. Now, create an EC2 instance role **AWSSTAR-INSTANCE-PROFILE**, which should have access to S3 and CodeDeploy.
6. We have to create a launch configuration and an Auto Scaling group. To do that, Go to **Launch Configuration** in the right side of the EC2 console:

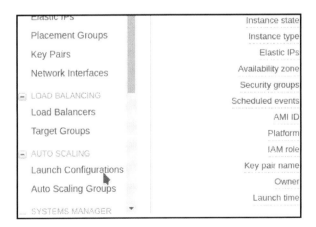

7. Click on **Create Launch Configuration**:

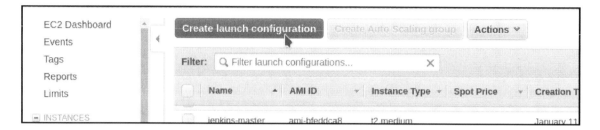

8. Select the **AMI** that we created by going to My AMIs section:

9. Then, select the instance type (`t2.micro` will be enough for the sample app). Post that, mention the configuration details, such as **Launch Config Name** as **AWSSTAR-LC**, IAM Role that we just created **AWSSTAR-INSTANCE-PROFILE**, in **Advanced Details** IP Address Type, and click on **Assign a Public IP address to every instance**. Then, click on **Next: Add Storage**:

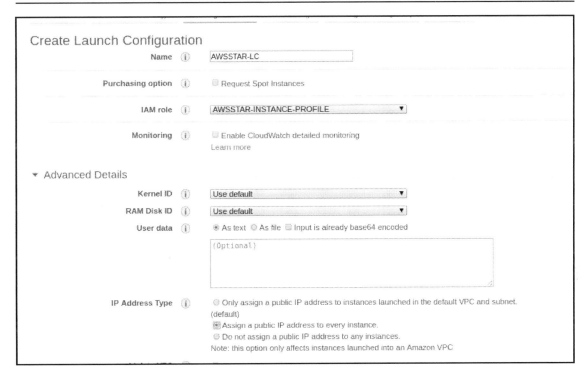

10. Select the required storage and configure **Security group** (make sure port 3000 should open for your Machine IP from where you will be accessing the application). **Review the Configuration** and click on **Create Launch Configuration**.

11. Once the launch configuration is created, select the **Launch Configuration** and then click on **Create Auto Scaling Group**:

12. Enter the **Group name** of Auto Scaling as **AWSSTAR-LCGN**, set the group size as **2**, mention VPC in the **Network** parameter, select a proper subnet (Public), and then click on **Next: Configure Scaling Policies**:

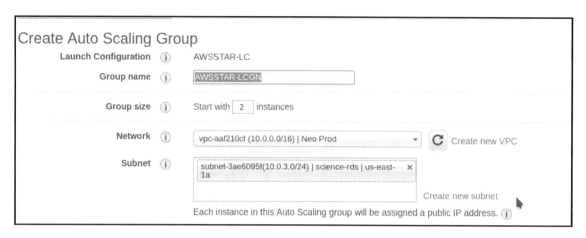

13. Now, we have to configure the scaling policy. In the scaling policy, we have to set the **Metric type** as **Average CPU Utilization** and **Target Value** as **70**. We also need to mention the minimum (which should be one) and maximum size of the group (basically, max number of instance). So if the CPU utilization will go above 70%, then the instance will automatically scale up using Launch Config. After that, click on **Next: Configure Notifications**:

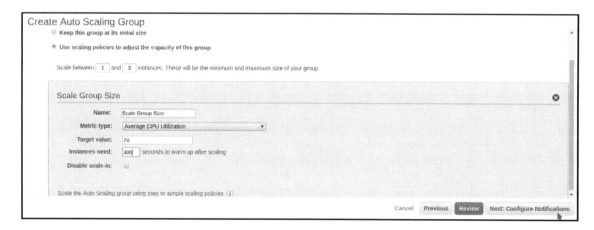

14. In the **Notification** section, we have to select the topic, for example, the status of instance of the Auto Scaling group. Then, SNS will send the notification to the subscribed mail ID with that topic. Click on **Add Notification**:

15. Select **Topic name** and click on **Next** to configure tags:

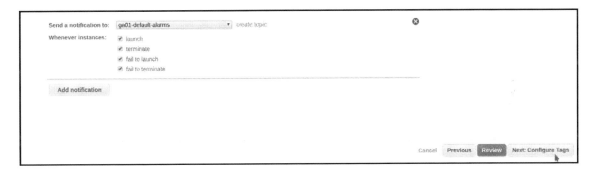

You can refer to `http://docs.aws.amazon.com/sns/latest/dg/GettingStarted.html` to create an SNS topic and understand how it works.

16. Configure the **Tags** and **review** it; post that, click on **Create Auto Scaling group**. Once we done with creating an Auto Scaling group, we can go to the EC2 console and see that one instance has been launched by Auto Scaling group, because we have given minimum value of instance as 1 during configuring Auto Scaling group:

17. Remember, the instance name given to instances launched with the AS group will not be mentioned, so we have to identify it through the instance ID of the instance present in the AS Group:

18. Once we are done with creating an Auto Scale Group, the next part is to create an AWS CodeDeploy Application with the Auto Scaling Group that we just created.

Creating AWS CodeDeploy application using the Auto Scaling group

In this recipe, we will be creating a CodeDeploy application, which will deploy the application in Auto Scaling Group. Here, CodeDeploy will be triggered via Jenkins, so before mentioning the details of CodeDeploy, we need to set up CodeDeploy.

Getting ready

First of all, we should have an Auto Scaling group, in which the instance should have a proper role attached, which we had already created in the previous section.

We also need to create CodeDeploy Service Role, which should have the policy to access the files from S3 and deploy it to the EC2 instance.

How to do it...

To create AWS CodeDeploy application, go to AWS Console and click on CodeDeploy in the **Developers Tool** section:

1. Click on **Create application**:

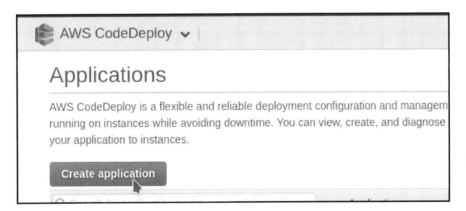

2. Then, fill the application name as **AWSSTAR-CD-AN** and the **Deployment group** name as **AWSSTAR-CD-GN**. Keep the deployment group in **In-Place Deployment** only.

3. In the **Environment configuration** section, we need to choose **Auto Scaling Groups**. Click on the **Name** dropbox, then we will see the Auto Scaling group that we created **AWSSTAR-LCGN**:

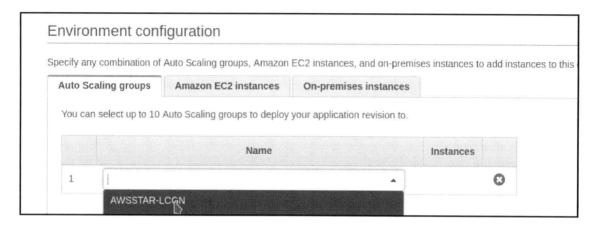

4. In **Deployment configuration**, select **CodeDeployDefault.OneAtATime** and then select the proper **Service role Arn,** which will allow CodeDeploy to access S3 and EC2 instances. Then, click on **Create Application**.

So, at this stage, we are done with configuring AWS services. Now, its time to setup the Jenkins Server and prepare it for the building and pipeline purpose. So, in the next section, we will be learning about setting up the Jenkins Server.

Setting up the Jenkins Server and installing the required plugins

In this recipe, we will be installing the Jenkins Server and necessary plugins. We need the Jenkins server to build the application and to push the artifacts to the S3 bucket to keep the multiple revisions for the rollback purpose. It will also push the deployable content to another S3 bucket, from where AWS CodeDeploy will pull the content and deploy it into a Auto Scaling group.

Getting ready

To set up Jenkins, we first need a server. Then, we have to install Java, which is required by Jenkins as a dependency. Post that, we will install Jenkins and install build tools related to an application, which is npm. After that, we have to install S3 and CodeDeploy-related plugins.

How to do it...

To setup Jenkins, we need perform the following steps:

1. Launch an EC2 instance (Amazon Linux, CentOS, or Red Hat) and run the following commands.
2. Update the system:

```
# yum update -y
```

3. Install Java and verify it:

```
# yum install java-1.8.0-openjdk
# java -version
```

4. Install NodeJS and npm (application-dependent package for building the application using Jenkins):

```
# yum install nodejs
# npm install -g forever
```

5. Install the Jenkins repository and its `gpg` key:

```
# wget -O /etc/yum.repos.d/jenkins.repo http://pkg.jenkins-
ci.org/redhat/jenkins.repo
# rpm -import http://pkg.jenkins-ci.org/redhat/jenkins-ci.org.key
```

6. Install Jenkins application:

```
# yum install Jenkins
```

7. Add Jenkins to system boot:

```
# chkconfig jenkins on
      Or
# systemctl enable jenkins
```

8. Start Jenkins:

```
# service jenkins start
      Or
# systemctl start jenkins
```

9. By default, Jenkins will start on port 8080; this can be verified via:

```
# netstat -antpul | grep 8080
```

10. Go to the browser and navigate to http://JenkinsServerIP:8080. You will see the Jenkins dashboard.

11. Now, follow the onscreen instruction and set up the Jenkins username and password. Install the suggested plugins at first.

12. Once you login to Jenkins with the username and password, click on **Manage Jenkins** present at the right side and then **Manage Plugins**:

1. Now, click on the **Available** tab and go to the filter search box. Install **s3 publisher plugin, Build Pipeline** as well as **AWS CodeDeploy Plugin for Jenkins**.

> Set up a Postfix Relay through Gmail so that the Jenkins server will be able to send the email. For the reference, you can visit `https://www.howtoforge.com/tutorial/configure-postfix-to-use-gmail-as-a-mail-relay/`.

Now, our Jenkins server is ready to get integrated with AWS services components. So in the next recipe, we will integrate all the AWS services with Jenkins and create a pipeline.

Integrating Jenkins with all of the AWS developers tools

In all the previous recipes, we configured AWS services and the Jenkins server. Now, it's time to integrate Jenkins with all of the tools of AWS that we had configured earlier and achieve the use-case or scenario. So whenever the latest code will be checked in the master branch of the repository (`CC-AWSSTAR-APP`), then based on the cron or Poll SCM parameter, Jenkins will get trigger. Jenkins will pull the latest code from the repository to its workspace. Then, it will run the commands which is mentioned in the build step of it. So basically, Jenkins will start building the code. Once the build will take place successfully, it will trigger an email. Post that, it will upload the build artifact in one of the S3 bucket (awsstar-s3-code), where revisions will be placed. Then, again the artifact will be uploaded to another S3 bucket (awsstar-s3-bucket) in zipped manner. Then, Jenkins will trigger CodeDeploy, which will pull the deployable content from awsstar-s3-bucket and deploy to the AWS Auto Scaling group.

Getting ready

Before starting integration of all the services with Jenkins, let's list out the name of the service components:

- CodeCommit repository: `CC-AWSSTAR-APP` (`https://git-codecommit.us-east-1.amazonaws.com/v1/repos/CC-AWSSTAR-APP`)
- S3 Buckets: awsstar-s3-code, awsstar-s3-bucket

- Auto Scaling group: AWSSTAR-LCGN
- AWS CodeDeploy application name: AWSSTAR-CD-AN
- AWS CodeDeploy group name: AWSSTAR-CD-GN

First of all, we have to configure the system in Jenkins and put access key and secret key of IAM user that should have S3 full access or else you can create a IAM role which will have fill access to s3, later attach that role to the instance. We also need to configure the email address. Then, we to create a credential by entering the HTTPS Git username and password.

We have to break the entire workflow in three stages.:

- The 1st stage will pull the code, build and create an artifact of it.
- The 2nd stage will upload the artifact to the S3 bucket.
- The 3rd stage will trigger the CodeDeploy application.

Once the AWS CodeDeploy application will be triggered, it will deploy the latest revision of the application to the Auto Scaling group.

How to do it...

Before moving ahead, we again need to make sure that the resources we created and configured should belong to the same AWS region.

1. First of all, we have to set up the access key and secret key of the IAM user or allow the IAM role in Jenkins so that Jenkins can upload the artifact to the buckets. To do that, we need to click on **Manage Jenkins** and then **Configure System**:

2. Once we click on **Configure System**, another page will open, where we have to scroll down and search for the **Amazon S3 profiles** section. When we we get to that section, there will be a button **Add**. Click on that; it will ask the value of a field **Profile name** which will be **AWSSTAR-S3-BUCKET Access key and Secret key**. Enter these details and click on **Save**, else if you have IAM role attached to the instance, then click on the checkbox of **Use IAM Role**:

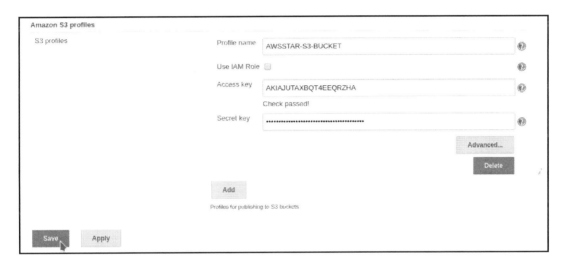

3. Now, we have to create a job as **AWSSTAR-CI-CD-Stage1,** and for that, we have to click on **New Item** on the left side of the sc:

4. Once we click on **New Item**, we will get another page where we have to enter the job name as **AWSSTAR-CI-CD-Stage1** and click on **Freestyle Project** and then **OK**:

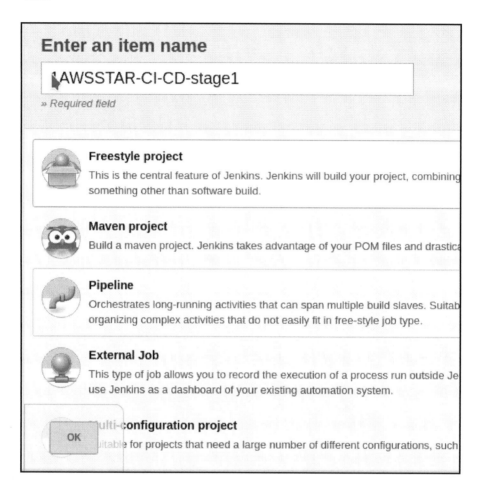

5. Then, we will get the configuration page of Job. In the **Source Code Management** section, we have to click on the radio button of **Git**. Before entering the Git URL, we need to first create credentials, so click on the **Add** button on the right side of credentials. Now, click on **Jenkins**:

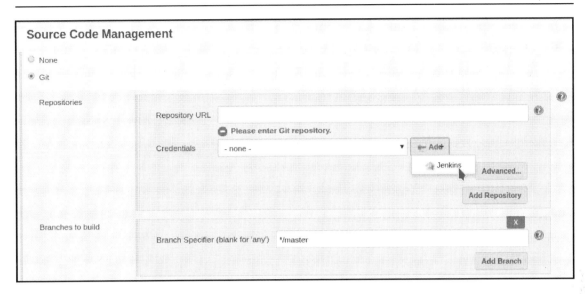

6. Once we click on **Jenkins**, the we will get one page where we have to enter the HTTPS Git **Username** and P**assword** and click on **Add**. In this, we added the credentials of CodeCommit repository:

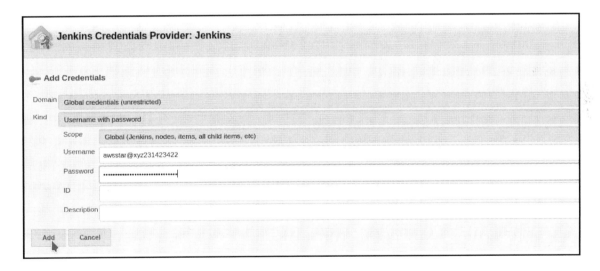

7. Then, we need to pass the Git URL of the **CC-AWSSTAR-APP** in the URL section and select the credentials:

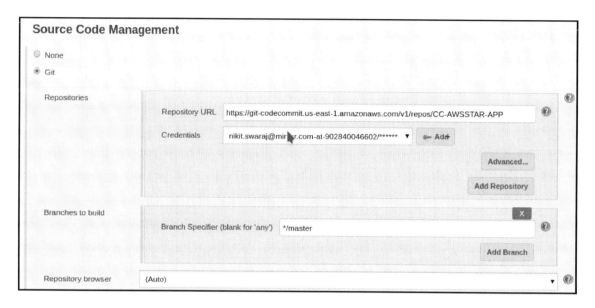

8. Set up the **Poll SCM** timing; right now, for a fast demo I have given ***** . This means every time it will poll for any changes in the repository:

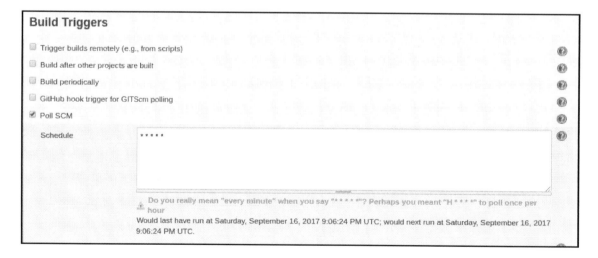

9. After that, we have to mention build steps in shell, so to get shell box where we can mention shell commands, we need to click on **Add build step** and then **Execute shell**:

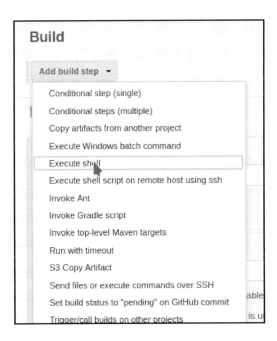

10. Once we click on **Execute Shell**, we will get a text field where we can write shell commands. In this box, we will put our build commands:

```
npm install
npm run build
```

11. These commands will run in the `workspace` folder, where our application will present:

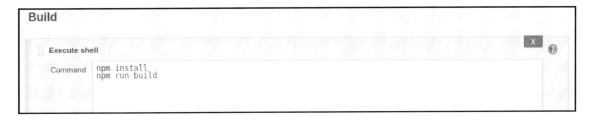

12. Once we set up our build step, then we have to set up **Post Build** step. In this step, we have to select three steps in which one is **Archive the artifacts** and enter the value ∗∗/∗for all the files and folder recursively. Another step is **Build other projects**. In the **Projects to build** text field, we have to mention the Stage2 job (Next job) and select **Trigger only if build is stable**. The third step is regarding **E-mail notification**. In **Recipients**, we have to mention the email ID which will send the status of the job. After that, click on **Save**:

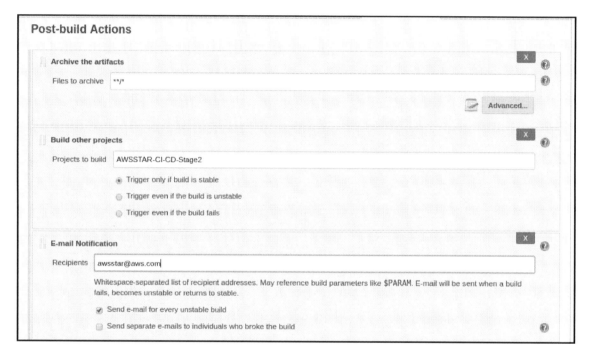

13. Once we are done creating Job 1 as **AWSSTAR-CI-CD-Stage1**, then we create Job2 **AWSSTAR-CI-CD-Stage2**. In the same way, click on **New Item**, mention **job name**, select f**reestyle project,** and then click on **OK**.

14. After that, go to build step of Job2 and click on **Copy artifacts from another project**. Mention the name of Job1 **AWSSTAR-CI-CD-Stage1** and select **Latest successful Build**. In **Artifacts to copy**, we have to give ** means all files and folders:

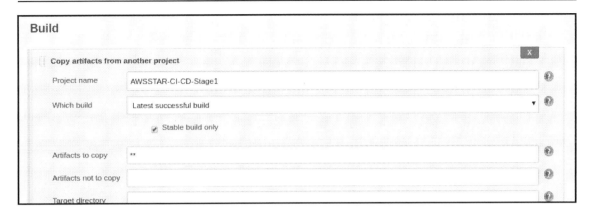

15. In the **Post-build Actions** step, we perform four steps, in which, the first is to **Publish artifacts to S3 bucket**. In this one, we have to give a **Profile name** similar to the one we set during configuring system **AWSSTAR-S3-BUCKET**. In the **Destination bucket,** we have to put that bucket name which will store revisions of application code and that is **awsstar-s3-code.** We need to give a proper **Bucket Region** 'us-east-1' (in our case):

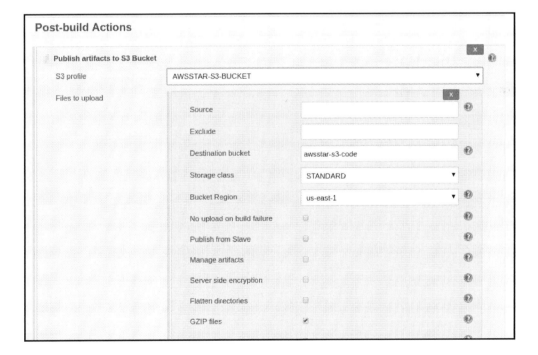

16. The next three steps is the same as previous Job1 Post Build. Here also we have to mention **Build another projects** and we have to give the name of third job as **AWSSTAR-CI-CD-Stage3**:

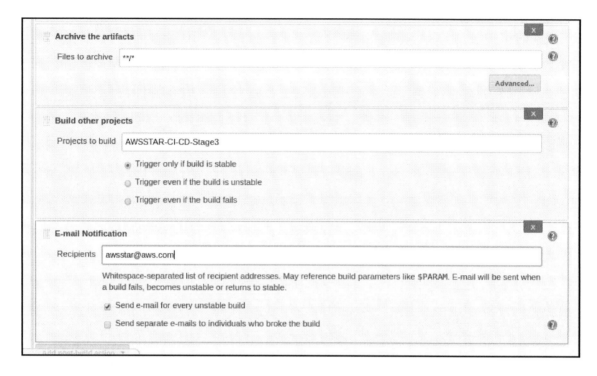

17. Once we are done creating Job2, it is time to create Job3 as **AWSSTAR-CI-CD-Stage3**. In the build section of Job3, we have to Copy artifacts from another project, where the project name is Job2 as **AWSSTAR-CI-CD-Stage2** and give ★★ in the artifacts to copy section:

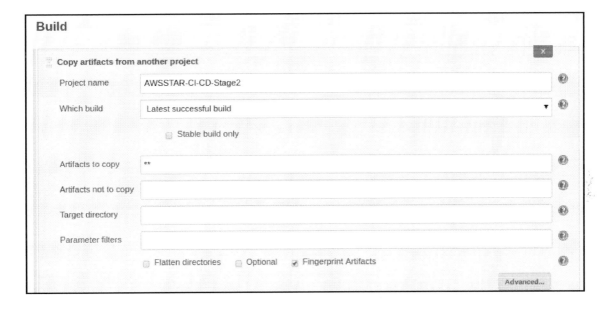

18. In the post-build section, we need to select **Deploy an application to AWS CodeDeploy**. We have to mention **CodeDeploy application name AWSSTAR-CD-AN**. **Deployment Group 'AWSSTAR-CD-GN', Deploy Config 'CodeDeployDefault.OneAtATime', Region 'US_EAST_1' S3 bucket 'awsstar-s3-bucket', include files '**'**. Click on the radio button of **Deploy Revision** and use **AccessKey and SecretKey**. Enter the key of an IAM user who will have access to run CodeDeploy. After that, click on **Save**:

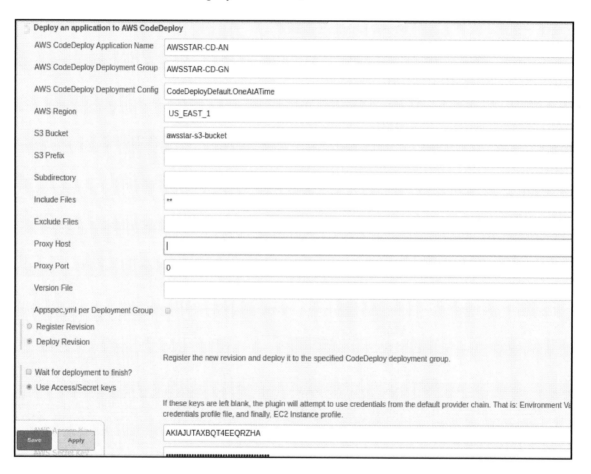

19. Until now, we are done configuring Jobs. Next, click on the + sign to create a **View** and give it a pipeline shape:

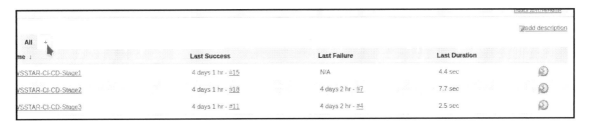

20. After clicking on **+,** we need to fill two entries, **Name** as **AWSSTAR-CI-CD-STAGES** and **Select initial job** as **AWSSTAR-CI-CD-Stage1**. Then, click on **OK**. We will be able to see **Build Pipeline**. Then click on **Run**, to run the pipeline:

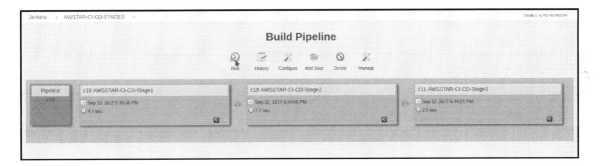

21. Once you run the pipeline, it will follow the work process that was described previously. This means it will upload the artifacts to **awsstar-s3-code**. We can see that the bucket gets populated with the latest code:

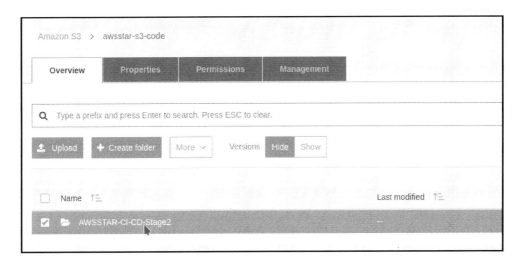

22. We can also see that deployable content will also be uploaded to **awsstar-s3-bucket**:

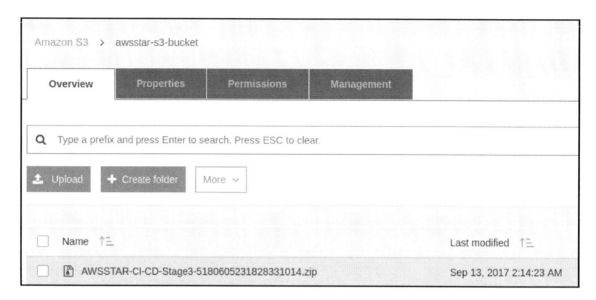

23. After that, if we see the deployment status in CodeDeploy, we will see somethings like this, if everything goes well:

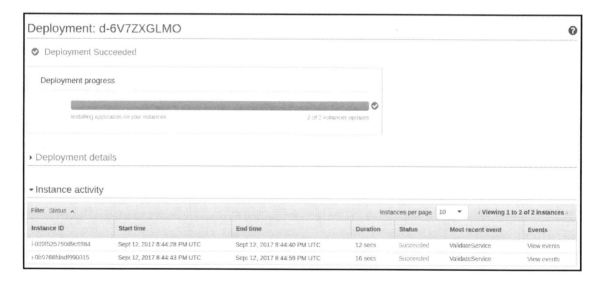

24. In the preceding screenshot, we can see that the application got deployed in two instances. So, these instances are a part of the Auto Scaling Group. CodeDeploy deploys the code in each instance one by one.

25. Now if you will hit `http://ServerIP:3000`, you will be able to access the application:

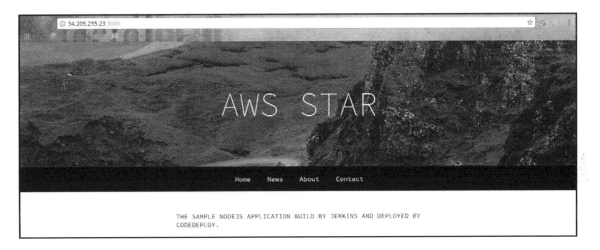

26. Now if I would hit the second instance of the Auto Scaling group, again we will get the same site:

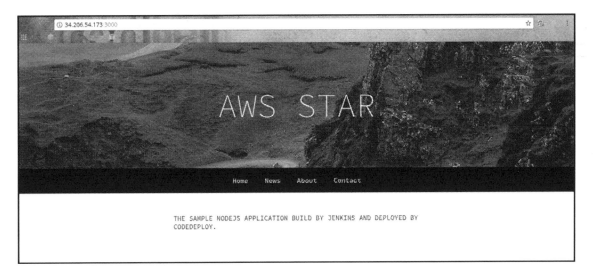

27. Now, if the third instance will get launched by the AS group, CodeDeploy will take care of that and deploy the application on that as well.

It's proven that teams and organizations which adopt continuous integration and continuous delivery practices significantly improve their productivity. With AWS CodeDeploy with Jenkins, it is an awesome combo when it comes to automating the app deployment and achieving CI and CD.

5
Understanding Microservices and ECS

In this chapter, we will be covering the following recipes:

- Understanding microservices and their deployment
- Playing around with Docker containers
- Setting up AWS ECR and pushing an image into it
- Understanding ECS and writing task definitions and services

Introduction

Microservices is the latest buzzword in the field of software architecture. This architecture is basically getting lots of attention. But before diving deep into it, let's first understand the alternate architecture; then, it will make sense to compare with it and see the use case.

Alternate and traditional architecture is known as **monolithic architecture**. In an enterprise, whenever we develop any application, it provides all the features and functionalities that meet business requirements, so all these hundreds of features and functionalities are piled or grouped in a single monolithic application. A monolithic application is built as a single piece or unit.

In microservice architecture, all the program components are independent of each other and loosely coupled and are standalone applications of their own. These components communicate with each other by service discovery, RMI, push messaging, or restful web services.

Understanding microservices and their deployment

Microservices is basically the variant of **service-oriented architecture (SOA)** that breaks the entire application into service components. These services will serve the request by communicating with each other through service discovery or **Remote Method Invocation (RMI)**:

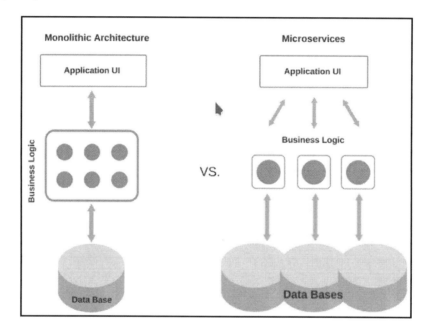

Difference between monolithic and microservice architecture

The characteristics of microservice-based applications are as follows:

- Service enabled, independently running components
- Each service has its own functionalities
- Components using simple communication channels such as service discovery, REST protocol, or messaging protocol
- Decentralized stack, that is, every component can have its own development stack and way of deployment

- Decentralized Data Storage and Management, where each business logic service has its own databases, as you can see in the preceding diagram
- Updating the revision of one component will not affect another, since every component is independent

Designing microservices

While developing a software application, either you develop it from scratch using the microservices architecture or you convert the existing applications into microservices. While developing, it's very important that you properly decide the size, scope, and capabilities of the microservices. This may be the toughest situation when you implement the microservices architecture in practice.

There are some misconceptions and key concerns, which are related to the scope, capabilities, and size of a microservice.

The team size or the number of lines of code are irrelevant metrics. Developers have lots of discussion on finalizing the microservice's size, depending on the line of code, its implementation, or the size of team. However, these are not practical and considered as lousy metrics, because developers can develop services with less code.

Micro is a confusing term; this leads most developers to think that they need to make the service as small as possible, but this is not true at all.

Some of the designing guidelines are as follows:

- **Properly scoped functionality**: The first and most important element of a microservice is to find out the requirement and assign what it should do and what should be the breadth of its functionality.
- **Exposing API**: Once we have multiple independent services, we should think about the communication of these microservices with each other.
- **Traffic management**: Once the service is up, a heavy traffic situation requires management; this is one of the design criteria for microservice.
- Unlike service in SOA, a given microservice should have very few operations or functionalities and a simple message format

Deployment of microservices

When it comes to the deployment of the microservices architecture, it plays a critical role and should have following requirements:

- It should have the ability to deploy or undeploy other services independently
- It should be able to scale at each microservice level
- It should build and deploy microservices quickly
- A failure in one microservices should not affect any of the other services

There are some orchestration tools for the better deployment of microservice application. They are as follows:

- Docker swarm
- Kubernetes
- Mesos
- AWS ECS

In this chapter, we will see how we can deploy microservices applications using AWS ECS; but before that, we must know how to work with Docker containers.

Playing around with Docker containers

Before indulging with Docker, let's take a look into containers.

Containers

Containers are kernel level virtualization, unlike hypervisor virtualization, where one or more independent machines run virtually on physical hardware via an intermediation layer. Containers run the user space on top of an operating system's kernel. Some of the containerization technologies are LXC and FreeBSD Jails. Now, let's take a look at Docker.

Docker

Docker is a containerization tool that runs on the top of libcontainer, and in the previous version, it used LXC as the default execution environment. It provides native API and command-line client binary Docker. Docker is a client-server application. The Docker client talks to the Docker server or daemon, which, in turn, does all the work. You can run the Docker daemon and client on the same host or connect your local Docker client to a remote daemon running on another host.

The core components of Docker are as follows:

- Docker client and Server
- Image
- Registry
- Containers

Images

Images are the building blocks of the Docker world. You launch your containers from images. They are the "build" blocks of Docker's lifecycle, and are in the layered format, using Union filesystems, which is built step-by-step using a series of instructions.

Registry

Registry is a place where your Docker images are stored such as Docker Hub. There are two types of registries: public and private. The public registries store the images which are available to all, that is, public. Private registries are used by the enterprises that do not want to expose their images to the public.

Containers

Containers are runtime instance of your image. They are launched from images and can contain one or more running processes.

It's a myth that people still think that Docker is a containerization technology, but it's not. It is a containerization tool, which is built on top of some libraries libcontainer or LXC. So, we can say that libcontainer or LXC is a containerization technology.

Getting ready

Docker Inc. basically provides two types of Docker Engine, one is EE (Enterprise Edition) and the other is CE (Community Edition). Of course EE has some price with additional benefits, while CE is free of cost. Here, we will play with the Community Edition Docker engine on CentOS7.

Installation of Docker engine

1. Install dependencies:

```
# yum install -y yum-utils device-mapper-persistent-data lvm2
```

2. Set up the repository:

```
# yum-config-manager --add-repo
https://download.docker.com/linux/centos/docker-ce.repo
```

3. Install the Docker engine:

```
# yum install docker-ce
```

4. Start the Docker service and enable the Docker service at boot time:

```
# systemctl enable docker
# systemctl start docker
```

5. Verify the version of Docker and whether it is installed correctly by running the `hello-world` image:

```
# docker -v
# docker run hello-world
```

Run Docker as a non-root user

1. To run Docker as a non-root user, you have to add your user in the `docker` group.

2. Create a `docker` group if there isn't one:

```
$ sudo groupadd docker
```

3. Add your user to the `docker` group:

```
######Mention UserName is place of $USER######
$ sudo usermod -aG docker $USER
```

4. Log out and log back in so that your group membership is re-evaluated. If you are on the EC2 machine, then carry out a reboot (stop and start is not required).

Now, we will have to be aware of the following activities with Docker containers before going ahead with the microservice deployment:

- Run containers, persistence storage
- Expose port
- Create an image using Dockerfile and push it to Docker Hub

How to do it...

1. Search and pull images from the Docker Hub (image registry):

```
# docker search < image name: tag >
```

Here, `tag` denotes version. If we won't give the tag, then Docker by default considers it as the latest version. In the following screenshot, it shows that we are searching the image of Ubuntu:

```
[root@localhost ~]# docker search ubuntu
INDEX        NAME
docker.io    docker.io/ubuntu
docker.io    docker.io/rastasheep/ubuntu-sshd
docker.io    docker.io/ubuntu-upstart
docker.io    docker.io/ubuntu-debootstrap
docker.io    docker.io/torusware/speedus-ubuntu
docker.io    docker.io/nuagebec/ubuntu
docker.io    docker.io/nickistre/ubuntu-lamp
```

2. Once we get the image name then we will pull it in our local machine:

```
# docker pull <image name: tag>
```

```
[root@localhost ~]# docker pull ubuntu
Using default tag: latest
Trying to pull repository docker.io/library/ubuntu ...
latest: Pulling from docker.io/library/ubuntu

75c416ea735c: Pull complete
c6ff40b6d658: Pull complete
a7050fc1f338: Pull complete
f0ffb5cf6ba9: Pull complete
be232718519c: Pull complete
Digest: sha256:a0ee7647e24c8494f1cf6b94f1a3cd127f423268293c25d924fbe18fd82db5a4
```

After pulling the image, let's try to see what all images are there in our system:

```
# docker image
```

```
[root@localhost ~]# docker images
REPOSITORY          TAG        IMAGE ID        CREATED        SIZE
docker.io/ubuntu    latest     d355ed3537e9    5 days ago     119.2 MB
```

Running a container

1. Now that we have an image in our system, so let's try to run a container:

```
# docker run -it ubuntu:latest /bin/bash
```

2. We pass two command line flags: -i and -t. The -i flag keeps STDIN open from the container, even if we're not attached to it. This persistent standard input is one half of what we need for an interactive shell. The -t flag is the other half and tells Docker to assign a pseudo-tty to the container we're about to create. This provides us with an interactive shell in the new container:

```
[root@localhost ~]# docker run -it ubuntu:latest /bin/bash
root@1557ac7f4894:/#
```

3. Here, you can perform entire operations, such as installing packages and running program. To get out of the container, press the following command:

```
# exit
```

4. You will come out of the container, but the container will be in the EXITED status. In this status, you won't be able to get inside the container until and unless you start it. If you want to get out of container, but still want the container to be up and running then press the following:

```
Ctrl p + q
```

5. To check the status (Running/EXITED) of containers, enter the `ps` command:

```
# docker ps
```

6. This command will show you the running containers only. So to get the list of all containers, whether it is in the running or EXITED status, hit the following command:

```
# docker ps -a
```

```
[root@localhost ~]# docker ps -a
CONTAINER ID    IMAGE            COMMAND        CREATED          STATUS
66b647917669    ubuntu:latest    "/bin/bash"    15 minutes ago   Exited (0) 12 minutes ago
6b02b366e1ad    ubuntu:latest    "/bin/bash"    16 minutes ago   Up 16 minutes
```

In the preceding image, we can see the list of two container with the container ID, which is `66b647917669` in its exited state and `6b02b366e1ad` in its up and running state.

Starting the stopped container

In the previous screenshot, we got a list of all the containers irrespective of STATUS.

Let's say if you get out of the container by the `exit` command and the container is in the exited status, then to get back inside the container, we have to follow the following steps:

1. Start the container.
2. Attach your shell to that container:

```
# docker start <container ID> or
# docker start <container_name> (Assigning container name is
mentioned in next heading)
```

3. In the preceding screenshot (output of `docker ps -a`), we had a stopped container with the container ID `66b647917669`, so we will start it. To attach to that container, we use the following code:

```
# docker attach <container ID/Name>
```

```
[root@localhost ~]# docker start 66b647917669
66b647917669
[root@localhost ~]# docker attach 66b647917669
root@66b647917669:/#
```

We can see that we entered in the container, which was stopped earlier.

Assigning a Name to a container

Syntax: `docker run -it --name <container_name > <image:tag> <entrypoint>`

```
# docker run -it --name webapp ubuntu:latest /bin/bash
```

Press *Ctrl P+Q* after that when you enter `docker ps`, then in the **NAME** section, you will see `webapp`.

Creating daemonized containers

1. Daemonized containers don't have an interactive session and are ideal for running applications and services in the background:

Syntax: `docker run -it -d --name <cont_name> <image:tag> <entrypoint>`

2. We've used the `docker run` command with the `-d` flag to tell Docker to detach the container to the background:

```
# docker run -it -d --name webapp ubuntu:latest /bin/bash
```

3. After that for troubleshooting, if you want to get inside the container, then run the following command:
   Syntax: `docker attach <container ID/Name>`

```
# docker attach webapp
```

```
[root@localhost ~]# docker run -it -d --name webapp ubuntu:latest /bin/bash
bf57830bbf74dd4da967503762ecc62545c588b331edf85210b9d3e171f2a45a
[root@localhost ~]# docker attach webapp
root@bf57830bbf74:/#
```

4. To stop a daemonized container we have to run the following command:

```
# docker stop <container ID/Name>
```

5. So, in this case:

```
# docker stop webapp
```

Exposing ports of a container

To access the application running inside the container, we can hit the private IP of the container in the host machine where the container is running, but what about to access it outside of the host machine, cause we generally map the URL of the application with the Public IP of the host machine.

1. We need to map the container port with the host port so that when we the hit public IP of the host machine, we should get the application running inside the container:

```
Syntax: docker run -it -d -p <host port>:<container port> <image>
<entry point>
```

2. Here we have specified a new flag, –p. The –p flag manages which network ports Docker exposes at runtime. When you run a container, you can specify a specific port on the Docker host that maps to a specific port on the container:

```
# docker run -it -d -p 80:80 nginx
```

```
[root@localhost ~]# docker run -itd -p 80:80 nginx
Unable to find image 'nginx:latest' locally
Trying to pull repository docker.io/library/nginx ...
latest: Pulling from docker.io/library/nginx

e6e142a99202: Pull complete
8c317a037432: Pull complete
af2ddac66ed0: Pull complete
Digest: sha256:72c7191585e9b79cde433c89955547685db00f3a8595a750339549f6acef7702
5a7d74db223b2702d7654fc900d58b27866ddb8512a6e158fdf4539417d4cb16
[root@localhost ~]# curl -I http://localhost
HTTP/1.1 200 OK
Server: nginx/1.13.1
Date: Tue, 27 Jun 2017 20:07:57 GMT
Content-Type: text/html
Content-Length: 612
Last-Modified: Tue, 30 May 2017 13:03:46 GMT
Connection: keep-alive
ETag: "592d6db2-264"
Accept-Ranges: bytes
```

In the preceding screenshot, we can see that while creating a container with the image and exposing port of it, when we entered `curl localhost` on the host machine, it gave the output that ran inside the container.

Managing persistent storage with Docker

Data volumes are designed to persist data, independent of the container's lifecycle. Docker, therefore, never automatically deletes volumes when you remove a container, nor will it "garbage collect" volumes that are no longer referenced by a container.

Adding a data volume

Syntax: `docker run -it -v <local_mount_point>:<container_mount_point> <image> <entrypoint>`

```
# cd /root/DevOps
# touch file{1..10}.txt
# ls /root/DevOps
# docker run -it -v /root/DevOps:/tmp ubuntu /bin/bash
```

```
[root@localhost ~]# ls /root/DevOps/
file10.txt  file1.txt  file2.txt  file3.txt  file4.txt  file5.txt  file6.txt  file7.txt  file8.txt  file9.txt
[root@localhost ~]# docker run -it -v /root/DevOps/:/tmp ubuntu /bin/bash
root@3030dd413478:/# ls /tmp/
file1.txt  file10.txt  file2.txt  file3.txt  file4.txt  file5.txt  file6.txt  file7.txt  file8.txt  file9.txt
root@3030dd413478:/#
```

The preceding command first lists the files of the local directory, and after mounting it to container mount point, it lists the files of the container mount point. We can see that both local and and container directory include the same file, because the container mounted its folder with the local host machine folder.

Getting details of a container

To know the IP details of a container, either you can go inside the container and perform `ip a`, or we can do the following.

The `docker inspect` command will interrogate our container and return its configuration information, including names, commands, networking configuration, and a wide variety of other useful data:

```
# docker inspect <container ID/Name>
```

```
[root@localhost ~]# docker inspect webapp
[
    {
        "Id": "bf57830bbf74dd4da967503762ecc62545c588b331edf85210b9d3e171f2a45a",
        "Created": "2017-06-27T15:49:28.384467503Z",
        "Path": "/bin/bash",
        "Args": [],
        "State": {
            "Status": "running",
            "Running": true,
            "Paused": false,
            "Restarting": false,
            "OOMKilled": false,
            "Dead": false,
            "Pid": 5368,
            "ExitCode": 0,
            "Error": "",
            "StartedAt": "2017-06-27T15:49:29.215500652Z",
            "FinishedAt": "0001-01-01T00:00:00Z"
        },
```

1. To get the IP details, we can enter the command as follows:

```
# docker inspect webapp | grep IPA
```

```
[root@localhost ~]# docker inspect webapp | grep IPA
              "SecondaryIPAddresses": null,
        "IPAddress": "172.17.0.2",
                  "IPAMConfig": null,
              "IPAddress": "172.17.0.2",
```

2. Delete a container:

```
# docker rm -f <container ID/Name>
```

3. Delete an image:

```
# docker rmi -f <Image ID/Name:tag>
```

Containerize your application using Dockerfile

Containerizing the application basically means to create the image along with the source code and later run the container of that image. We create the Image using two methods.

- The docker commit command
- The docker build command with a Dockerfile

The `docker commit` method is not currently recommended, as building with a Dockerfile is far more flexible and powerful.

The Dockerfile uses a basic DSL with instructions for building Docker images. We then use the `docker build` command to build a new image from the instructions in the Dockerfile:

1. Let's create an `Application` folder where the application, as well as Dockerfile, resides:

```
# mkdir app
# cd app
# echo "<h1> Worked Successfully </h1>" > index.html
# vi Dockerfile

    FROM nginx:latest
    MAINTAINER XXXXX "devops@msp.com"
    ADD . /usr/share/nginx/html
    RUN service nginx restart
    EXPOSE 80
```

2. Now that we have a sample web page and a Dockerfile, let's try to build the image.
   Syntax: `docker build -t <image name>:`

```
# docker build -t webapp
```

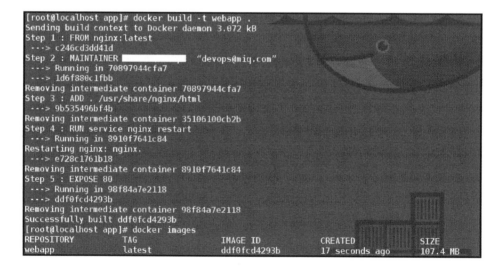

3. Once we build the image and try to list the images that are present in our local machine, we will be able to see the new image name that we have built.

4. As soon as we have the image, let's try to run the container of it:

```
# docker run –itd –p 80:80 webapp:latest
```

```
[root@localhost app]# docker run -itd -p 80:80 webapp:latest
2b9ec122e9fedf6a2aa83920bbacad10e05e4e0300cc7b79dbd895d1c1e2a16a
[root@localhost app]# curl localhost:80
<h1> Worked Successfully </h1>
```

Now we have a sample web app in a containerized manner.

Push the image to Dockerhub

Once we have built the image, it's time to push it to the registry Docker Hub:

1. Login to Docker Hub (if you don't have a Docker Hub account, create one by hitting `https://hub.docker.com/`):

```
# docker login
```

```
[root@localhost ~]# docker login
Login with your Docker ID to push and pull images from Docker Hub. If you don't have a Do
o create one.
Username:
Password:
Login Succeeded
```

2. After successful login, push the image to the Docker Hub. But before that, tag that image and then push it:

Syntax: `docker tag <image_name> <username>/<image_name>:<version>`

`docker push <username>/<image_name>:version`

```
[root@localhost ~]# docker tag webapp        /webapp:latest
[root@localhost ~]# docker push        /webapp:latest
The push refers to a repository [docker.io/     /webapp]
914573421982: Pushed
b198c8333a61: Pushed
87823f21b793: Mounted from library/nginx
1c3fae42c500: Mounted from library/nginx
54522c622682: Mounted from library/nginx
latest: digest: sha256:32a888443456f0bf02ff83542e9ad9411ff8fb13f2014b826e643d95eb8f3d1c size: 1362
```

You can view your newly created Docker image in Docker Hub account. This was all about getting us ready to move forward and play with container management services such as Kubernetes and ECS. Before moving ahead and using ECS, which is a container management service provided by AWS, we should know the private registry used by ECS, which is ECR. In the next recipe, we will learn about ECR.

Setting up AWS ECR and pushing an image into it

Amazon EC2 Container Registry (**Amazon ECR**) is a Docker registry service managed by AWS. ECR is scalable, secure, and reliable. ECR supports private Docker repositories with resource-based permissions using IAM so that specific users or AWS EC2 instances can access repositories and images. Using ECR is a bit different than using a Docker hub in terms of authenticity and permissions. The following are some components of Amazon ECR:

- **Registry**: The Amazon ECR registry is provided to each AWS account (as of writing this book, it is available in 12 regions only; for now, it means that it's not available in Mumbai, Seoul, and Sau Paulo). We can create repositories in the registry and store an image in that repository.
- **Authorization Token**: To access the ECR, the Docker client needs to authenticate to Amazon ECR registries as an AWS User before it can push and pull images. We can authenticate to ECR using the AWS CLI get-login command (we will learn about it in detail later).
- **Repository**: An Amazon ECR image repository contains Docker images.
- **Repository policy**: We can control access to the repositories and the images using the repositories policy.
- **Image**: We can push and pull Docker images to our repositories, and use these images locally in our development machine or use them in the task definition file.

Now, its time to set up ECR and push a Docker image in ECR.

Getting ready

To play around with ECR, make sure you should take care of these things:

- Docker must be installed in your machine or server

- AWS CLI should be installed and configured with the access and secret keys of an IAM user, which should have AmazonEC2ContainerRegistryPowerAccess and AmazonEC2ContainerServicePowerAccess policies (we need AmazonEC2ContainerServicePowerAccess cause ECR comes under the section of AWS ECS service).

If preceding things are taken care off, we need to do the following:

- Create a repository in ECR
- Authenticate your Docker client with AWS ECR
- Tag your Docker image with the repository details
- Push the image to ECR

How to do it...

To create a repository in ECR, we need to follow the steps mentioned as follows:

1. Go to the AWS console and click on **EC2 Container** lying in the **Compute** section. After that, we will get a screen similar to the following (if you haven't used ECS before). Then, click on **Get Started**:

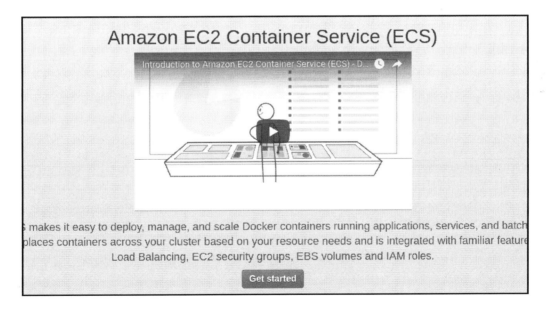

2. When we click on **Get started**, we get a screen where we are asked to **select options to configure**. In the two check boxes, uncheck the first checkbox, because we are not going to configure and deploy a sample application onto an ECS cluster. After that, click on **Continue**:

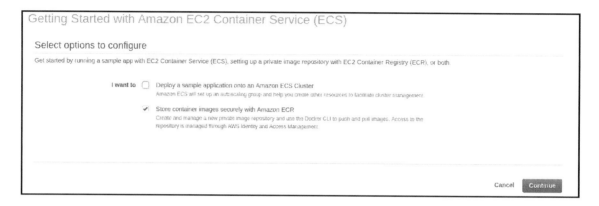

3. Once we click on **Continue**, we will get a screen where we have to enter the repository name `awsstar`. Post that, click on **Next step**:

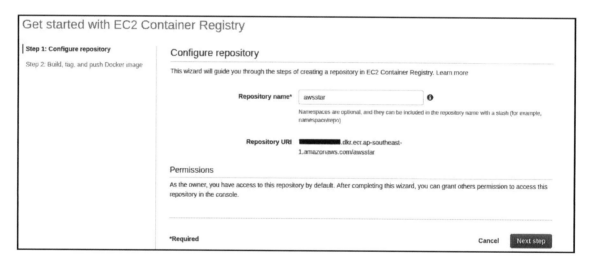

4. Once we click **Next Step**, we will have our new and empty repository in place:

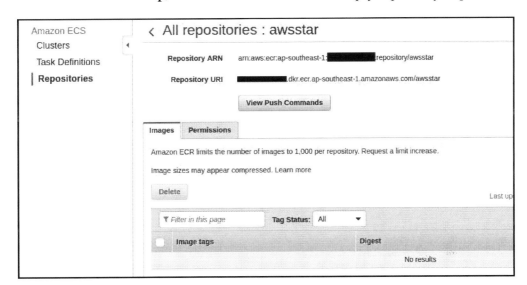

You can read the instruction by clicking on **Push Commands**. These commands will also be written to authenticate your Docker client with AWS ECR.

To authenticate Docker client with ECR

Once we have our repository in place in AWS ECR, and assuming AWS CLI is installed in the server from where the Docker client is authenticating and pushing the image, we need to perform the following steps:

1. We need to retrieve the `ecr login` credentials by entering the following command:

```
aws ecr get-login --no-include-email
```

2. Once we run the preceding command, we will get the ECR Docker Registry Login credentials. If you check the output of your command, it will be `docker login -u Username -p PasswordString ECRRegistryURL`:

```
root@awsstar:~# aws ecr get-login --no-include-email
docker login -u AWS -p
eyJwYXlsb2FkIjoiYW5FRXRRPVE5sc0pxODVxOGQ3VkI1bUlqeVJlT1FJZHppFd0JMaVVBdWs0RVZ
TaFlDRWRRZd0JUSEtFODY0QUEyMkFYMVVXSkkwwM3ZXeFpqam5EU3E1QnpENVFHHcHhScmZuQWRZVE
xrTE1BaUpscnnBaVXhWSE5HQ3hCVHZaVVBsRERyRHVUYy9LMHc2WEdRSTdtbjk0cXXJPVXdyajZnT
```

```
WJ4NmYzSDlSeGEvdmU0aUcvTkh0ZStOS0RRdk8zZUltSE1QZGRKdHdGcHpVSG1McUdWQ0habTV2
bUhMbTlQZGxvUk9DRnNlaaG5QM2g1eVNkTGo0Smp1U1VJYUZrUysya1Bk=
https://7xxxxxxxx6.dkr.ecr.ap-southeast-1.amazonaws.com
```

3. Now, copy the output of `aws ecr get-login` and paste it in the terminal-like command to authenticate. Then, we will get a **Login Succeeded** output at the end, meaning that our Docker client lying in our server is connected with the ECR Docker Registry and it will be able to push or pull any Docker image to or from the AWS ECR Registry:

```
root@awsstar:~# docker login -u AWS -p
eyJwYXlsb2FkIjoiYW5FRXRRPVE5sc0pxODVxOGQ3VkI1bUlqeVJlT1FJZHppd0JMaVVBdWs0RVZ
TaFlDRWRRZd0JUSEtFODY0QUEyMkFYMVVXSkkwwM3ZXeFpqam55EU3E1QnpENVFFHcHhScmZuQWRZVE
xrTE1BaUpscnnBaVXhhWSE5HQ3hCVVHZaVVBsRERyRHVUYy9LMHc2WEdRRSTdtbjk0cXJJPVXdyajZnT
WJ4NmYzSDlSeGEvdmU0aUcvTkh0ZStOS0RRdk8zZUltSE1QZGRKdHdGcHpVSG1McUdWQ0habTV2
bUhMbTlQZGxvUk9DRnNlaaG5QM2g1eVNkTGo0Smp1U1VJYUZrUysya1Bk=
https://7xxxxxxxx6.dkr.ecr.ap-southeast-1.amazonaws.com
Login Succeeded
```

Once we have a proper authentication between the Docker client and AWS ECR, it's time to push our image to the AWS ECR repository; but before that, we need to tag the image with the repository name of AWS ECR.

 The credentials generated by AWS for authentication will expire after 24 hours. So for further use, you again have to generate the credentials. You can use the ECR-Credential helper so that you do not need to generate the credentials every time, the ECR-Credential helper will take care of it. You can refer to `https://github.com/awslabs/amazon-ecr-credential-helper` for more info.

Tagging your Docker Image with the repository details

Let's say we have one image that we built initially in the previous recipe *Playing Around with Docker Containers* using Dockerfile and we gave it the name `webapp`, so we will tag that image.

1. First of all, verify whether the image is present in our system:

```
root@awsstar # docker images
REPOSITORY TAG     IMAGE ID      CREATED        SIZE
webapp     latest  e064290c666d  1 weeks ago    108.3 MB
nginx      latest  da5939581ac8  2 weeks ago    108.3 MB
```

2. Now, we have to tag the image webapp; however, tagging for ECR is different than tagging for Docker Hub that we did in the previous recipe. We need to tag the image in the following manner:

Syntax: `docker tag <image name>:<tag> <ecr registry url>/<repository>:<tag>`

```
root@awstar # docker tag webapp:latest 77xxxxxxx6.dkr.ecr.ap-
southeast-1.amazonaws.com/awsstar:Webapp_Latest
```

3. Now if we check the image present in our system, we will find one additional image with the tag that we had given:

```
root@awsstar # docker images
REPOSITORY        TAG      IMAGE ID      CREATED                SIZE
7xxxxxxx6.dkr.ecr.ap-southeast-1.amazonaws.com/awsstar Webapp_Latest
e064290c666d    40 minutes ago          108.3 MB
 webapp           latest e064290c666d   40 minutes ago         108.3 MB
 nginx            latest da5939581ac8   2 weeks ago            108.3 MB
```

It's time to push the Docker image to the ECR.

Pushing the image to ECR

1. To push the image we need to run the following command:

```
root@awstar # docker push 7xxxxxxx6.dkr.ecr.ap-southeast-
1.amazonaws.com/awsstar:Webapp_Latest
   The push refers to a repository [774250464776.dkr.ecr.ap-
southeast-1.amazonaws.com/awsstar]
   64d272edf6b2: Pushed
   110566462efa: Pushed
   305e2b6ef454: Pushed
   24e065a5f328: Pushed
   Webapp_Latest: digest:
sha256:4891595608d19d003ea528ad6a8c9b90ac5dbbdadd3ea8d0ce9fd6dc37fc33f5
size: 1155
```

2. We can see that image got pushed, now we have to verify this with the ECR console:

We can see that we have one image with the tag **Webapp_Latest** in `awsstar` repositories. Now that we saw how to use ECR, we are all set to use ECS and its components. In the next recipe, we will see how we can use the AWS ECS service with the help of task definition and service files.

Understanding ECS and writing task definitions and services

Amazon EC2 Container Service (**ECS**) is a container orchestration service. It is highly scalable and a fast container management service that helps manage a containerized application that is deployed in the cluster of EC2 instances. Basically, Amazon ECS lets you launch and stop container-based applications with simple API calls and allows you to get the state of your cluster from a centralized service. It also gives you access to many familiar Amazon EC2 features. ECS handles fault tolerance by itself, which means we don't have to worry about that when designing our infrastructure using ECS.

Amazon ECS takes care of container running inside the cluster. It schedules the placement of containers across your cluster, based on your resource needs and availability requirements. ECS eliminates the worry about scaling your management infrastructure or need for you to operate your own cluster management and configuration management systems.

Here are the core components of AWS ECS:

- **Container instance**: It's nothing but just a fancy word for an EC2 instance. Basically, each container instance is host to one or more Docker containers. All the container instances run the ECS agent and are registered into a cluster. Those instances should have a proper IAM role with the required permissions because they make calls to the ECS service. When an instance is registered by an ECS cluster, it will update the status to ACTIVE and the agent connection status to TRUE. If both the statuses are ACTIVE and TRUE, the container instance will be available to run tasks sent by ECS:

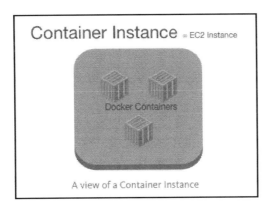

- **Cluster**: A **cluster** is a logical grouping of Container instances. Each container instances in a cluster runs the ECS agent, which allows instances to connect to the cluster. A cluster can contain multiple container instances, which means different tasks can be performed inside the same cluster. A region in the AWS account can have multiple ECS clusters at the same time, but a container can be part of one cluster's container instance at a time. While creating a new cluster, we must keep the following things in mind:
  - **EC2 instance type**: This is the instance type a container instance should have. It will affect the number of tasks that can run inside a cluster.

- **Number of instances**: This is the number of instances that should be launched. All the instances should be launched using the ECS AMI.
- **EBS Storage**: The amount of GB storage that is attached with our instances.
- **Networking**: This is the VPC that should get selected. Make sure that VPC should have two subnets in different AZs.
- **Key pair**: The key pair is required to access instances via SSH.

- **Task definitions:** As mentioned before, each container instance hosts one or more Docker containers inside it. To run these Docker containers inside the container instance, we need to provide a configuration file to define how the container will run and how much resource will it take and many more. So basically, that Configuration file is know as Task definition. It is required to run docker containers inside ECS. The following parameters are the most common while configuring a task definition:
  - The Docker image to be used
  - The CPU is and the memory usage limit
  - Ports needed to map from container to the instance
  - Commands the container should run when started
  - The env variable to pass to the container
  - The volume to be passed to the container

The preceding parameters are usually passed with the Docker containers, but apart from that, we can also mention AWS-specific features, such as IAM roles, and so on. The following is a sample example of the empty task definition:

```
{
"family": "",
"taskRoleArn": "",
"networkMode": "",
"containerDefinitions": [
{
"memory": 1024,
"cpu": 100,
"links": ["mysql"],
"portMappings": [
{
"hostPort": 8080,
"containerPort": 8080,
"protocol": "tcp"
}
],
```

```
"essential": true,
"name": "CONTAINER_NAME",
"environment": [
{
"name": "JAVA_OPTS",
"value": "-Xms64m -Xmx256m"
},
],
"image": "PATH_TO_THE_DOCKER_IMAGE",
"logConfiguration": {
"logDriver": "awslogs",
"options": {
"awslogs-group": "LOG_GROUP",
"awslogs-region": "LOG_REGION",
"awslogs-stream-prefix": "LOG_PROJECT"
}
}
}
]
}
```

- **Service**: We know how containers are defined and where it will be hosted, but the question is how and who manages the containers lifecycle? Who manages the number of tasks (running container) per task definition. So for this, AWS provides something called **service**. The ECS service allows to maintain the number of instance of task definition in an ECS cluster. A major role of service is to maintain the exact or desired number of instances running. Let's say for some reason if a task stops or fails, then at that moment of time, the service scheduler will take care of it. This means it will launch another instance for replacement and keep the same number of instances active. Whenever new tasks are launched, the service will try to balance them across AZs. The balancing strategy considers the following criteria:

  - Find out which container instances will be able to support task definition. Based on that, the service will check whether those container instances have enough resources such as memory, CPU, and available ports to run the task definition.

  - When we have those container instances filtered by the preceding step, the EC2 service will sort them from the least used Availability Zones to the most used ones. The Availability Zone with fewer container instances will have priority over others.

  - When we have the best Availability Zone with the fewer container instances, the EC2 service will place the task in the optimal place.

Now using the preceding components, we will be creating an ECS cluster and deploying a static application.

Getting ready

We will use the following steps to deploy a static application in an ECS cluster.

- Create an ECS cluster
- Create a task definition
- Run the task using task definition in an ECS cluster
- Verify the container of the application running inside the container instance
- Verify the application is up and running

How to do it...

So first of all we need to setup an ECS cluster. To set up ECS cluster use the following steps:

1. Go to the AWS Console and click on **EC2 Container Service** residing in the **Compute** section. Once you click on it, you will get the following screen (if you are using ECS for the first time), then click on **Get Started**:

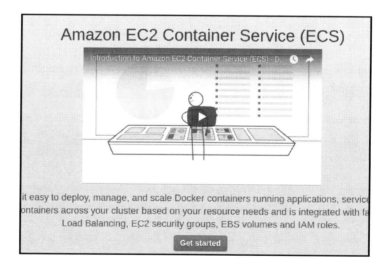

2. A page appears where we will be asked to choose **Deploy a sample application** and **Store container images**. If you select both the options and click on **continue**, a wizard comes and let you go through the whole setup: creating a repository, setting up a cluster, and deploying an application inside it. Click on **cancel** and go ahead, because we will set up a cluster separately and create a task definition so that we will get clear picture and concept:

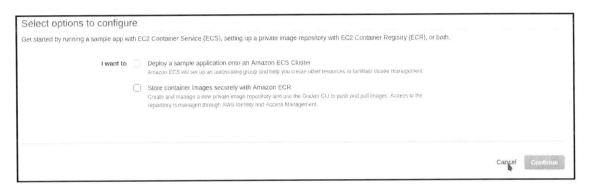

3. Now, we will get the ECS console that has three sections to the left, and those sections are cluster, task definition, and repositories. By default we will be in **Cluster** section. So we need to click on **Create Cluster**:

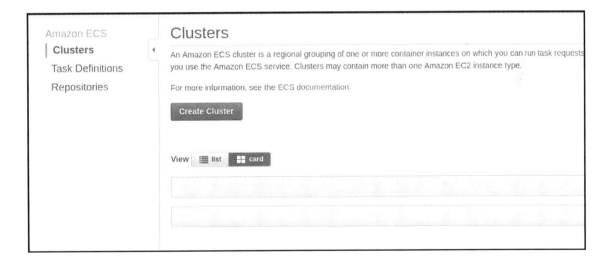

4. After clicking on **Create Cluster,** we will get a screen, where we have to fill up the following details:

    1. **Cluster name**: AWSSTAR
    2. **Provisioning Model: On-Demand Instance**
    3. **EC2 instance type: t2.medium**
    4. Number of instances: 1
    5. **EBS storage (GiB)**: 22 (Min)
    6. **Key pair**- Select your key pair name through which you can SSH into the container instance:

5. **VPC**: Either you can create a new VPC or you can select your own VPC and concerned subnets. Here, we select **Create a new VPC**.

6. **Security group**: Either you can select **Create a new Security Group** or you can select your own Security Group. Here, we select **Create a new Security Group**.

7. **Container instance IAM role**: Either you can select **Create new role** or you can create an ECS role.

8. Once you have completed filling all the required fields, click on **Create**:

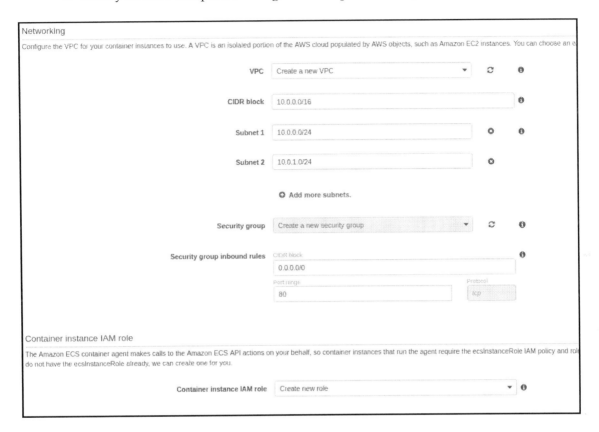

9. After clicking on **Create cluster**, we will be seeing a Launch status page. So basically, AWS at the backend runs a Cloudformation Stack, which sets up everything:

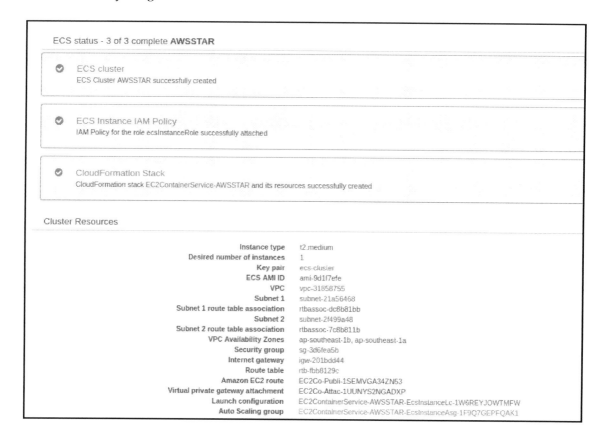

ECS status - 3 of 3 complete **AWSSTAR**

✓ ECS cluster
ECS Cluster AWSSTAR successfully created

✓ ECS Instance IAM Policy
IAM Policy for the role ecsInstanceRole successfully attached

✓ CloudFormation Stack
CloudFormation stack EC2ContainerService-AWSSTAR and its resources successfully created

Cluster Resources

Instance type	t2.medium
Desired number of instances	1
Key pair	ecs-cluster
ECS AMI ID	ami-9d1f7efe
VPC	vpc-31858755
Subnet 1	subnet-21a56468
Subnet 1 route table association	rtbassoc-dc8b81bb
Subnet 2	subnet-2f499a48
Subnet 2 route table association	rtbassoc-7c8b811b
VPC Availability Zones	ap-southeast-1b, ap-southeast-1a
Security group	sg-3d6fea5b
Internet gateway	igw-201bdd44
Route table	rtb-fbb8129c
Amazon EC2 route	EC2Co-Publi-1SEMVGA34ZN63
Virtual private gateway attachment	EC2Co-Attac-1UUNYS2NGADXP
Launch configuration	EC2ContainerService-AWSSTAR-EcsInstanceLc-1W6REYJOWTMFW
Auto Scaling group	EC2ContainerService-AWSSTAR-EcsInstanceAsg-1F9Q7GEPFQAK1

10. Now while creating the ECS cluster, AWS launches Container Instance in the Auto Scaling group. You can see the name of Auto Scaling group in the cluster resources of the preceding image. Once you click on the **Launch Configuration** of AWSSTAR, you will be redirected to the Launch Configuration page and there we can see that a Launch Configuration is created:

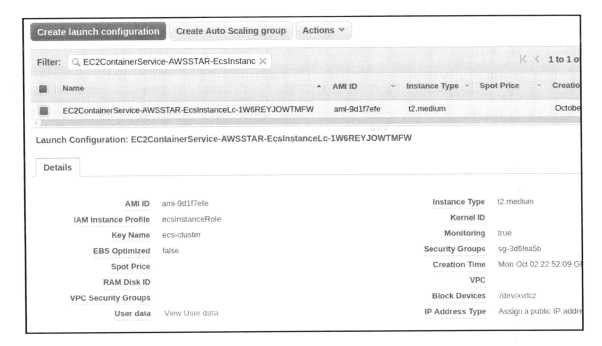

11. If we click on **View User data**, we will see a `bash` command which assigns every instance launched with the launch configuration to the AWSSTAR ECS cluster:

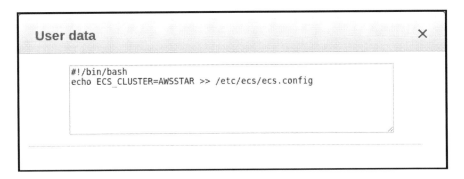

12. Again, let's go back to **ECS Launch status** and click on **View Cluster**. Then, we can see an ECS **Cluster: AWSSTAR** is in the **ACTIVE** status. We can also see that a container instance is attached with the cluster:

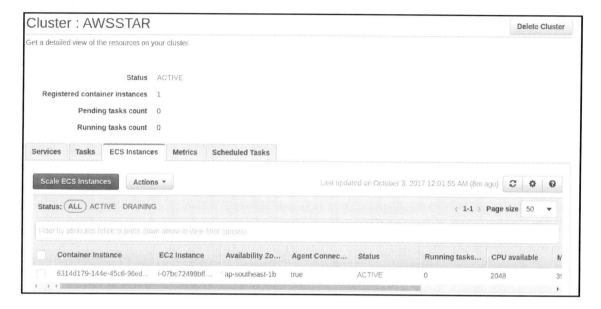

This was all about creating an ECS cluster. Now, let's create a task definition.

To create a task definition, we have to perform the following actions:

1. Go to the ECS console, click on **Task Definition** (left side), and then click on **Create new Task Definition**:

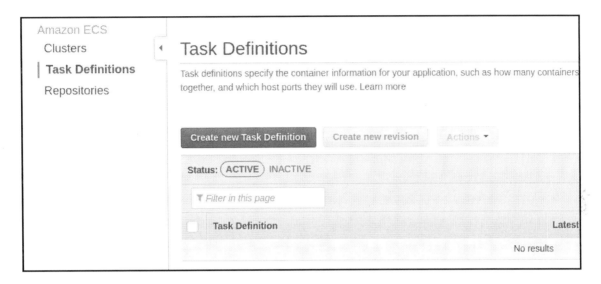

2. After clicking on **Create new Task Definition,** we have to fill all the parameter values:
   - **Task Definition Name**: httpd
   - **Task Role**: **None** (for now)
   - **Network Mode**: **Bridge**

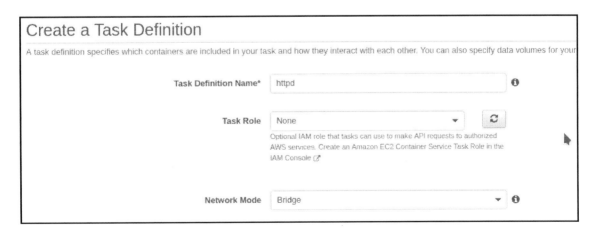

3. Now in the **Container Definition** section, we will be clicking on **Add Container** and then a slider will come where we have to fill the following details:

- **Container Name**: webserver
- **Image**: httpd (if you are simply putting Image name without repo, it will fetch it from DockerHub instead of ECR)
- **Memory Limit**: Hard Limit-128MB. If you specify a hard limit memory, your container will be killed if it attempts to exceed that limit. If you specify a soft limit memoryReservation, ECS reserves that amount of memory for your container; however, the container can request up to the hard limit, if specified, or all of the available memory on the container instance, whichever is reached first. If you specify both, the hard limit must be greater than the soft limit.
- **Port Mapping**: HostPort 80 -> ContainerPort 80

4. Then, click on **Add**:

1. Once we are done adding the container, scroll down and click on **Create**. Then, we will have a task definition **httpd:1**:

Now once we are done with creating, let's run tasks using the task definition.

To run tasks on Container Instance, we have to perform the following actions:

1. Go to the ECS console and click on **Task Definition** (left most); then, we will get a task definition httpd that we just created earlier. Click on **checkbox of httpd** and then click on **Actions**. Now, select **Run Task**:

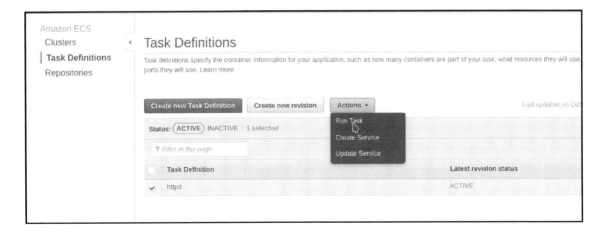

2. After Clicking on **Run task**, we will get another page where we have to fill the following information:

- Cluster: AWSSTAR
- Number of tasks: 1
- Task Group: Leave blank because we are creating it for the first time.
- Placement Templates: AZ Balanced Spread (this template will spread tasks across availability zones and within the availability zone spread tasks across instances)

3. Click on **Run Task**:

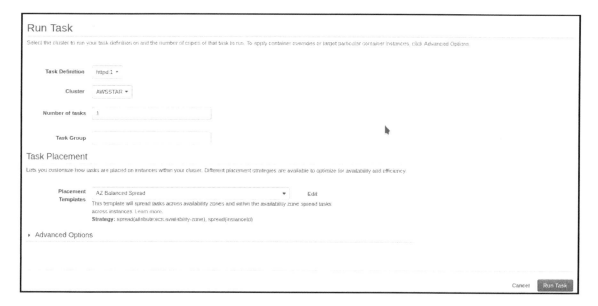

4. Then, we will be redirected to the ECS cluster as **AWSSTAR**, and in the **Tasks** tab of the cluster, we can see that there will be one task running. Now the **Last status** is RUNNING:

Since the task is running inside the container instance, let's verify all things are running inside the container instance.

Verifying containers inside the Container instance

To check the status of containers inside the Container instance, we need to ssh inside **Container instance** using its public IP.

1. Click on **Instance ID** below the EC2 **Instances** tab, then we will be redirected to the EC2 console; from there, we can fetch the public IP:

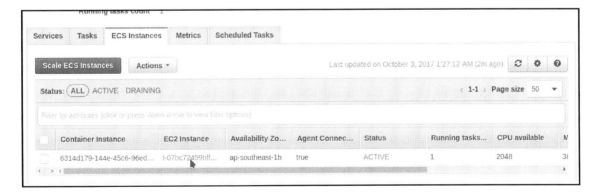

2. The following image shows the EC2 instance public IP:

3. Now, open your system terminal and use the key pair try to ssh into this EC2 instance or **Container instance**. (Before that open port 22 in the **Security group** of that EC2 instance.)

4. Once we get inside the instance, carry out `docker ps`, which will show two containers running. The first container has been triggered and run by task definition, and another one is `ecs-agent`, which will run by default:

5. Here we can verify that the HTTPD container is running inside the container instance. Now, it's time to verify the application. To verify the application we can simply hit the public IP of the instance:

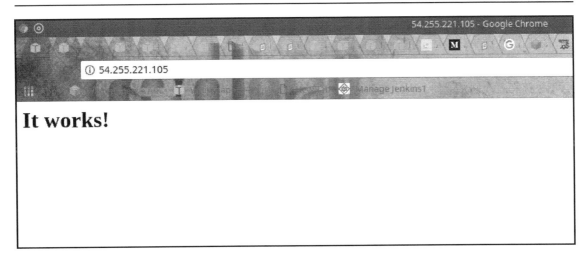

It shows the output in the browser. In this way, we can work around with ECS. Now, we are all setup for achieving CI/CD for microservices using ECS and developer tools of AWS.

6

Continuous Deployment to ECS Using Developer Tools and CloudFormation

In this chapter, we will cover the recipes to build a pipeline for continuous deployment of the containerized application to AWS ECS using CodeCommit, CodeBuild, CloudFormation, and CodePipeline:

- Understanding the architecture and workflow
- Setting up the infrastructure to host the application
- Setting up CodeCommit for our application source
- Creating a CodeBuild project for the build stage
- Understanding the inside content of helper files (BuildSpec.yml, Dockerfile, and CF template)
- Creating a CodePipeline using CodeCommit, CodeBuild, and CloudFormation

Introduction

This chapter is all about continuous deployment of a containerized application to AWS ECS using developers tools of AWS and CloudFormation. Once we are done with the previous chapter, it's a good time to go ahead and implement a CI/CD Pipeline which will build the application and deploy it into the staging or production environment.

This chapter assumes that one should know basics of the following things:

- AWS developers tools (Chapters 1 to 4)
- Basic knowledge of AWS services, such as Auto Scaling, ELB, and IAM (although the steps will be performed to achieve these in a pipeline)
- AWS ECS, Docker, and understanding Dockerfile
- Linux

Understanding the architecture and workflow

Consider the following scenario:

We have a Maven-based Java application in a CodeCommit repository master branch (assume its the final, tested and latest code which is production ready). This application will get build by CodeBuild and then will be containerized. Once it will get containerized, it is then deployed on servers. The web servers are set up on AWS. As a part of the architecture, the servers are part of the ECS cluster and featured with Auto Scaling and serving under the load balancer. Every time a new feature is developed, we have to manually run the build and deploy the image in ECS. But don't you think that it will take more time to do this? We should automate it and leave the hurdles behind. Before that, let's see our web server infrastructure diagram.

How to do it...

The following is the architecture diagram of infrastructure that will server the web application:

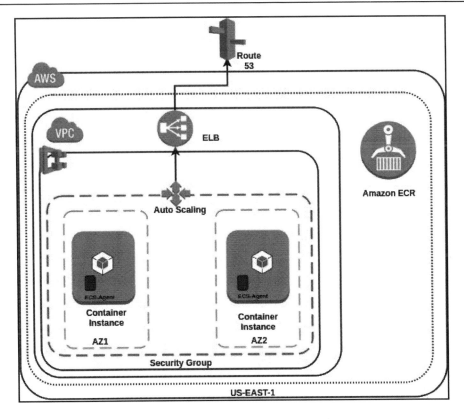

Steps to achieve the preceding infrastructure is mentioned here:

1. Set up an ECS cluster with a minimum of two container instances (the reason will be explained in the implementation).
2. ECS runs the CloudFormation stack to create cluster due to which the container instance will spin up with Auto Scaling, so there is no need to set up Auto Scaling separately.
3. Create a classic ELB and register the existing instances into it. Edit the Auto Scaling group of ECS and update it with the classic ELB.
4. Once the ECS cluster is registered with the classic LoadBalancer, give the ELB DNS a value of the CNAME record on the URL record set in route 53.
5. Post that, create an Amazon ECR, which will store the Docker images.

In this chapter, we are using a classic LoadBalancer, but you can also use ALB and the dynamic Port feature. To know more about this, visit `http://www.tothenew.com/blog/dynamic-port-mapping-in-ecs-with-application-load-balancer/`.

How it works...

Here we will see the workflow through the architecture diagram, which is given as follows:

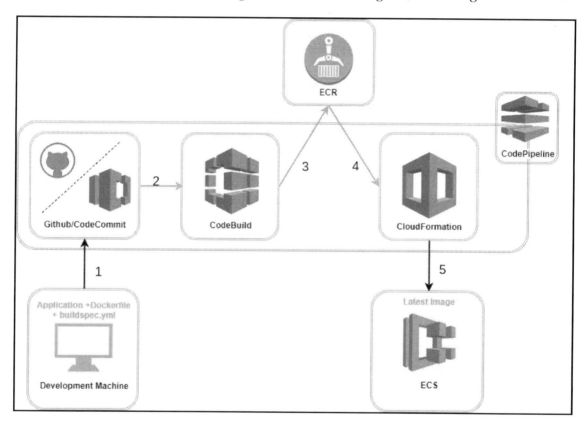

According to the preceding diagram, the workflow will be in the following manner:

1. Let's start with the application, which is in the development or staging environment and ready for production. So, developers will push the code in the master branch of the repository. It can be either on GitHub or CodeCommit (in this chapter we are using CodeCommit). Along with the application, the Dockerfile, Buildspec.yml, and CloudFormation template are also in the root directory.

2. Now CodeCommit is a part of CodePipeline, and in CodePipeline we have other tools integrated, which will also get triggered. When developers push the application code in CodeCommit, the *Source* stage of pipeline will begin to run. The *Source* stage also produces an output artifact called **MyApp**. This artifact will be considered as an input artifact for the next stage *Build*.

3. After some time in the *Source* Stage, the *Build* stage will get triggered automatically. In this stage, CodeBuild is integrated, so it will run the build process using BuildSpec.yml file. In this file, developers have given Dockerfile to build the image and push it to ECR. So in the build step, we are basically building the application and containerizing it, as well as pushing it into ECR. Here, the Build stage produces an output artifact **MyAppBuild** .

4. After the build stage, the *Deploy* stage comes into the picture. It is integrated with CloudFormation, which will use the CloudFormation template to create or update a stack. The responsibility of the stack is to create a task definition and service, and assign it to the ECS cluster.

5. In this manner, ECS will start running the task; meaning, it will pull the image form ECR and start running it.

In this way, the entire pipeline will work, but these were only the implementation steps. There will be lots of tweaks and turns while implementing these steps. First of all, we have to set up the infrastructure, according to the infrastructure diagram.

Setting up the infrastructure to host the application

In this recipe, we will be setting up scalable and fault tolerant Infrastructure to deploy the containerized application.

Getting ready

To set up the infrastructure according to the diagram in the previous recipe, we have to perform the following operations:

1. Create an ECS cluster with a minimum of two instances.
2. Create a classic load balancer and register the ECS instance into that ELB.
3. Also, edit ECS Auto Scaling and update the newly created load balancer in it.
4. Create an Amazon ECR repository, which will store the containerized application image.

How to do it...

To set up the infrastructure, a detailed explanation and implementation is provided here:

Creating an ECS cluster

1. To create an ECS cluster, go to the AWS console and click on the EC2 container engine in the
   Compute section. After that, click on **Create Cluster** and fill or select the following information.
   - Cluster name: ECS-ECSAPP
   - Provisioning model: On-demand instance
   - Instance type: t2.small (for this application its sufficient)
   - Number of instances: 2
   - Storage: 22 (minimum)
   - KeyPair: Select any key pair, which will allow you to SSH inside the container instance
   - Keep the networking section as it is if you want to create a new VPC and Security group, else you can select your VPC, Subnet, and Security group
   - Container instance IAM role: Create new role

2. After filling these details, click on **Create**, which will start creating the ECS cluster by running the CloudFormation stack at the backend:

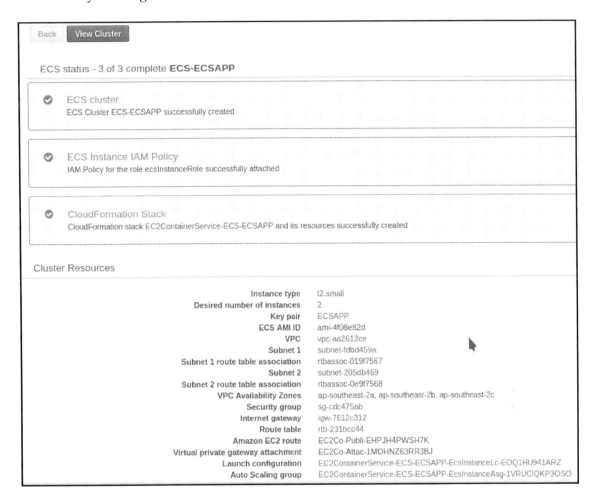

3. Now, let's take a look at the instance status of the ECS cluster. Click on **View Cluster** and go to the ECS **Instances** tab:

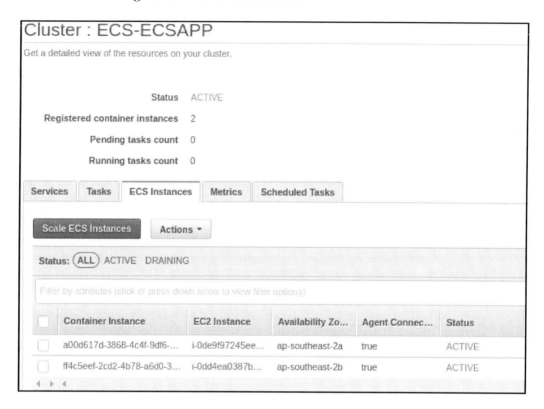

4. Both the instances are in the **Active** state. Now, let's create a load balancer and register the instances.

Creating a Load Balancer (Classic ELB)

A load balancer basically distributes incoming application traffic across multiple EC2 instances in multiple availability zones. This increases the fault tolerance of your applications. Elastic load balancing detects unhealthy instances and routes traffic only to healthy instances.

1. To create a load balancer, go to the EC2 console, click on **Load Balancers** in the **Load Balancing** section at the left side. After that, click on **Create Load Balancer**:

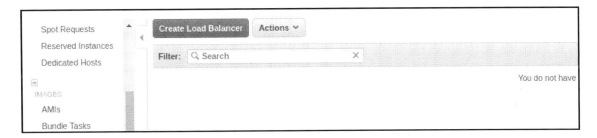

2. Once we click on **Create Load Balancer**, we will land on another page, where we will be asked to choose the load balancer type. Here, we pick Classic ELB, because we need network layer routing and not application layer routing:

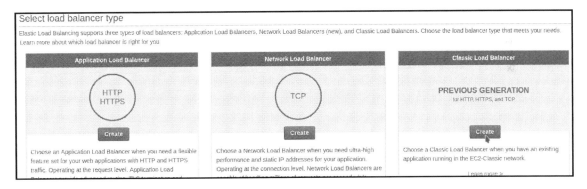

3. After choosing **Classic Load Balancer**, we will enter the **Load Balancer** wizard, in which the first step is to define load balancer. Here, we have to enter or select the following information:
   - **Load Balancer name**: LB-ECSAPP
   - **Create LB Inside**: We have to select the same VPC in which the ECS Cluster Instances lies.

- **Listener Configuration**: LB Port 80 should listen to Instance Port 80.
- Select both the available subnets. Basically two subnets in different availability zones provides higher availability for your load balancer. After that, click on **Next: Assign Security Groups**:

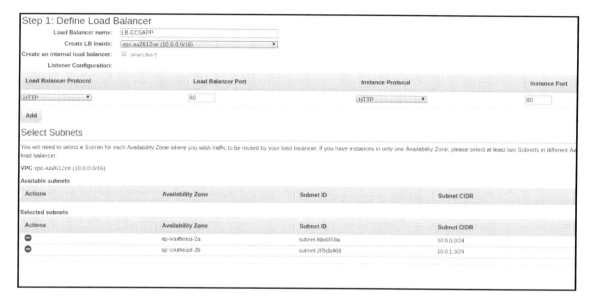

4. Once we click on **Next: Security Group**, we will move to step 2. Select the existing security group, which was created by ECS:

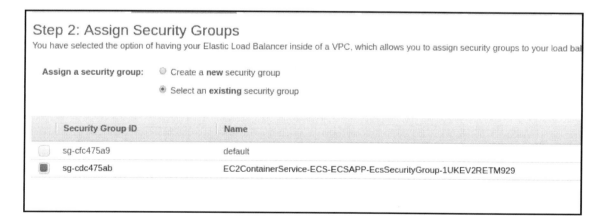

5. After that, click on **Next: Configure Security settings.** In this step, we can upload the SSL certificate, which will improve our load balancer security.

We haven't given port 443/https in the LB port, because we don't need it now. But, it's always a good practice to use either the HTTPS or the SSL protocol for your frontend connection. Click on **Next: Configure health check**. Here, we can fill the information as seen in the following image and click on **Next: Add EC2 Instances**:

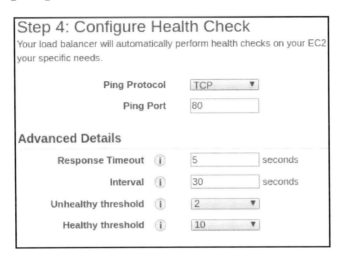

6. Once we click on **Add EC2 Instances**, we will get Step 5, where we have to select both the instances created by the ECS cluster. Then, click on **Next: Add Tags**:

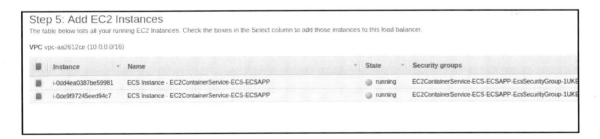

7. After that, we have to give some tags names and values. Post that, click on **Review**; after reviewing, click on **create**. Then, we will have a load balancer with two instances registered with it, but both instances will be in and out of services, because there is no application running and serving on port 80 in container instances, which basically fails the condition of health checks:

8. Once we are done with creating the load balancer, let's register the Auto Scaling group created by ECS cluster.

Register Auto Scaling with Load Balancer

1. It's very simple and straightforward to add an Auto Scaling group to Load Balancer. First, go to the Auto Scaling console from the EC2 console, and select the Auto Scaling group created by ECS. After that, click on **Action** and then **Edit**:

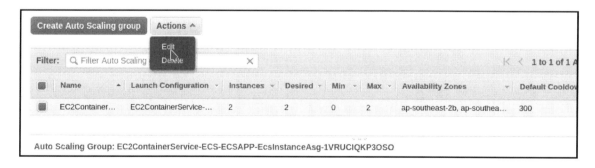

2. Once we click on **Edit**, then scroll down, and click on the **Load Balancers** section. Automatically, our recently created ELB will come. We have to select that and click on **Save**:

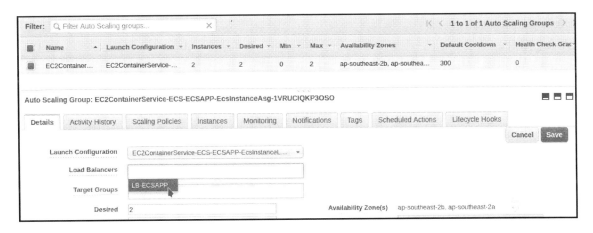

We registered the Auto Scaling group with a Load Balancer. Now, it's time to create an ECR Repository.

Creating an Amazon ECR

To create an ECR repository, go to Amazon EC2 Container Registry and click the **Repository** section at the left-most corner. After that, click on **Create Repository** and mention **Repository name** as `ecr-ecsapp`, and then click on **Next step** and we will have our ECR repository:

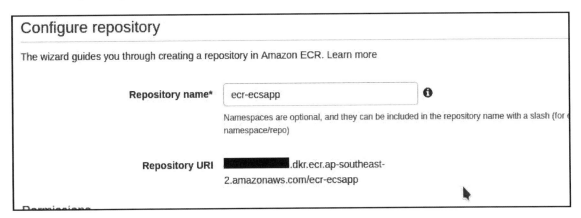

Until now, we basically set up the infrastructure. Now, it's time to create a pipeline.

Setting Up CodeCommit for our application source

In this recipe, we will clone the application code along with helper files (BuildSpec.yml + Dockerfile + CF template) from GitHub and will mirror it to the CodeCommit repository.

Getting ready

We will be performing the following operations:

- Creating a repository **CC-ECSAPP** in CodeCommit
- Cloning the GitHub URL, which has the application code along with the mirror option
- Then we will, push the same cloned application code into the CodeCommit repository **CC-ECSAPP**

How to do it...

First, create a CodeCommit repository named CC-ECSAPP as follows:

1. Go to the AWS console and click on **CodeCommit**, lying in developers tools.
2. Click on **create new repository** and mention the repository name and description. Then, click on **Create repository**:

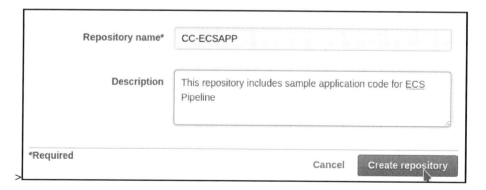

3. Now, clone the URL `https://github.com/awsstar/Sample-App-ECS-Pipeline.` `git` with the mirror option, and then again, push the same into the CodeCommit repository `CC-ECSAPP`:

```
root@awsstar:~# git clone --mirror
https://github.com/awsstar/Sample-App-ECS-Pipeline.git transferFolder
    Cloning into bare repository 'transferFolder'...
    remote: Counting objects: 31, done.
    remote: Compressing objects: 100% (19/19), done.
    remote: Total 31 (delta 1), reused 31 (delta 1), pack-reused 0
    Unpacking objects: 100% (31/31), done.
    Checking connectivity... done.
    root@awsstar:~# cd transferFolder/
    root@awsstar:~/transferFolder# git push https://git-codecommit.ap-
southeast-2.amazonaws.com/v1/repos/CC-ECSAPP --all
    Username for 'https://git-codecommit.ap-southeast-2.amazonaws.com':
iamuser-at-2xxxxxxxx6
    Password for 'https://iamuser-at-2xxxxxxxx6@git-codecommit.ap-
southeast-2.amazonaws.com':
    Counting objects: 31, done.
    Delta compression using up to 4 threads.
    Compressing objects: 100% (20/20), done.
    Writing objects: 100% (31/31), 11.20 KiB | 0 bytes/s, done.
    Total 31 (delta 1), reused 0 (delta 0)
    To https://git-codecommit.ap-southeast-2.amazonaws.com/v1/repos/CC-
ECSAPP
      * [new branch] master -> master
```

4. Now, we can see that we have the application code in the CC-ECS repository:

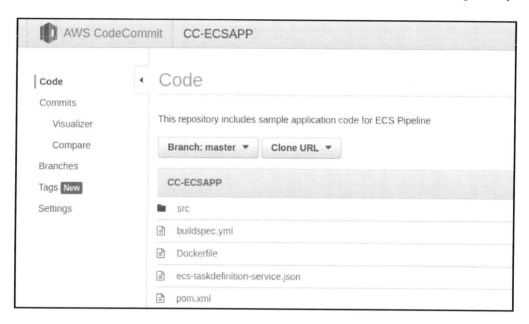

The helper file in the repository still needs some information related to your resource name. So, this is not a final push to the repository. We will tweak helper files at the end while running the pipeline.

Creating a CodeBuild project for the build stage

In this recipe, we will create a CodeBuild project, which will build the image and push it to ECR using BuildSpec.yml.

Getting ready

We will be carrying out following operations to create a CodeBuild project `CB-ECSAPP`:

- Create a CodeBuild project with the name `CB-ECSAPP` and integrate it with the CodeCommit.
- While selecting build environment, we need to select Ubuntu OS and runtime as Docker because while in the build process, the docker image will get build and for that, the build environment should have a docker client installed.

Let's go ahead and create a build project for the build stage of pipeline.

How to do it...

To create a build project, which will be integrated in the pipeline, we have to perform the following steps:

1. Go to the AWS console, and click on **CodeBuild,** which lies in the **Developer Tools** section.
2. After that, click on **Create Project** and fill or select the following details:
   - **Project name**: CB-ECSAPP
   - **Source provider**: AWS CodeCommit
   - **Repository**: CC-ECSAPP
   - Environment image: Use an image managed by AWS CodeBuild
   - OS: Ubuntu
   - Runtime: Docker
   - Version: aws/codebuild/docker:1.12.1
   - Build specification: Use the buildspec.yml in the source code root directory
   - Artifact Type: None (cause it's already mentioned in BuildSpec.yml)
   - Service Role: Create a service role in your account (later, you have to attach the EC2 Container Registry access Policy with this role)

3. After filling the preceding details, review it and click on **Save**:

Until here, we created a CodeCommit repository and a CodeBuild project. Now, we have to create a CloudFormation stack; but before that, we need to understand what actually is written inside helper files.

Understanding the inside content of helper files (BuildSpec.yml, Dockerfile, and CF template)

In this recipe, we will see and understand what's there inside the helper files. We will analyze the flow of the BuildSpec.yml file and how it is basically creating image of the application and pushing it to ECR. Post that, we will understand Dockerfile. Then, we will understand how CloudFormation carries out its magic. Post that, we will update the helper files with our resource name.

How to do it...

The build stage of CodePipeline is integrated with CodeBuild, and here Codebuild is using BuildSpec.yml as the build command reference file. CodeBuild will pull the latest application code in the build environment, and then create an image of it. While creating image using Dockerfile it also builds the application using mvn. It means the build of application code takes place inside the Dockerfile only. Let's understand it in detail.

Here we have a `BuildSpec.yml` file:

```
version: 0.2
env:
 variables:
 AWS_DEFAULT_REGION: "MENTION YOUR REGION"
 AWS_ACCOUNT_ID: "MENTION YOUR ACCOUNT ID"
 IMAGE_REPO_NAME: "MENTION YOUR ECR REPO NAME"
 IMAGE_TAG: "latest"
phases:
 pre_build:
 commands:
 - sudo apt-get update -y && apt-get install jq -y
 - echo Logging in to Amazon ECR...
 - $(aws ecr get-login --region $AWS_DEFAULT_REGION)
 build:
 commands:
 - echo Build started on `date`
 - echo Building the Docker image...
 - docker build -t $IMAGE_REPO_NAME .
 - docker tag $IMAGE_REPO_NAME:$IMAGE_TAG
$AWS_ACCOUNT_ID.dkr.ecr.$AWS_DEFAULT_REGION.amazonaws.com/$IMAGE_REPO_NAME:
$IMAGE_TAG
 post_build:
```

```
commands:
- echo Build completed on `date`
- echo Pushing the Docker image...
- docker push
$AWS_ACCOUNT_ID.dkr.ecr.$AWS_DEFAULT_REGION.amazonaws.com/$IMAGE_REPO_NAME:
$IMAGE_TAG
- tmp=$(mktemp) && SHA=$(docker inspect YOURREPOURI:latest | jq -c
'.[0].RepoDigests' | sed 's/[][]//g' | sed 's/"//g') && jq -r --arg SHA
"$SHA"
'.Resources.TaskDefinition1.Properties.ContainerDefinitions[0].Image=$SHA'
ecs-taskdefinition-service.json > "$tmp" && mv -f "$tmp" ecs-
taskdefinition-service.json
artifacts:
 files:
 - ecs-taskdefinition-service.json
 discard-paths: yes
```

1. In the variable section, we can see some variable region, account ID, ECR-repo-name and tag. These variables will be used in the build phases of this file.

2. In the pre-build phase, we are updating the environment and installing jq, which is needed during JSON manipulation. After that, the docker client of the build environment is authenticating itself with the ECR repository.

3. In the Build phase, the Docker image is created using Dockerfile, which was present in the application root directory. After that, the image is getting tagged with the repository and the latest tag.

4. In the post-build phase, the docker image is uploaded to the Amazon ECR repository. After that, we fetch the RepoDigest of the latest image and update it into the CloudFormation template. So when CloudFormation will update the stack, it will update the latest image in the task definition.

In this way, `BuildSpec.yml` helps CodeBuild to carry out its process. Now, let's discuss Dockerfile:

```
FROM maven:3.5.0-jdk-8
RUN apt-get update -y && apt-get install mongodb-server -y
ADD . /App
WORKDIR /App
RUN mvn package -DskipTests
EXPOSE 8080
ENTRYPOINT service mongodb start && java -jar target/my-first-app-1.0-
SNAPSHOT-fat.jar
```

1. In the Dockerfile, we are using the base image as maven and the version is 3.5.0 with JDK8. The image distribution is Debian, meaning we can use an apt package manager to install any package.

2. In the second step, we install dependencies, which is the mongodb server.

3. After that, we add the application code lying in the build environment to `App` folder.

4. Post that, we change the directory to `App` and run `mvn package`, which will basically build the application.

5. Then, exposing port `8080`, means our application is running on port `8080`.

6. The entry point means when the container will get launched; at that moment of time, the command will get executed. Here, we are starting the mongodb server service and running the application:

> In the preceding Dockerfile, there is something which is not written in the best way. We should try to keep our Docker image as small as possible (but required things must be there). But, here while building the application, we are leaving everything (src, target, and layouts) as it is, meaning the build artifact as well the application code. However, in production machine, we only require the build artifact to run the application (in our case, we only need target folder, but the rest of the files and folder are also there). To solve this kind of issue, we can use a multistage Docker build. This means, you can build applications in one image and copy the artifact in the other image. Upload the final image to the registry. To know more about multistage Docker build, visit `https://docs.docker.com/engine/userguide/eng-image/multistage-build`.

Let's see what is inside the CloudFormation template:

```
{
  "AWSTemplateFormatVersion":"2010-09-09",
  "Parameters": {
  "Tag": {
  "Type": "String",
  "Default": "latest"
  },
  "DesiredCount": {
  "Type": "Number",
  "Default": 1
  },
  "Cluster": {
  "Type": "String",
  "Default": "YOURECSCLUSTER"
  },
  "Repository": {
  "Type": "String",
  "Default": "YOUR ECR REPO NAME"
  }
```

```
},
"Resources": {
"Service": {
"Type": "AWS::ECS::Service",
"Properties": {
"Cluster": { "Ref": "Cluster" },
"DesiredCount": { "Ref": "DesiredCount" },
"TaskDefinition": { "Ref": "TaskDefinition1" }
}
},
"TaskDefinition1": {
"Type": "AWS::ECS::TaskDefinition",
"Properties": {
"ContainerDefinitions": [
{
"Name": "awsstar-app-ecs",
"Image": "YOURREPONAME:latest",
"Cpu": "1",
"PortMappings": [
{
"ContainerPort": "8080",
"HostPort": "80"
}
],
"Memory": "512",
"Essential": "true"
}
]
}
}
}
```

This file is responsible for creating task definition and services, which will be assigned to an ECS cluster. In the post-build section of `BuildSpec.yml`, we are modifying one key of this file and that is the image. We replace the value of the key Image with the RepoDigest of latest image. In the next run, CloudFormation will update the stack.

Now, let's gather all the resource information and update the helper files:

```
AWS_DEFAULT_REGION: "ap-southeast-2"     (You can choose your own region)
AWS_ACCOUNT_ID: "YOUR AWS ACCOUNTID"
IMAGE_REPO_NAME: "ecr-ecsapp"
YOURREPOURI:
```

We will modify the `BuildSpec.yml` file first:

```
version: 0.2
env:
 variables:
 AWS_DEFAULT_REGION: "ap-southeast-2"
 AWS_ACCOUNT_ID: "2xxxxxxxx6"
 IMAGE_REPO_NAME: "ecr-ecsapp"
 IMAGE_TAG: "latest"
phases:
 pre_build:
 commands:
 - sudo apt-get update -y && apt-get install jq -y
 - echo Logging in to Amazon ECR...
 - $(aws ecr get-login --region $AWS_DEFAULT_REGION)
 build:
 commands:
 - echo Build started on `date`
 - echo Building the Docker image...
 - docker build -t $IMAGE_REPO_NAME .
 - docker tag $IMAGE_REPO_NAME:$IMAGE_TAG
$AWS_ACCOUNT_ID.dkr.ecr.$AWS_DEFAULT_REGION.amazonaws.com/$IMAGE_REPO_NAME:
$IMAGE_TAG
 post_build:
 commands:
 - echo Build completed on `date`
 - echo Pushing the Docker image...
 - docker push
$AWS_ACCOUNT_ID.dkr.ecr.$AWS_DEFAULT_REGION.amazonaws.com/$IMAGE_REPO_NAME:
$IMAGE_TAG
 - tmp=$(mktemp) && SHA=$(docker inspect 2xxxxxxxx6.dkr.ecr.ap-
southeast-2.amazonaws.com/ecr-ecsapp:latest | jq -c '.[0].RepoDigests' |
sed 's/[][]//g' | sed 's/"//g') && jq -r --arg SHA "$SHA"
'.Resources.TaskDefinition1.Properties.ContainerDefinitions[0].Image=$SHA'
ecs-taskdefinition-service.json > "$tmp" && mv -f "$tmp" ecs-
taskdefinition-service.json
artifacts:
 files:
 - ecs-taskdefinition-service.json
 discard-paths: yes
```

Dockerfile will remain the same as it is. But, we need to modify some value in the `cs-taskdefinition-service.json` file. These values are mentioned as follows:

```
ClusterName: ECS-ECSAPP
Repository: ecr-ecsapp
Image: 2xxxxxxxx6.dkr.ecr.ap-southeast-2.amazonaws.com/ecr-ecsapp:latest
```

After making these changes, push it to the `CC-ECSAPP` repository. Now, we are ready to set up CodePipeline.

Creating a CodePipeline using CodeCommit, CodeBuild, and CloudFormation

In this recipe, we will create a CodePipeline, in which we will be integrating our existing CodeCommit repository and CodeBuild project. We will also integrate CloudFormation as a deploy stage.

Getting ready

We will be using the following resources to integrate with the CodePipeline:

- CodeCommit: **CC-ECSAPP**
- CodeBuild: **CB-ECSAPP**
- CloudFormation: **CF-ECSAPP**

How to do it...

1. To set up CodePipeline project, go to AWS console, and click on **CodePipeline** in the **Developer Tools** section. Then, click on **Create pipeline**, and we will land to step 1, which will ask **Pipeline name**. After mentioning the pipeline name as **CP-ECSAPP**, click on **Next step**:

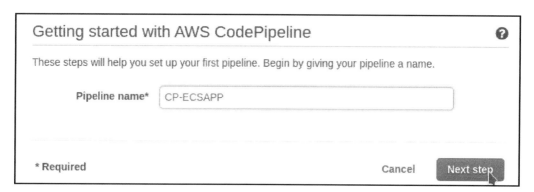

2. The next step will take us to the Source Stage of CodePipeline, where we will be asked to mention the Source provider. In the source provider, we need to select CodeCommit, because our source code lies in CodeCommit. After selecting CodeCommit, we have to provide **Repository name** and branch and then click on **Next step**:

 CodePipeline will use Amazon CloudWatch Events to detect changes in CodeCommit.

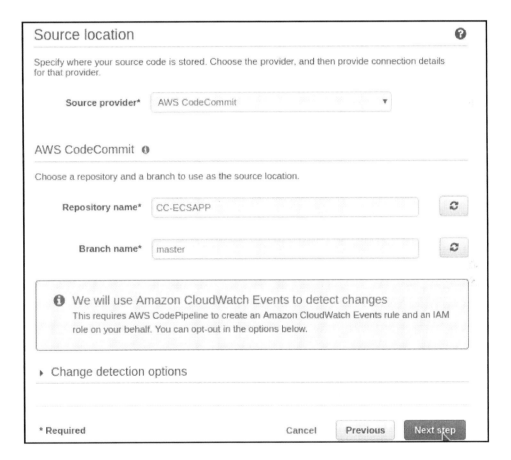

3. In the next step, we will select CodeBuild as **Build provider** and then select our existing CodeBuild project as **CB-ECSAPP**. After that, click on **Next Step** to configure the **Deploy** stage:

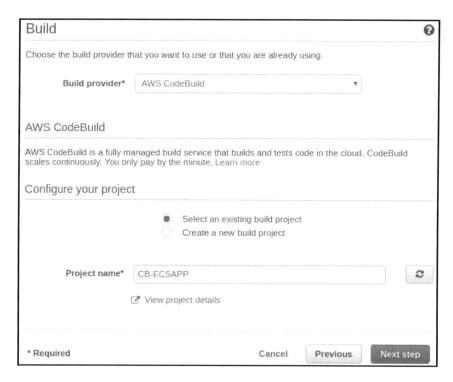

4. Now in the deploy stage, we have to select the deployment provider, which is CloudFormation in our case. After selecting CloudFormation, we have to select or fill additional information about CloudFormation:

- **Action mode**: Create or update stack (in the first run of pipeline, it will create the stack, and in the next run, it will update it)
- **Stack name**: CFT-ECSAPP
- **Template file**: ecs-taskdefinition-service.json (one of helperfile name).
- **Configuration file**: Leave empty, cause all the configuration is already mentioned in the helper file.
- **Capabilities**: **CAPABILITY_IAM**
- **Role name**: Select or create the role name (Role should have the permission of ECS, EC2, S3, CodeCommit), which can be assumed by AWS CloudFormation.

5. After that, click on **Next Step**:

6. We have to create a service role and later select it. Then, review your pipeline and click on **Create Pipeline**. This is how our pipeline will look. Click on **Release change** to start the pipeline:

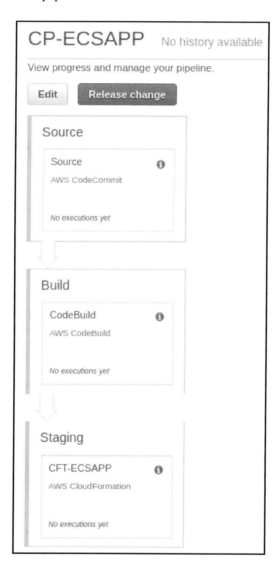

7. Once we trigger the pipeline, source stage will rescan the CodeCommit and trigger CodeBuild. We can check the activities of CodeBuild:

Build

Build ARN	arn:aws:codebuild:ap-southeast-2:230367374156:build/CB-ECSAPP:01603aec-8568-4503-919f-2fe3362ca48d
Build project	CB-ECSAPP
Source provider	AWS CodePipeline
Repository	
Start time	6 minutes ago
End time	6 seconds ago
Status	Succeeded
Initiator	CP-ECSAPP

▸ Build details

Phase details

	Name	Status	Duration
▸	SUBMITTED	Succeeded	
▸	PROVISIONING	Succeeded	25 secs
▸	DOWNLOAD_SOURCE	Succeeded	4 secs
▸	INSTALL	Succeeded	
▸	PRE_BUILD	Succeeded	32 secs
▸	BUILD	Succeeded	3 mins, 15 secs
▸	POST_BUILD	Succeeded	1 min, 18 secs
▸	UPLOAD_ARTIFACTS	Succeeded	
▸	FINALIZING	Succeeded	4 secs
▸	COMPLETED	Succeeded	

8. We can also verify that latest image that got pushed to Amazon ECR:

9. After successful execution of the build stage, deploy stage will get triggered, means CloudFormation will start creating stack and performing its task:

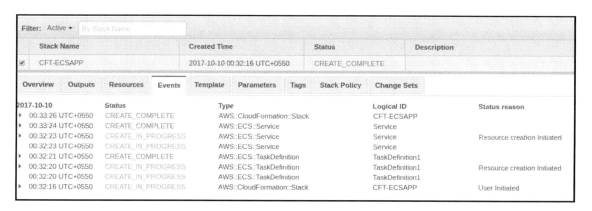

10. Now if we will hit the ELB DNS, we will get the following webpage:

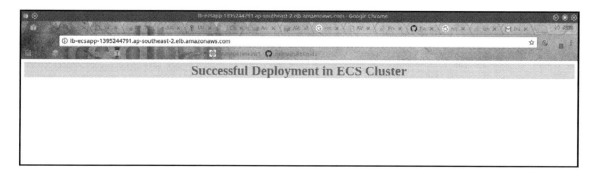

11. Now again if we will change in the source code and again push the code in master branch of `CC-ECSAPP` repository, the pipeline will trigger automatically and it again does its work and updates the latest change in the ECS cluster.

You can change the code of `src/main/java/io/vertx/blog/first/MyFirstVerticle.java` in line 61 to see the change.

In this chapter, we used only AWS-related services; but if your code resides in GitHub (mostly used), then you can follow this blog by AWS to set up the CI/CD pipeline `https://aws.amazon.com/blogs/compute/` `continuous-deployment-to-amazon-ecs-using-aws-codepipeline-aws-` `codebuild-amazon-ecr-and-aws-cloudformation/`. This blog also has the same concept that we followed previously.

7

IaC Using CloudFormation and Ansible

Infrastructure as Code (**IaC**), as the term sounds, is a management of infrastructure (which includes networks, virtual machines, load balancers, and connection topology) in a descriptive model (such as JSON or YAML). This chapter is all about setting up your infrastructure. Since we are using AWS, we would like to automate our infrastructure using CloudFormation and Ansible. The following are the recipes that we will be covering in this chapter:

- AWS CloudFormation and writing the CloudFormation template
- Creating a production-ready Web application infrastructure using CloudFormation
- Automation with Ansible
- Creating an AWS infrastructure using the Ansible EC2 dynamic inventory

Introduction

Managing infrastructure is a process which is associated with software engineering. Enterprises usually have racks hardware; they used to install OS and configure application on top of it to fulfill their technology requirements. With the involvement of Cloud technologies, the on-demand provisioning of VMs, networking, and storing components becomes a lot more easier.

The only problem here is that the provisioning of such infrastructures is done manually by infrastructure managers or DevOps guys, and the manual processes have certain disadvantages, which are mentioned as follows:

- The manual process requires more human capital, which forces a company to endure higher cost to meet important business needs.
- Humans are error prone, which makes inconsistency in infrastructure provisioning, leading to deviations from configuration standards.
- Manual process are slow, which can limit the speed at which your organization can release new version of an application.
- Making documentation and repeating the same task again and again will not be efficient.

IaC provides solutions to these deficiencies by providing automation to the provisioning process. Instead of performing manual steps, administrators and developers can provision the infrastructure using the configuration file. This configuration is treated as a software code.

These files can include sets of rules to provision resources such as compute, storage, network, as well as application services. IaC increases the speed and agility of infrastructure deployments.

There are lots of great tools in the market having some advantage and disadvantages over others. The tools which are booming in the market right now are AWS CloudFormation and Terraform. Since this book is all about AWS, we will be see how to use CloudFormation and set up its infrastructure in one go.

 Terraform is a great IaC tool by Hashicorp Inc. and supports almost all leading Cloud technologies such as AWS, Azure, GCP, OpenStack, and more, whereas CloudFormation is restricted only for AWS.

AWS CloudFormation and writing the CloudFormation template

AWS CloudFormation is a free infrastructure automation service provided by Amazon Web Services. This service helps the customer to set up their infrastructure on AWS, in an easy and automated manner. This service helps you spend less time on managing the resources and more time on focusing on your applications. You can create a CloudFormation template where you can put all the resources that you want to provision (for example, EC2, RDS, and so on) and submit it to the CloudFormation service. Then, this service will take care of provisioning those resources for you. You don't have to create anything and figure out what's dependent on what. There are a couple of scenarios where AWS CloudFormation can help.

Simplify Infrastructure Management: Let's say we have a scalable web application that might use EC2, ELB, and RDS. Normally, what you can do is provision all these resources manually and then later configure all these resources to work together. Post that, you can setup your application on that. All these tasks add up to the complexity and time before you get your web application up and running. Later if you want to delete the application and its resources, you have to manually delete all the resources which are additional time taking.

When we write all the resources which are required to set up a web application in a CloudFormation template and create a stack (we will discuss about stack later), CloudFormation will take care of provisioning all the resources automatically. It will also configure the resources to work together. The best part of it is, if you want to delete the application and its resources, then you simply have to delete the stack. All the resources created by the stack will be deleted automatically.

Replicate your infrastructure: Let's say you have one application up and running in one region (`us-east-1`), and if your application needs additional availability for HA, then you may have to replicate your application into multiple regions so that if one region becomes unavailable, the end users can still be able to access your application from another region. Now the challenging factor in replicating your application is that you have to replicate the same resources as well.

When you use CloudFormation, you can reuse the template in all the regions to setup your resources fast and consistently.

Track and control changes to your infrastructure: Let's say you have setup your infrastructure using the CloudFormation template and want to upgrade your resource incrementally, for example, you might change to a higher performing instance type in your Auto Scaling group. If any problem occurred after that, roll back your infrastructure to the previous or original settings. To roll back, you have to carry out the operation manually, and for that, you not only have to remember which resources were changed but also you have to know what were the original settings.

So whenever you provision your infrastructure with the CloudFormation template, it describes what all the resources will be provisioned and with what settings. Since these templates are text files, you can simply track the differences in your template to track the changes you made in the infrastructure.

Terms and concepts related to AWS CloudFormation

When you use the AWS CloudFormation service, you will deal with templates and stacks. You will create a template file in which you will describe your resources and its properties. When you will create a stack using that template file, CloudFormation will provision the resources that were mentioned in the template.

 A **CloudFormation template** is a file which is written in the JSON and YAML format. You can save these files in any extensions, such as `.yaml`, `.json`, `.cft`, or `.txt`. In this template, we basically mention all the resources that you want to provision. Using this template file, AWS CloudFormation builds your resources.

You can write the CloudFormation template in JSON as well as YAML.

For YAML

```
AWSTemplateFormatVersion: "2010-09-09"
Description: A sample template
Resources:
  MyEC2Instance:
    Type: "AWS::EC2::Instance"
    Properties:
      ImageId: "ami-2f726546"
      InstanceType: t1.micro
      KeyName: testkey
      BlockDeviceMappings:
```

```
DeviceName: /dev/sdm
Ebs:
  VolumeType: io1
  Iops: 200
  DeleteOnTermination: false
  VolumeSize: 20
```

For JSON

```json
{
  "AWSTemplateFormatVersion" : "2010-09-09",
  "Description" : "A sample template",
  "Resources" : {
    "MyEC2Instance" : {
      "Type" : "AWS::EC2::Instance",
      "Properties" : {
        "ImageId" : "ami-2f726546",
        "InstanceType" : "t1.micro",
        "KeyName" : "testkey",
        "BlockDeviceMappings" : [
          {
            "DeviceName" : "/dev/sdm",
            "Ebs" : {
              "VolumeType" : "io1",
              "Iops" : "200",
              "DeleteOnTermination" : "false",
              "VolumeSize" : "20"
            }
          }
        ]
      }
    }
  }
}
```

Both the previous mentioned templates will create the same resource and that is the EC2 server.

Stack: When you write resources in a template, you create a stack in CloudFormation using the template to provision the resources. So basically, a stack is a single unit through which you can manage related resources. If you want to create, update, or delete your resources, then you have to do it by creating, updating, and deleting stack.

Change sets: If you want to make some changes to the live or running resources in a stack, then you have to update the stack. You can update the stack by generating a change set; this means you have to provide the latest template with a change in the change set. After that, it will show you what all the resources will be provisioned or changed. Post reviewing and confirmation, it will update the resources.

When you create a stack to provision the resources, AWS CloudFormation makes underlying service calls to AWS to provision your resources. CloudFormation can perform only actions that you have permission to carry out. For example, to create an EC2 server using CloudFormation, you should have proper permission to create the EC2 server.

This was some theoretical concepts; now, let's see how you can write a CloudFormation template from scratch.

How to do it...

In this recipe, we will see how to write a CF template and then learn how to create a stack using that CF template via the CloudFormation console.

Writing a CF template

To provision and configure your resources with the CF template you must understand and know how to write a CF template. You can use the JSON or YAML format to write a CF template. You can use the CloudFormation designer or any text editor such as sublime or vim to create and save a CF template. You can choose any format (JSON or YAML) with which you are comfortable.

Since YAML provides comment features and JSON does not, I recommend the beginners to go for YAML. In this chapter, we will have examples using YAML-formatted CF templates only. If you are comfortable with JSON, then you can use the online YAML to JSON converter.

Let's see the syntax and structure of the template file which describes your AWS infrastructure:

```
---
AWSTemplateFormatVersion: "version date"

Description:
  String

Metadata:
```

```
     template metadata

Parameters:
  set of parameters

Mappings:
  set of mappings

Conditions:
  set of conditions

Transform:
  set of transforms

Resources:
  set of resources

Outputs:
  set of outputs
```

As you can see, the previous templates have some major sections, in which only one section is mandatory--Resources--and the rest is optional. You can write these sections in any order, but by best practice, it will be helpful if you use logical ordering. We will discuss all the sections one by one.

TemplateFormatVersion (optional): This section basically identifies the capabilities of the template. If you don't specify a value, then CloudFormation takes the latest and default value, which is 2010-09-09. We can write this section in the following manner:

```
AWSTemplateFormatVersion: "2010-09-09"
```

Description (optional): This section allows you to include some details or comments about the templates, for example:

```
Description: >
  This template will setup an EC2 server along with RDS.
```

Metadata (optional): This section is generally used to include arbitrary JSON or YAML objects, which provide additional information or details in the template, for example:

```
Metadata:
  Instances:
    Description: "This instance is for Webapplication"
  Databases:
    Description: "The database have 5GB storage only"
```

`Parameters` (optional): Although this section is optional, but it's very important. As the name sounds, with the help of the parameter section, you can pass custom values into your template when you create a stack. A parameter must contain a value and you can also specify a default value so that if you does not provide any value, it will take the default value, for example:

```
Parameters:
  ParameterLogicalID:
    Type: DataType
    ParameterProperty: value
```

- `ParameterLogicalID` : This is the name of the parameter of which you will pass the value.
- `DataType` : This is like a string or number.
- `ParameterProperty`, which are allowed by AWS are:
  - `AllowedPattern`
  - `AllowedValues`
  - `Default`
  - `ConstraintDescription`
- Each `ParameterProperty` has some value

For example, here we have taken the scenario of instance type, where we have mentioned the default value as t2.micro, and allowed couple of values. Now if you don't provide any value, then by default it will take t2.micro as instance type.

Defining parameters

```
Parameters:
  InstanceTypeParameter:
    Type: String
    Default: t2.micro
    AllowedValues:
      - t2.micro
      - t2.small
      - t2.medium
    Description: Pls Enter t2.micro,t2.small or t2.medium. By default it
  will take t2.micro as allowed values.
```

Using parameters

Within the same template, you can use the `Ref` intrinsic function to specify the parameter value in other parts of the template. The following snippet uses the the previous defined parameter `InstanceTypeParameter`:

```
Ec2Instance:
  Type: AWS::EC2::Instance
  Properties:
    InstanceType:
      Ref: InstanceTypeParameter
    ImageId: ami-3c47a355
```

There are some AWS-specific parameter types as well. For example, if you mention `AWS::EC2::AvailabilityZone::Name`, then the value of current AZ such as us-east-1 will be placed in the CloudFormation template. Similarly, there are many more AWS-specific parameters that exist.

Mapping (optional): The mapping section which is also optional, matches a key to a corresponding set of named values. Let's say if you want to set the values based on region, for example, if the region is `us-east-1`, then choose `ami-6fgsidg`, and if the region is `ap-southeast-1`, then choose `ami-xhdo9j`. Use the `Fn::FindInMap` intrinsic function to retrieve values in a map. The syntax of mapping is as follows:

```
Mappings:
  Mapping:
    Key1:
      Name: ValueX
    Key2:
      Name: ValueY
    Key03:
      Name: ValueZ
```

For example:

```
AWSTemplateFormatVersion: "2010-09-09"
Mappings:
  RegionMap:
    us-east-1:
      "64": "ami-641sde34"
    us-west-1:
      "64": "ami-c9c3478c"
    eu-west-1:
      "64": "ami-9fc2f643"
    ap-southeast-2:
      "64": "ami-67z28c34"
    ap-northeast-1:
```

```
        "64": "ami-8v03a89d"
Resources:
  myEC2Instance:
    Type: "AWS::EC2::Instance"
    Properties:
      ImageId: !FindInMap [RegionMap, !Ref "AWS::Region", 32]
      InstanceType: t2.micro
```

Here in `ImageId`, under property section, the value is retrieved by `!FindInMap`, it will go in the mapping section, then `RegionMap`, then search for the key which is region, then choose the value of the name `64`. Let's say if we are running the template from the `ap-southeast-1` region, the value of `ImageId` will be `ami-66f28c34`.

`Conditions` (optional): As the name sounds, it provides condition functionality in the CF template. For example, let's say you defined a parameter, `ENVTYPE`, and you have given a condition to provision the resource only when `ENVTYPE` is `dev`. If you pass `ENVTYPE` as staging, then it won't provision based on your condition. You can use the following function to apply condition:

- `Fn::And`
- `Fn::Equals`
- `Fn::If`
- `Fn::Not`
- `Fn::Or`

The following is the syntax of `Conditions` of the CloudFormation template:

```
Conditions:
  Logical ID:
    Intrinsic function
```

For example:

```
AWSTemplateFormatVersion: "2010-09-09"
Mappings:
  RegionMap:
    us-east-1:
      AMI: "ami-7f418316"
      TestAz: "us-east-1a"
    us-west-1:
      AMI: "ami-951945d0"
      TestAz: "us-west-1a"
    us-west-2:
      AMI: "ami-16fd7026"
      TestAz: "us-west-2a"
```

```
      eu-west-1:
        AMI: "ami-24506250"
        TestAz: "eu-west-1a"
      sa-east-1:
        AMI: "ami-3e3be423"
        TestAz: "sa-east-1a"
      ap-southeast-1:
        AMI: "ami-74dda626"
        TestAz: "ap-southeast-1a"
      ap-southeast-2:
        AMI: "ami-b3990e89"
        TestAz: "ap-southeast-2a"
      ap-northeast-1:
        AMI: "ami-dcfa4edd"
        TestAz: "ap-northeast-1a"
Parameters:
  EnvType:
    Description: Environment type.
    Default: test
    Type: String
    AllowedValues:
      - prod
      - test
    ConstraintDescription: must specify prod or test.
```
Conditions:
  CreateProdResources: !Equals [!Ref EnvType, prod]
```
Resources:
  EC2Instance:
    Type: "AWS::EC2::Instance"
```
    Condition: CreateProdResources
```
    Properties:
      ImageId: !FindInMap [RegionMap, !Ref "AWS::Region", AMI]
  MountPoint:
    Type: "AWS::EC2::VolumeAttachment"
    Properties:
      InstanceId:
        !Ref EC2Instance
      VolumeId:
        !Ref NewVolume
      Device: /dev/sdh
  NewVolume:
    Type: "AWS::EC2::Volume"
    Properties:
      Size: 100
      AvailabilityZone:
        !GetAtt EC2Instance.AvailabilityZone
Outputs:
  VolumeId:
```

```
Condition: CreateProdResources
Value:
   !Ref NewVolume
```

In the preceding template, we defined a `Condition` called `CreateProdResources` and the logic is if the `EnvType` parameter is `prod`, then it's `true`. Now, this condition has been used in the `Resource` section of the EC2 instance. If you pass the value of `EnvType` as `prod`, it will create the resource, that is, launch the EC2 instance; if you will pass test, then it won't.

`Resources` (required): This is the required and important section, where you mention which resources you want to provision such as EC2, S3 RDS, and so on.

The following is the syntax of the `Resources` section:

```
Resources:
   Logical ID:
      Type: Resource type
      Properties:
         Set of properties
```

The resource type in the type directive will identify the type of resources you are declaring to provision, for example, `AWS::EC2::Instance` declares an EC2 instance.

For example:

```
Resources:
   MyEC2Instance:
      Type: "AWS::EC2::Instance"
      Properties:
         ImageId: "ami-2f726546"
```

The preceding example will provision an instance with `ami-2f726546`.

`Output` (optional): This section provides the output value of resources that you declared to create. You can use these values to import into other stacks as well.

The following is the syntax of the `Output` section:

```
Outputs:
   Logical ID:
      Description: Information about the value
      Value: Value to return
      Export:
         Name: Value to export
```

For example:

```
Outputs:
  BackupLoadBalancerDNSName:
    Description: The DNSName of the backup load balancer
    Value: !GetAtt BackupLoadBalancer.DNSName
    Condition: CreateProdResources
  InstanceID:
    Description: The Instance ID
    Value: !Ref EC2Instance
```

The preceding snippet will provide the value of `ELD DNS Name` as the output and also the instance ID of an EC2 instance.

This was all about how to write a basic CF Template; now, let's create a stack using the CF Template via the CF Console.

Creating stack using the CF template

In this recipe, we will create a stack using the CF template. First, fetch the CF template from this link `https://github.com/awsstar/CF-Templates.git` and use `EC2firstExample.yaml` to create a stack. This template will provision an EC2 instance using the default VPC and its subnet. It will also create a Security Group. After launching the instance, it will install HTTPD and pass some data in the `index.html` file. This template also requires a key pair needs to be created earlier. To do this, we have to perform the following steps:

1. Go to the AWS console and click on **CloudFormation** in the **Management** section. Then, you will get a page as follows. Click on **Create Stack**:

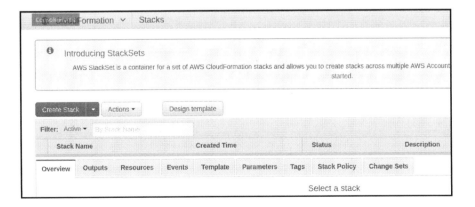

2. Once you click on **Create Stack**, you will land up on another page where you will be asked to select the template. You can also design a template by clicking on **Design Template**. Here, you have to click on the radio button of **Upload a temple to Amazon S3** and then **Choose file**. Now, select the template that you have fetched from GitHub, post that, click on **Next**:

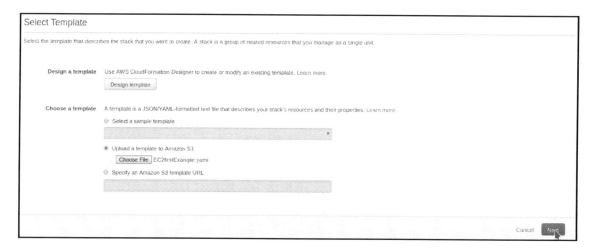

3. When you click **Next,** you will be asked to give a stack name as an identifier and fill two parameters. Now, these parameters appeared because we mentioned these parameters in the CF template. The following is the snippet of the parameter:

```
Parameters:
  InstanceType:
    Description: "Enter t2.micro or m1.small. Default is t2.micro."
    Type: "String"
    Default: "t2.micro"
    AllowedValues:
      - "t2.micro"
      - "m1.small"
  KeyName:
    Description: "Enter an existing EC2 KeyPair. Default is MyEC2Key"
    Type: "String"
    Default: "MyEC2Key"
```

4. The page that we got while giving stack a name is as follows:

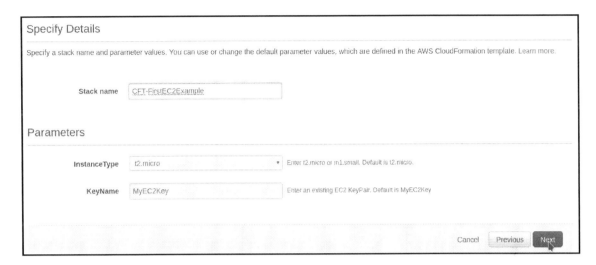

5. Click on **Next**. You will be asked to create some tags, and then you have to select the role. Make sure that the role should have appropriate permission to create and delete the resources. After selecting the role, click on **Next**:

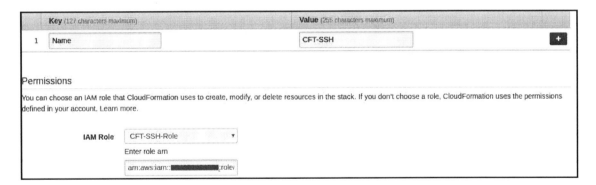

6. Post that, you will get a review page; after reviewing, click on **Create**. Now, you will be able to see that CloudFormation will start provisioning the resource and status of stack will be **CREATE_IN_PROGRESS**:

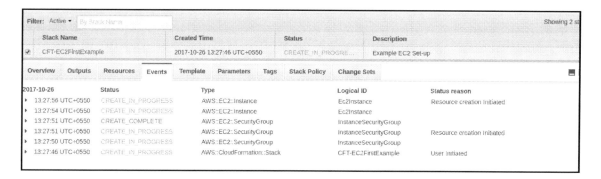

7. After some time, the status of stack will change from **CREATE_IN_PROGRESS** to **CREATE_COMPLETE**:

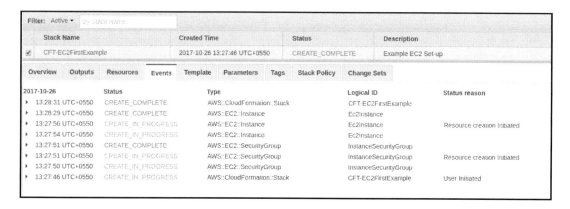

8. Now, click on the **Resources** tab to the left of the **Events** tab. You will see the resources that are provisioned here:

You can SSH the instance using a keypair. You can also hit the public IP of the instance and see the webpage.

Creating a production-ready web application infrastructure using CloudFormation

In this recipe, we will create a production-ready web application infrastructure with CloudFormation. The architecture will look like the following diagram:

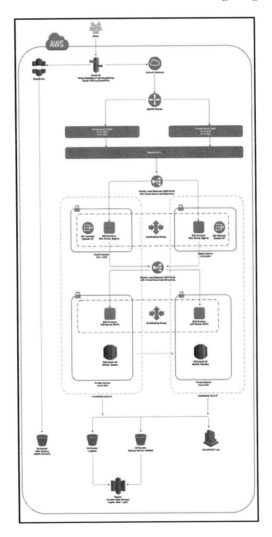

Getting ready

To achieve the preceding infrastructure, you need to clone this repository `https://github.com/awsstar/CloudFormation-WebApp-Architecture.git`. Post that, you have to create stack with it. The template will create the following AWS resources:

- Amazon IAM
- Amazon VPC
- Amazon EC2
- Amazon ELB
- Amazon AutoScaling
- Amazon CloudFront
- Amazon RDS
- Amazon S3
- Amazon Cloudwatch
- Amazon Route53
- Amazon Security Group & NACL

Before creating stack with the template, you should have following things:

- Your AWS account must have the limit to create all the resources mentioned earlier
- One EC2 key pair
- One Hosted Zone in Route53
- One installed certificate in ACM (AWS Certificate Manager)

You can create the stack in following region:

- US East (N. Virginia)
- US East (Ohio)
- US West (N. California)
- US West (Oregon)
- Asia Pacific (Tokyo)
- Asia Pacific (Singapore)
- Asia Pacific (Sydney)

How to do it...

The repository that you cloned contains nested templates, which does the following:

- A VPC with public and private subnets
- The EC2 instance with high availability deployed across two AZs and scalable with Auto Scaling group
- NAT gateways to handle outbound traffic
- An application load balancer for the public subnets to handle inbound traffic
- Centralized logging with Amazon Cloud watch
- Create S3 buckets for ELB Logging and webhosting static content
- Multi AZ database for Production environment

You can launch multiple stacks in three different env: test, dev, and prod. Now once you cloned the repository, you have to do the following things:

1. Change the ARN value of the certificate and enter the suitable values according to your AWS Account in the `Master.yaml` file. The following is the snippet and the text with the bold needs to be replaced with your certificate ARN:

```
RegionMap:
    us-east-1:
        # AMI Instance - Amazon Linux AMI 2016.09.1 (HVM), SSD Volume
Type - ami-dc9339bf (Free tier eligible)
        AMI: "ami-0b33d91d"
        # AStorage - The storage class to which you want the object to
transition.
        AStorage: "GLACIER"
        # Update with your own cert ARN HERE!
        # Assuming you have already upload to AWS Certificate Manager
        CertARN: "arn:aws:acm:us-east-
1:902840046602:certificate/1df4b43e-3d80-4c13-bc8b-0892ee346847"

    us-east-2:
        AMI: "ami-c55673a0"
        AStorage: "GLACIER"
        CertARN: "arn:aws:acm:us-east-
1:902840046602:certificate/1df4b43e-3d80-4c13-bc8b-0892ee346847"

    us-west-1:
        AMI: "ami-165a0876"
        AStorage: "GLACIER"
        CertARN: "arn:aws:acm:us-east-
1:902840046602:certificate/1df4b43e-3d80-4c13-bc8b-0892ee346847"
```

2. Now, create an S3 bucket in your account and upload the files which are present in the `infrastructure` directory of the repository:

```
# aws s3 cp --recursive infrastructure/* s3://YOUR_BUCKET_NAME
```

3. Go to the AWS CloudFormation console and click on **create stack**. Post that, upload the `Master.yaml` file from your computer where you have to clone the repository and make the certificate ARN change. Then, click on **Next**:

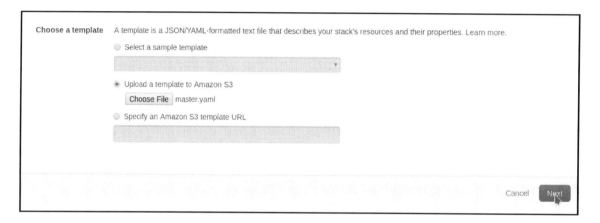

4. Once you click on **Next**, you will land on a new page, where you have to fill the stack name and parameter details.
    1. **Stack name**: Here you can give only three values, because it will affect the stack. The template is written in such a manner that it will pick the stack as the environment name. So, you are allowed to give only three values; they are `prod`, `test`, and `dev`.
    2. **PMHostedZone**: You have to enter an existing hosted zone that already exists in your AWS account.
    3. **PMInstanceType**: Choose the instance type.
    4. **PMKeyName**: Enter the name of existing key pair.
    5. **PMOWNIP**: You have to enter your office or home IP so that it won't be open for all.
    6. **PMTemplateURL**: Here, you have to give the bucket path where you have uploaded the templates of the `Infrastructure` folder and the path should be in this manner `https://s3.amazonaws.com/bucket-name`. Then, click on **Next**:

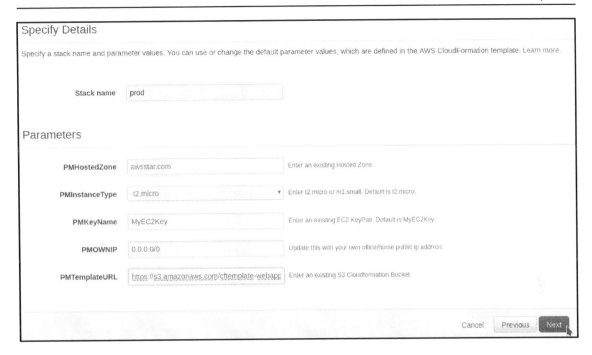

Specify Details

Specify a stack name and parameter values. You can use or change the default parameter values, which are defined in the AWS CloudFormation template. Learn more.

Stack name: prod

Parameters

PMHostedZone	awsstar.com	Enter an existing Hosted Zone.
PMInstanceType	t2.micro ▼	Enter t2.micro or m1.small. Default is t2.micro.
PMKeyName	MyEC2Key	Enter an existing EC2 KeyPair. Default is MyEC2Key.
PMOWNIP	0.0.0.0/0	Update this with your own office/home public ip address
PMTemplateURL	https://s3.amazonaws.com/cftemplate-webapp	Enter an existing S3 Cloudformation Bucket.

Cancel   Previous   Next

5. Post that, give **Tags** a name, and select the **Role** which should have the permission for all the resources mentioned previously. After that, click on **Next** and you will get a review page. After reviewing, click on the checkbox of **capabilities section**, and then click on **Create.**

6. Then, you will get stack console where you can see the progress of the stack creation:

7. Once your stack will get the status **CREATE_COMPLETE**, you can check all the resources.

 There are lots of sample solution templates provided by AWS, which can help you understand and create CF templates more (`http://docs.aws.amazon.com/AWSCloudFormation/latest/UserGuide/sample-templates-applications-us-east-1.html`).

Automation with Ansible

If you are a DevOps or a System Administrator, who wants to be a DevOps, then you must know at least one configuration management technology. Ansible is one of the most popular configuration management tool, which can perform configuration changes at the server level, as well as it is good for infrastructure automation.

Ansible is a simple, agentless, and powerful open source IT automation tool. It has the following functionality:

- Provisioning
- Configuration management
- Application deployment
- Continuous delivery
- Orchestration

Ansible is associated with Open Source leader Red Hat Inc. So, it has very fast growth in terms of development and pull request. Ansible has the following features:

- **Agentless**: To run the Ansible playbook (configuration or template) on a destination server, you don't need any agent to be installed.
- **Need only SSH and Python**: Ansible communicates with the destination server with SSH and converts the Ansible playbook into Python script at the backend. It then uploads the Python script to the destination server and runs it. So, it's necessary that destination should also have SSH and Python, which comes with Linux by default.
- **Everything is YAML**: The Ansible playbook is written in the YAML format, so its very easy to understand and write the configuration in the YAML format.
- **Structure is flexible**: Ansible has a flexible structure and allows including multiple roles and playbooks in a single playbook.
- Encryption and security built-in.
- Full Power at the CLI (Open Source).
- **More features in tower**: Ansible has an enterprise version Ansible tower, which provides more features and functionalities.
- It maintains Idempotency.
- It has a push-based strategy, means change will happen at the destination end, only when you want to apply it on the destination server.

Workflow

The following image shows the architecture of Ansible:

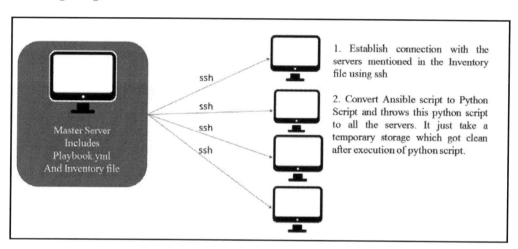

Installation

It's simple to install Ansible:

```
# yum install python-pip -y
# pip install ansible
------Check version--------
# ansible --version
ansible 2.4.0.0
  config file = None
  configured module search path = [u'/home/nikit/.ansible/plugins/modules',
u'/usr/share/ansible/plugins/modules']
  ansible python module location = /usr/local/lib/python2.7/dist-
packages/ansible
  executable location = /usr/local/bin/ansible
  python version = 2.7.12 (default, Nov 19 2016, 06:48:10) [GCC 5.4.0
20160609]
```

How to do it...

In this recipe, you will first understand how to write an Ansible playbook and then we will try to deploy a web server in a remote instance using Ansible.

File structure and syntax

Ansible requires two most important files, which are known as playbook and inventory file.

Playbook: These are expressed in the YAML format and have a minimum of syntax, which is not to be a programming language or script, but rather a model of a configuration. Each playbook includes one or more "plays" in a list. The goal of a play is to map a group of hosts to some well-defined roles and tasks. A task is nothing but a call or operation, which applies on group of hosts. The following is the syntax of the `Playbook.yaml` file:

```
---

- hosts: webserver
  sudo: yes
  remote_user: ec2-user
  tasks:
      - name: Updating System
        yum: name=* state=latest
```

In the previous playbook, two directives are important, first is `hosts` and second is `tasks`. Task will be applied on the hosts. In the preceding example, the task of updating the system will be assigned to the hosts group `webserver`. This group can have many servers or a single server inside it. These things are described in the inventory file.

 Inventory file: The inventory is a file which includes the remote server IPs and its credentials. Playbook runs on inventory files. The inventory file can have multiple groups. Each group has its own group server's IP.

For example:

```
[Dev]
45.27.98.102
23.56.34.223
34.54.63.67

[Prod]
45.98.204.34
12.24.353.23
```

If hosts directive `Playbook.yaml` has value Dev, then whatever the tasks written in `Playbook.yaml` will be applied to all the three IPs under the `Dev` group, similarly for `Prod`.

This was basic syntax and structure of an Ansible, and trust me there are lots of more interesting thing to do with Ansible. Check the official documentation of Ansible for advance syntax and structure (`http://docs.ansible.com/ansible/latest/index.html`).

Deploying a web server using Ansible

You can perform this example either on your local machine or a server. I would recommend to perform this operation on a server, that will take you through all the things required to set up. First launch an EC2 machine in a public subnet and make sure you open the SSH port from wherever you will be running your Ansible playbook.

1. Create a file in your server from where you will initiate the playbook:

```
# vi playbook.yaml

---

- hosts: servers
  sudo: yes
# You should give your remote server user name
  remote_user: ec2-user
  tasks:
      - name: Updating System
        yum: name=* state=latest
      - name: Install EPEL-repo
        yum: name=epel-release state=latest
      - name: Install nginx
        yum: name=nginx state=latest
      - name: start the service
        cmd: systemctl start nginx
```

2. Now, create the inventory file. You can give any name to this inventory file:

```
#vi hosts

[servers]
ansible_ssh_private_key_file="/path/to/your/sshkey.pem"
ansible_host="YOURIP"
```

3. Now to run the playbook, we can use the following command:

```
# ansible-playbook playbook.yml -i hosts
```

4. This command will go to the remote server and install Nginx package and start the service of Nginx. After that, hit the public IP, and you will get the Nginx welcome page.

Creating an AWS infrastructure using the Ansible EC2 dynamic inventory

Ansible is not only used for configuration management but also for infrastructure automation. It has more than 100 modules to support the AWS infrastructure. The only reason for not recommending Ansible for infrastructure automation is that it does not support rollback or delete function automatically; you have to write the playbook for the creation of the infrastructure as well as the deletion. So, writing the playbook for both the functionalities is bit painful. For small infrastructures in the testing and development environment, you can create a small Ansible playbook.

Now, let me give you a scenario. Suppose you have the requirement to launch an instance and install some packages on top of it in one go, what would be your approach be? You know that to install anything inside a server you should first mention the IP in the inventory file. But how can you put the IP of an instance which is created dynamically. This means you will write a playbook, which will launch an instance. Then fetch the IP of instances, put that IP in your inventory file, and then continue with your installation of package inside the instance.

So fetching the public or private IP of a dynamically or recently launched instance got easy by the EC2 dynamic inventory. This is the reason for using a dynamic inventory, because by default, Ansible does not store metadata of resource of AWS, like CloudFormation does.

In this recipe, we will first setup dynamic inventory pre-requisites. Then, we create an infrastructure which includes a VPC, Security Group, EC2 instance and ELB. Post that, we will install webserver inside the EC2 instance. All these things will happen with a single run of the Ansible playbook.

Getting ready

IP updation inside the inventory file after the dynamic launch of instance can be achieved by the EC2 dynamic inventory management. To setup dynamic inventory management, you need two files:

```
https://raw.githubusercontent.com/ansible/ansible/devel/contrib/inventory/ec2.
py
https://raw.githubusercontent.com/ansible/ansible/devel/contrib/inventory/ec2.
ini
```

An `ec2.py` file is a Python script, which is responsible for fetching details of the EC2 instance, whereas the `ec2.ini` file is configuration file which is used by `ec2.py`. For example, if you mention private IP in `ec2.ini`, then while executing `ec2.py`, it will show you private IP. To use these files, your system should have the following packages:

- Python-pip & Boto
- jq
- GNU sed (it comes by default with Linux)

Now, you have to perform the following settings in your system:

- Download the IAM user credentials (AWS access key and AWS secret key). That IAM key should have the permission to create the resources that is mentioned previously in the main heading section.
- Install `awscli` and configure it with the IAM key that you just downloaded.
- Download `ec2.py` and `ec2.ini` and make it globally available because we will use these files in the helper script. The role of the helper script is to run the `ec2.py` script and get the IP. Once you get the IP, update the inventory file:

```
    # wget
https://raw.githubusercontent.com/ansible/ansible/devel/contrib/inven
tory/ec2.py
    # wget
https://raw.githubusercontent.com/ansible/ansible/devel/contrib/inven
tory/ec2.ini
    # chmod a+x ec2.py && chmod a+x ec2.ini
    ####We are Copying the files to /usr/bin/ to make it globally
available###
    # cp -rvpf ec2.* /usr/bin/
```

- Install Boto and verify `ec2.py` by running it:

```
# pip install boto
###Verify by running it. It will take some time, so wait a little
bit####
# ec2.py --list
```

- Download Json Parser jq:

```
# wget http://stedolan.github.io/jq/download/linux64/jq
# chmod a+x jq && cp -rvpf jq /usr/bin
```

Now, you are good to run the playbook.

How to do it...

If you have the preceding pre-requisites in place, then clone this repository. `https://github.com/awsstar/Ansible-Infra-Automate.git` . This repository includes three files and a folder:

```
# git clone https://github.com/awsstar/Ansible-Infra-Automate.git
# cd Ansible-Infra-Automate
# ls
dynamic.sh hosts playbook.yml roles
```

File `dynamic.sh` is a shell script which is called inside Ansible playbook to fetch the IP of latest launched server with tag `server1` and update it in `hosts` inventory file. Before running the playbook, you have to make the following changes in the files and then you can use it:

1. First of all you have to create EC2 keypair in your AWS account and copy that key into the directory `Ansible-Infra-Automate`. Then edit `hosts` file and replace your keyname in place of `KEY.PEM`:

```
[local]
localhost
[servers]
server1 ansible_ssh_private_key_file="{{ playbook_dir }}/KEY.PEM"
ansible_host="54.198.202.93"
```

2. After that, you have to modify the `playbook.yml` file by replacing some variables:

```
- hosts: localhost
  connection: local
  become_method: su
  gather_facts: yes
  vars:
      keypair: "YOUR_EXISTING_KEY"
      image1: "YOUR_AMI_ID"
      region: "us-east-1"
      #Prefix for naming
      prefix: "CHOOSE_ANY_NAME"
      az: "us-east-1b"
      inst_name1: "server1"
      security_group: "CHOOSE_ANY_NAME"

  roles:
    - VPC
    - INSTANCES
    - UPDATEIP
- hosts: servers
  sudo: yes
  remote_user: ec2-user
  roles:
    - UPDATEHOST
```

3. You have to mention the name of your existing key pair give the `ami-id`, preferably `CentOS/Redhat/AmazonLinux`, because to install webserver on the server is mentioned with the yum command.

4. Post that, give the prefix value so that if your subnet will create then name will be like `prefixValue_public_subnet`. After that, give any name to the security group.

5. Post that, edit the `roles/INSTANCES/tasks/main.yml` file and mention your certificate ARN so that ELB should support https.

6. Once you are done editing the files, hit the following command to setup the infrastructure:

```
# ansible-playbook playbook.yml -i hosts
```

7. Now, this will create the whole infrastructure in a couple of minutes. Later, you can hit ELB DNS and then you will get Nginx welcome page.

 If you face any issue with this Ansible playbook, then raise the issue, I will be happy to help you.

8

Automating AWS Resource Control Using AWS Lambda

This chapter is all about AWS Lambda, which is also known as **Function as a Service**. After the introduction of Lambda service by AWS in 2014, the emergence of serverless computing has dramatically risen in popularity. In this chapter, the following recipes will be covered which are related to audit compliance and automation with AWS resources:

- Creating an AMIs of the EC2 instance using AWS lambda and CloudWatch
- Sending notifications through SNS using Config and Lambda
- Streaming and visualizing AWS CloudTrail logs in real time using Lambda with Kibana

Before moving ahead with the implementation of recipes, let's discuss something about lambda.

Introduction

AWS Lambda is a service which was launched by AWS in 2014 at re:Invent; since then, it revolutionized the serverless application landscape. Lambda basically provides runtime or environment for your function or code to execute. It executes the function on your behalf and takes care of provisioning and managing resources, which will be needed for your function to run. These resource configurations will be asked to you while you create a lambda function.

When a Lambda function is invoked, it launches a container at the backend with the configuration that you provide during the creation of the Lambda function. Initially, it will take some time to provision and bootstrap a container; after that, it will run the code which will be mentioned in the Lambda function. Once your code completes its execution, the container will be destroyed after a while. You can also deploy a static application in Lambda.

Right now, AWS Lambda supports the following runtime:

- NET Core 1.0.1 (C#)
- NodeJS
- Java
- Python

This was the introduction to AWS Lambda. Now, let's see how to use Lambda in action.

Creating an AMIs of the EC2 instance using AWS lambda and CloudWatch

In the era of Cloud and DevOps, maintaining multiple copies of your data will save you whenever there is something wrong with the server. A backup of your data is important, because you can restore your lost data using it. In AWS, you can take a backup of EBS. You can automate the backup of EBS using any custom script, which will use `ec2 api` and take a snapshot of the same. Earlier, we used to keep that script in any server and schedule it using cron; but now, we use lambda instead of server where we keep our script of taking a backup of EBS. Using lambda will remove the need of another server, which was needed to run the script on cron basis. Having EBS backup, means the snapshot is good, but if you have multiple EBS volumes attached to an instance, then it's recommended to take the AMI of the instance. During instance failure or disaster, instance recovery with the AMI will be faster in comparison with EBS. So, let's see how we can implement this using Lambda.

Getting ready

Scenario: Let's say we have some instance and want to create an AMI of it. The condition is that we want some specific instance to have their AMI, for example, production servers.

Solution: We can write a script to take the AMI of the instance in which there is one tag key **Backup,** whose value should be **Yes**. Then, it will take the AMI of that instance.

I already have a script which will cover this scenario. You have to clone it first and save it in your local machine (`https://github.com/awsstar/Serverless-Lambda.git`). This repository includes a JSON file, which we will use in Lambda.

How to do it...

Let's first see how to enable tagging:

1. If you have cloned the repository, you have to tag the instance with key as `Backup` and value the as `Yes`. Click on the **Tags** tab then click on **Add/Edit tags**:

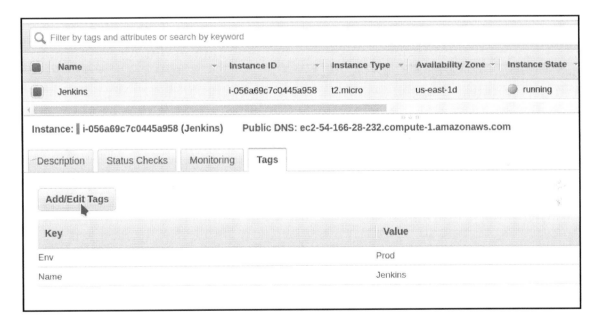

2. Once you click on **Add/Edit Tags**, you will get a small window. Click on **Create Tag**, then add key as `Backup` and value as `Yes`. Post that, click on **Save:**

3. Similarly, apply the same tag to all the instances for which you want to schedule the AMI.

This was all about creating a tag. Now, let's discuss the steps to create a Lambda function:

1. Go to the AWS Management Console and click on Lambda in the **Compute** section. You will land in new the Lambda console. Click on **Create a function:**

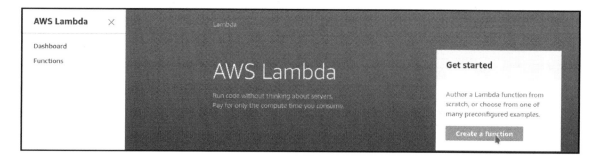

2. After that, click on **Author from scratch** so that you can create your own Lambda function:

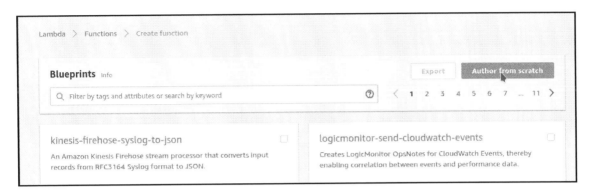

3. After that, you will get a new page. Give this function a meaningful name (in this case, I had given `functionAMI`). After that, select **Create a custom role**:

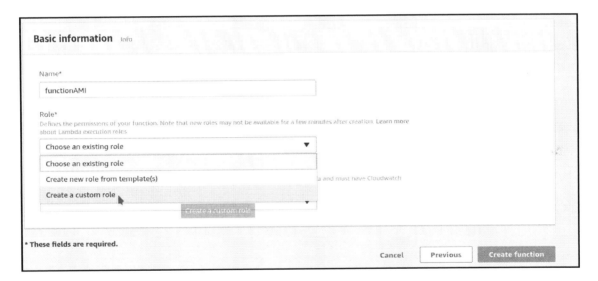

4. Once you select **Create a custom role**, you will be redirected to another page, where you have to create a role with a custom policy. Give this role a proper name (`functionAMIRole`) and click on **Edit** to edit the policy:

5. Remove the existing policy and paste the policy given as follows:

```
{
  "Version": "2012-10-17",
  "Statement": [{
    "Effect": "Allow",
    "Action": ["logs:*"],
    "Resource": "arn:aws:logs:*:*:*"
  }, {
    "Effect": "Allow",
    "Action": "ec2:*",
    "Resource": "*"
  }]
}
```

This policy has full access to EC2; you can limit the access by being specific.

6. Once you paste the policy in the custom role, click on **Save**. Then, go back to the Lambda page, select your newly created role, and then click on **Create function**:

7. Now, you will land to the Lambda code editor page, where you have to paste the content of the script that you cloned. After pasting the content, click on **Save**:

Edit the second line of script `aws.config.region` = `'YOUR REGION';`, if you are running it apart from `us-east-1`.

In the script, I used the three EC2 APIs:

- `describeInstances()`: This will describe the filtered instances, which have the key tag `Backup` and the value `yes`.
- `createImage()`: This will create the AMIs of the filtered instances.
- `createTags()`: This will assign the tags with key `DeleteOn` and the value `yes` to the created images, for another lambda function which will delete the AMI after some retention period.

To add trigger, you need to follow these steps:

1. Click on the **Triggers** tab. After that, click on **Add Trigger**:

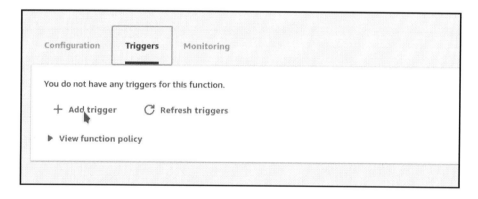

2. The trigger will invoke the lambda, based on the event that is scheduled. You will get a window where you have to select the source of the event. Here we have to select **CloudWatch Events,** which basically schedules the cron:

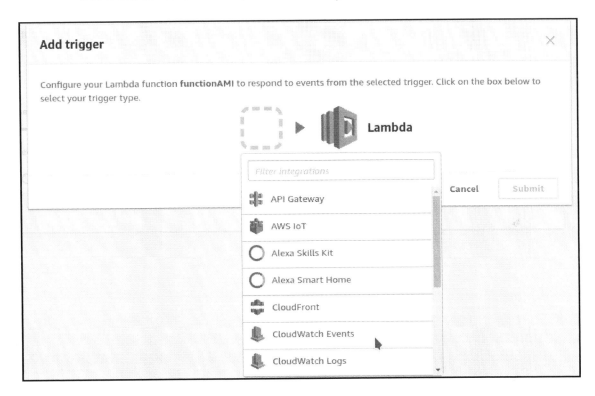

3. After that, in the **Rule** section, click on **Create a new rule**. Give a proper name to the rule in the **Rule name** textbox, mention **Rule description**.
4. In **Rule type** select **Schedule expression** to set the cron. After that, click the checkbox of **Enable Trigger**. Then, click on **Submit** to apply the trigger.

For demo purpose, I have provided a 5 minute interval. You can mention your time whenever you want to take the AMI, for example `cron(30 18 ? * MON-FRI *)`, this expression will take the AMI everyday from Monday to Friday midnight.

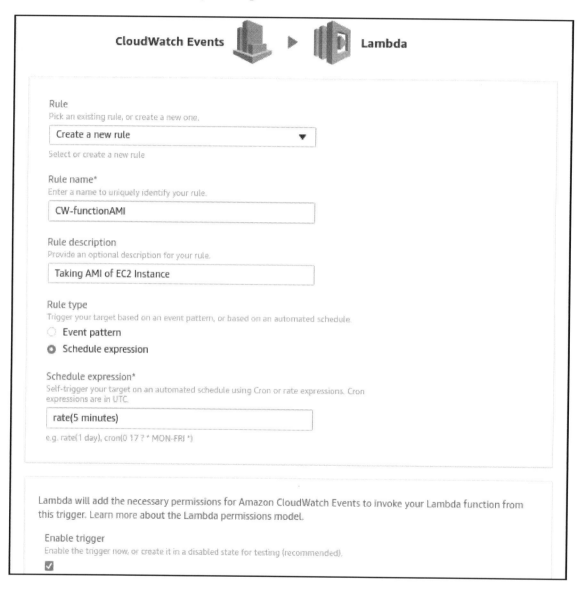

5. You can see that a trigger for the Lambda has been created:

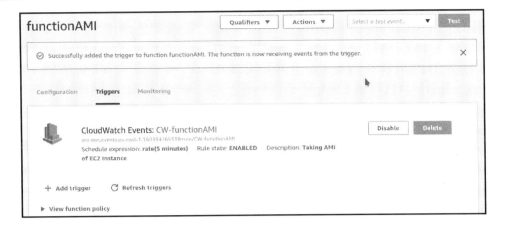

6. Now, Go to CloudWatch logs, you will be able to see the current logs like below image (shows creating AMIs of the Instance)

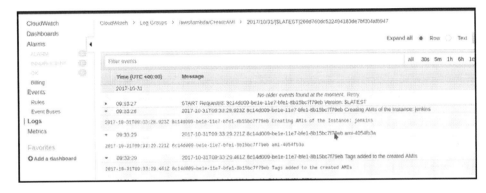

7. Now, go to the EC2 console and click on AMI at leftmost side, then you can see that AMI of your instances will be there:

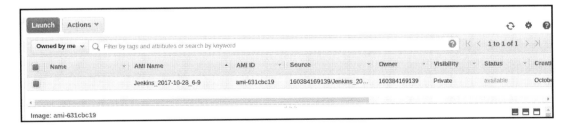

8. Now to delete the AMI, you have to carry out the same process. You have to change the script this time and use the `deleteAMI.json` file (search in the repository that you have cloned). This will delete all the AMI which will have the `DeleteOn` tag and the `yes` value,

Sending notifications through SNS using Config and Lambda

Enterprises generally have multiple teams and departments responsible for managing the infrastructure on AWS for their own products. It's very difficult to ensure or believe that the infrastructure will remain the same as it was setup. Some of the resources such as Security Group are very critical in terms of the security of the product. Right now, AWS does not provide 100% service to notify product owners of changes to the configuration of AWS resource. So, in this section of the chapter, we will implement a system which will notify the product owner whenever there will be any change in the security groups.

Scenario: Let's say Team A is the owner of a security group that allows HTTP traffic (port 80) from the public internet (0.0.0.0/0). They want to expose only the frontend or UI of the product, so they created this security group. Now, suppose Team B comes along and wants to allow the HTTP traffic to their resources, Team B saw that Team A's SG had already allowed HTTP, so they decided to use this SG. They also wanted to allow SSH connection on port 22. Due to some reason, they forgot to inform Team A about this new rule and failed to coordinate with them. Now, all of Team A's resources which were using that SG allows SSH access, without any communication with Team A. After some days or weeks, when the security audit takes place, Team A saw the rule that allowed SSH access, which is vulnerable, and removed the rule. Now, this caused connectivity issues for Team B, which resulted in confusion and problems in both teams.

Solution: If Team A had been notified that there is some change in SG, then there could have been less confusion, and both the teams could have avoided the problem. Now, let's see how we're going to implement this system.

Getting ready

AWS already provides us with a service called AWS Config, which solves 90% of what we need to implement in this system. **AWS Config** is a service that tracks resources and sends notification via SNS when changes occur. For small startups and companies, using only the Config service will suffice.

However, if your organization is big and has multiple teams and departments, receiving notifications for every change of resource of every team will be annoying. A team would want to receive a notification only when there is a change in their team resources.

They need certain procedures which will filter those notifications and only sends notifications that pertain to the specific team. This is a perfect scenario to use Lambda. Lambda functions can subscribe an SNS topic, allowing them to receive SNS messages from the AWS Config, and then filtering them so that only the changes that pertain to a team are sent.

We will perform the operation in the following manner to implement this system:

- Create an SNS topic for the admin who will receive notifications for all the changes in the resource, which is mentioned in AWS Config.
- Validate the email address of the owner of the Security Group. This email address will get the email only when there is a change in the owner's SG.
- Create an AWS Config rule.
- Create a Lambda function using the script `sgNotification.json` file (present in the cloned repository).
- Create an event trigger.

How to do it...

The following are the steps to create an SNS topic:

1. Go to the AWS console and click on **Simple Notification Service** under the **Messaging** section. You will get an **SNS dashboard**. Click on **Create Topic**:

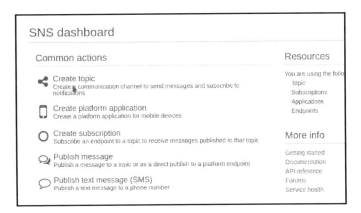

2. Once you click on **Create topic**, you will get a window where you have to provide **Topic name** and **Display name** and then click on **Create topic**:

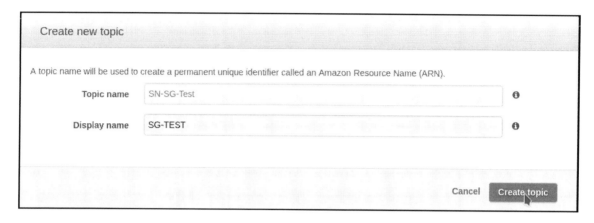

3. Once you will click on **Create topic**, then your topic will be created. After that you have to **Create subscription** with the admin email with respect to who can receive the changes of the resource. Click on **Create subscription**:

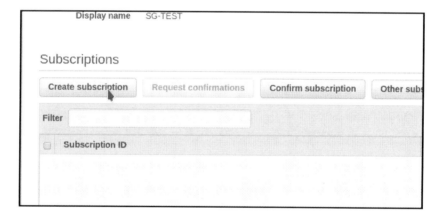

4. Once you click on **Create subscription,** a window will prompt where you have to choose the protocol and endpoint. In protocol, you have to choose **Email,** and in endpoint, you have to give the **admin email** address (in my case, it's `nixsrj@gmail.com`). Post that, click on **Create subscription**:

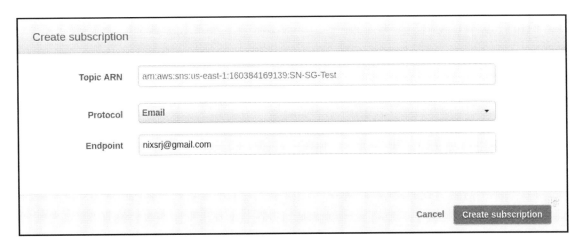

5. After that, your endpoint will wait for your endpoint email confirmation in the **Subscriptions** section. This means you will get an email to verify your email address:

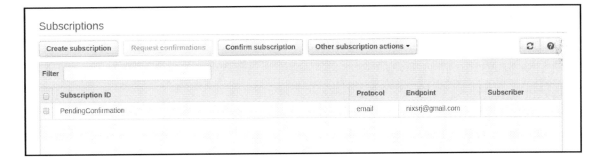

6. Verify your email address and click on **Confirm subscription**:

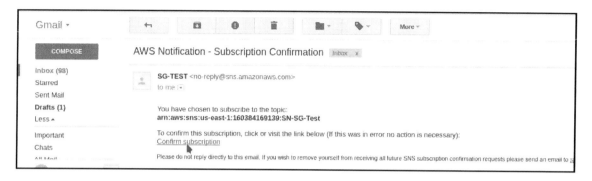

7. Once you confirm the subscription, then in the SNS dashboard, you can see that your **Subscription ID** will have an ARN:

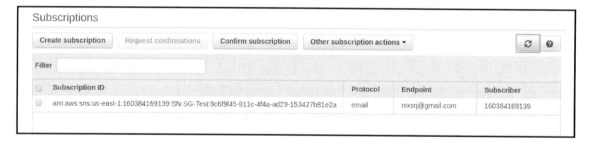

To validate the email address of the owner of a Security Group parform the following steps:

1. Go to AWS Console and click on **Simple Email service** in the **Messaging** section. Then, you will get an **SES Home** dashboard. Click on **Email Addresses** to the left side:

2. You will get another page where you have to click on **Verify a New Email Address**. After that, one window will appear where you have to enter owner's email address (in my case it's swarajnikit@gmail.com) to get verified. Now, click on **Verify This Email Address**:

3. A verification mail will be sent to the owner's email ID. After confirmation from the owner's end, the email will be verified:

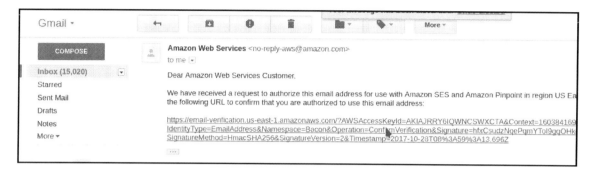

4. You can now see that the status of email is verified:

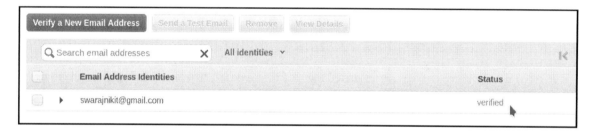

5. Similarly, verify the email address of the admin, because it will act as the originating address; this means a mail will be send from the admin to the owner's email. Here, we are considering the admin email address as `nixsrj@gmail.com`. Now, we will have two verified addresses:

Configuring the AWS Config service for AWS resources

1. Go to the AWS console and click on **Config** under the **Management** section. Then, you will get a **Config** dashboard. Go to **Settings** to the left corner of your screen and configure as follows:

    - Click on the checkbox of **Record all resources supported in this region.**
    - In the **Amazon S3 bucket** section, click on the radio button of **Create a bucket**. Then, in the prefix text field, give the bucket name (in my case, `aws-resources`).
    - In the **Amazon SNS topic** section, click on the checkbox of **Stream configuration changes and notifications to an Amazon SNS topic.** Then, click on the radio button of **Choose a topic from your account.** After that, select **Topic name** that we just created (**SN-SG-Test**):

2. Post that, select the role. You can click on the radio button of **Choose a role from your account** and select the default role and click on **Save**:

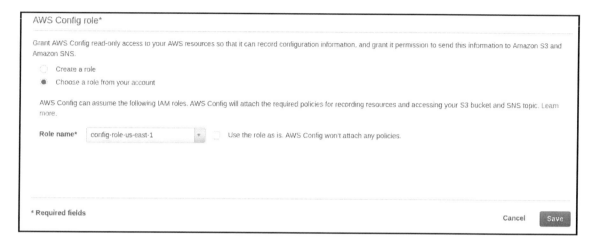

3. Make sure after clicking on **Save**, you will get the page where it says **Recording is on** after clicking on **Save**:

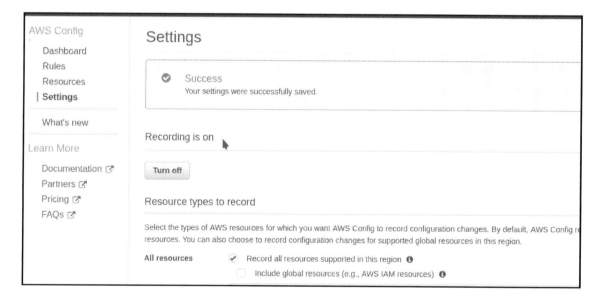

4. At this point of time, whatever the change you will carry out in your AWS account, the admin will get a notification like this:

But the admin still receives all the messages that are associated with the AWS account. Now, we have to filter it out and check the **Security Groups,** which has the **NotifyOnChange** tag that has the value set as **yes**. The **OwnerDL** tag has its value set as **OWNER'S_EMAIL** to get the notification. That will be filtered out and whatever email address is mentioned in the tag, gets an email from Config.

Creating a Lambda function

Here similarly, we have to go Lambda console, and create a new Lambda function using the code of the sgNotification.json file (present in cloned repository).

You have to modify the first line of script, where you have to enter the value of a variable, which accepts your "from" email address `var fromAddress = "YOUR FROM ADRRESS";`

Create a new role using the following policy:

```
{
  "Version": "2012-10-17",
  "Statement": [
    {
      "Effect": "Allow",
      "Action": [
        "logs:CreateLogGroup",
        "logs:CreateLogStream",
        "logs:PutLogEvents"
      ],
      "Resource": "arn:aws:logs:*:*:*"
    },
    {
      "Effect": "Allow",
      "Action": [
        "ses:SendEmail",
        "ses:SendRawEmail"
      ],
      "Resource": "*"
    }
  ]
}
```

Lambda needs this policy to create logs and sends the email to the owner's email address.

Creating a trigger

1. Click on **Add trigger** in the **Triggers** section of the Lambda function. Then, select **SNS** as the event source:

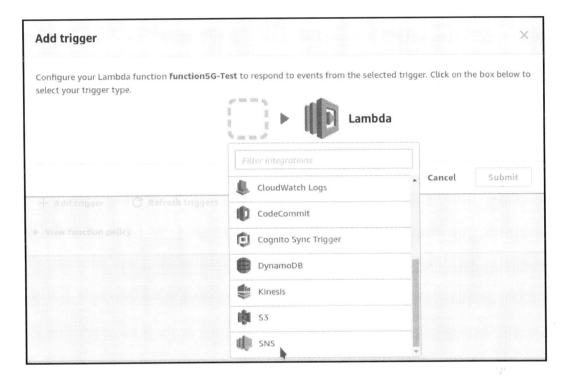

2. After that, select the newly created SNS topic (**SN-SG-Test**) as the source. Post that, click on checkbox to enable trigger and then click on **Submit** to apply the trigger:

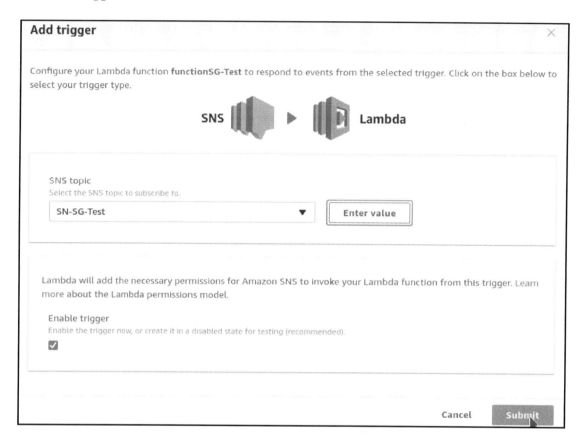

3. Now, let's test this implementation by creating any security group and giving the tag as mentioned earlier (**OwnerDL** and **NotifyOnChange**). Post that, update in the security group. In my case, I already have a security group, which had the **OwnerDL** and **NotifyOnChange** tags and the ID is **Security Group: sg-ec7e359e**:

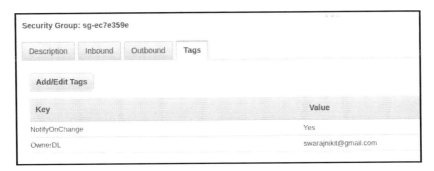

4. In inboud rules, I added the `1433` MS SQL port and opened it for MYIP. After some time, the owner (`swarajnikit@gmail.com`) got a mail from the admin (`nixsrj@gmail.com`) that **The security group sg-ec7e359e was changed**:

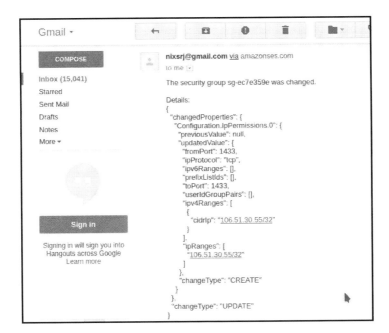

5. In the previous image, we can verify the ID is **Security Group: sg-ec7e359e** and the port 1433 that we had opened. In this way, the owner of the security group will be notified if there is any change in the security group.

Streaming and visualizing AWS CloudTrail logs in real time using Lambda with Kibana

AWS CloudTrail is a service provided by AWS, which records AWS API calls for your account and stores the log files in the S3 bucket. It will also give you the information related to the recent activity that took place in AWS account via the CloudTrail dashboard. This information includes the time of the API call, identity of the API caller, source IP address of API caller, the request parameters, and the response elements returned by the AWS service.

CloudTrail can give you a history of all the API calls for your account, whether the API calls have been made via Console, SDKs, CLI, or higher-level services such as CloudFormation. This record of history enables security analysis as well as compliance auditing and resource change tracking.

Understanding CloudTrail logs could become a bit challenging sometimes due to the following mentioned reasons:

- CloudTrail uploads the logs to S3 periodically, so keeping track of new files are bit tough.
- CloudTrail API activity console only shows the API activity to create, modify, and delete API calls. For read-only API activity, we should rely on Amazon S3 bucket or CloudWatch Logs.
- Streaming CloudTrail logs to CloudWatch is easy and straightforward when we click some buttons, but CloudWatch has limited capability when it comes to data visualization.

Now, the solution of the above pain lies in the below architecture diagram. This diagram shows how CloudTrail logs can be streamed in real time using CloudWatch, Lambda, and Amazon Elasticsearch service:

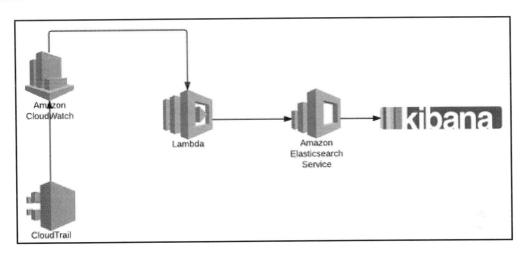

Elasticsearch is a highly scalable open-source full-text search and analytic engine. It allows you to store, search, and analyze big volumes of data quickly and in near real time, whereas Kibanas is an open source data visualization plugin for Elasticsearch. It provides visualization capabilities on top of the content indexed on an Elasticsearch cluster.

Workflow

The workflow of the system is triggered when CloudTrail starts sending a new log file to CloudWatch log group. Post that, the CloudWatch log group will stream the log file to Lambda and trigger the Lambda function. This function is written in Node.JS and carries out the log processing and stores the parsed data in Elasticsearch. After that, using index, data in Elasticsearch can be visualized through Kibana.

Getting ready

To implement the preceding system, we have to carry out the following operations in sequence:

1. Enable CloudTrail logs and configure CloudWatch in it.
2. Setup Amazon ElasticSearch.
3. Enable streaming of CloudWatch logs in Elasticsearch.
4. Configure Kibana.

How to do it...

In this section, we will be performing all the steps that we mentioned above

Enabling CloudTrail logs

1. Go to the AWS console and click on CloudTrail in the management section. You will get the CloudTrail dashboard. Click on **Create trail**:

Welcome to CloudTrail

With CloudTrail, you can view events for your AWS account. Create a trail to retain a record of these events. With a tra also create event metrics, trigger alerts, and create event workflows. Learn more

Create trail

Recent events

These are the most recent events recorded by CloudTrail. To view all events for the last 7 days, go to Event history.

2. Then, give a name (CT-AWS) to the **Trail name** and click on the radio button **Yes** of **Apply trails to all regions**. This will record all the activity of all regions. In **Read/Write events**, select **All** to capture all the events:

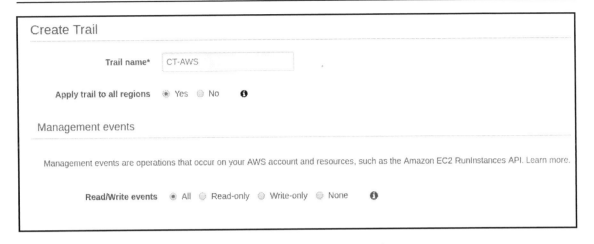

3. In the **Data events** section, click on the check box of the **Select all S3 buckets in your account**. If you do this, then you can record the S3 object-level API activity (for example, GetObject and PutObject) for individual buckets or for all current and future buckets in your AWS account. In the storage location section, click on **Yes** to **Create a new S3 bucket** and then give the name of S3 bucket (ct-aws). Post that, click on **Create** to create the trail:

4. After that, you will be redirected to the **Trails** dashboard where you can see your newly created trail with green tick as status. If you click on **CT-AWS,** then you will be redirected to the S3 bucket where you can see the stored logs:

Configuring CloudWatch

1. After configuring CloudTrail, click on the trail that you created in **CT-AWS**; scroll down and search for the CloudWatch section to configure. Click on **Configure**.

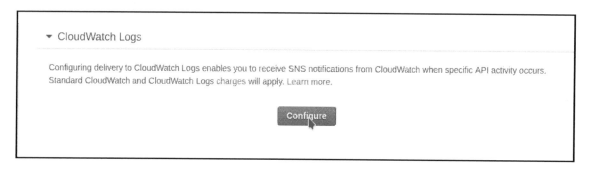

2. Give new name to the log group **CloudTrail/CT-AWS** and then click on **Continue**:

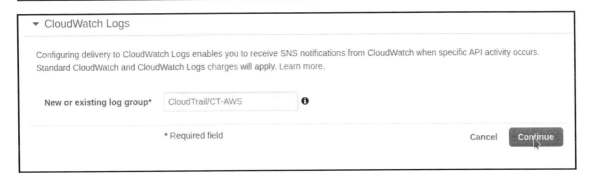

3. Once you will click on **Continue**, you will be redirected to the IAM page where it will ask for your permission to create a role on your behalf. This role will allow CloudTrail to create log group in CloudWatch. Click on **Allow**, and you will be redirected to the previous page:

4. In the preceding diagram, you can see that **Log group** is created **CloudTrail/CT-AWS**. Now to verify, go to the CloudWatch console, there you will find a new log group:

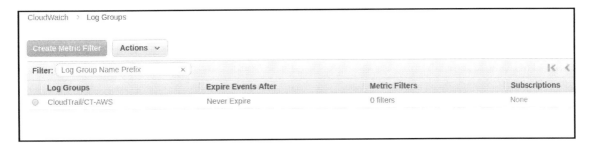

Creating Elasticsearch

1. Go to the AWS console, click on **Elasticsearch Service** under the **Analytics** section. You will get a welcome page, where you have to click on **Create a new domain**:

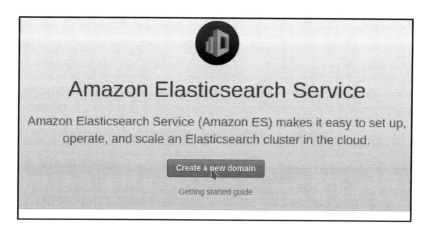

2. Give the name (`es-aws`) to your domain, which will be a part of your domain endpoint; then, click on **Next**:

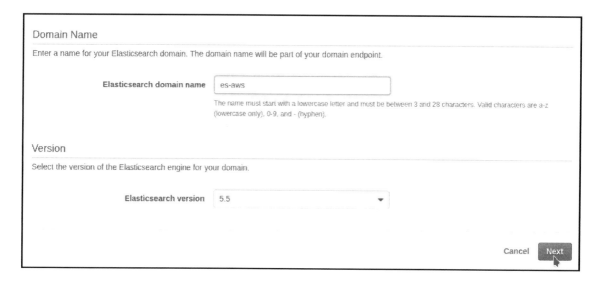

3. After that, mention the Instance Count 1 and select the instance type based on your choice, give the EBS storage size and then click **Next**.

4. You have to configure the access configuration, that is, network settings. Choose internet or VPC access.

   To enable VPC access, AWS will use private IP addresses from your VPC, which provides security by default. You control network access within your VPC using security groups. You can optionally add an additional layer of security by applying a restrictive access policy. Internet endpoints are publicly accessible. If you select public access, you should secure your domain with an access policy that only allows specific users or IP addresses to access the domain. Here, in my case, I am choosing **Public access.** I will restrict the access to my office/home IP, the reason is this Elasticsearch will not have any application data so it's not exposing the application in anyway.

5. Now, you have to set the access policy by clicking on **Select a template** and selecting **Allow access to the domain from specific IPs**:

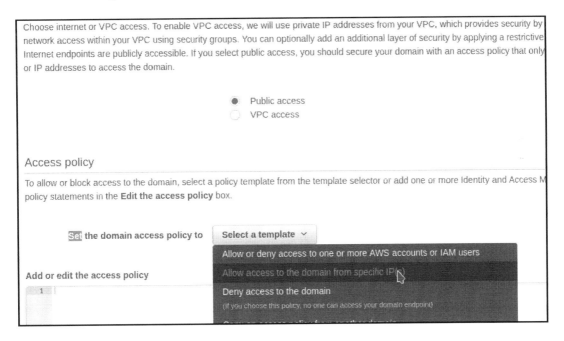

6. Once you will click on **Allow access to the domain from specific IP(s)**, a box will prompt where you have to enter your office IP so that the Elasticsearch endpoint can be accessible by the office IP only:

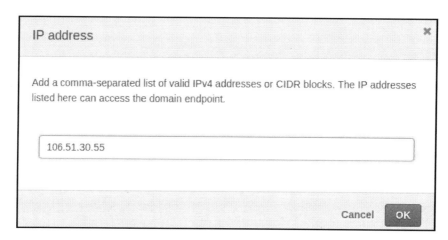

IP address ✕

Add a comma-separated list of valid IPv4 addresses or CIDR blocks. The IP addresses listed here can access the domain endpoint.

106.51.30.55

Cancel OK

7. Click on **OK**; then the access policy will be created automatically. Now, click on **Next** to get the review page:

Add or edit the access policy

```
 1 ▾ {
 2      "Version": "2012-10-17",
 3 ▾    "Statement": [
 4 ▾      {
 5          "Effect": "Allow",
 6 ▾        "Principal": {
 7            "AWS": "*"
 8          },
 9 ▾        "Action": [
10            "es:*"
11          ],
12 ▾        "Condition": {
13 ▾          "IpAddress": {
14 ▾            "aws:SourceIp": [
15                "106.51.30.55"
16              ]
17            }
18          },
19          "Resource": "arn:aws:es:us-east-1:160384169139:domain/es-aws/*"
20        }
21      ]
22    }
```

Cancel Previous Next

8. Once you review the page, click on **Create**, then you will see that Elasticsearch **Domain status** will be in **Loading**, means its spinning up an Elasticsearch instance for you:

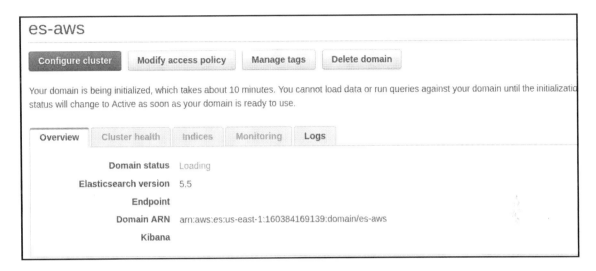

9. After sometime, when the domain status will become Active, you will get the endpoint of Elasticsearch and Kibana:

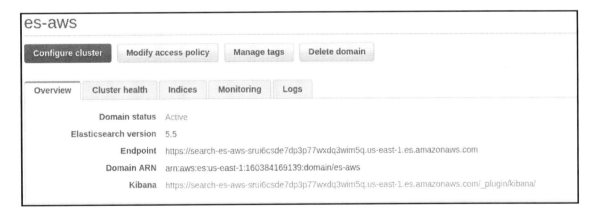

Now your Elasticsearch instance is up and running.

 To know more about Elasticsearch and how it works refer to `https://www.elastic.co/guide/index.html`.

Enabling the streaming of CloudWatch logs in Elasticsearch

1. Go to the AWS CloudWatch console and click on Logs at the left most; select the CloudTrail Log group that we just created earlier, and click on **Actions** and select **Stream to Amazon Elasticsearch Service**. This will stream all the CloudWatch logs to Elasticsearch:

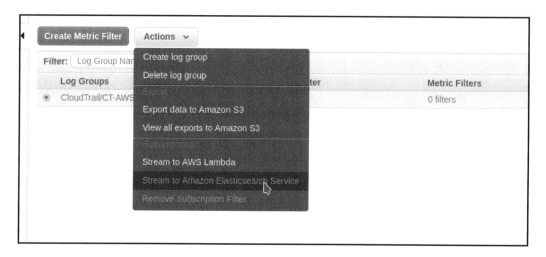

2. Now you will be askedt where the Elasticsearch exists, either in this account or another. Select the ES cluster created in your account:

3. We have to select **Lambda IAM Execution Role** and click on **Create new IAM role**, which will redirect you to IAM and create a new **lambda_elasticsearch_execution** role. After that, click on **Next**:

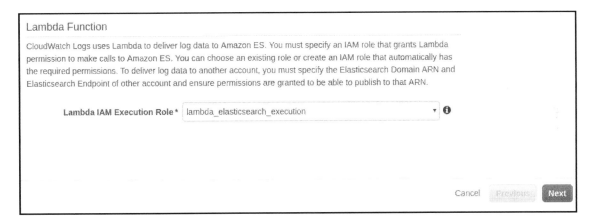

4. Select **Log Format** as **AWS CloudTrail** and click **Next** and then review it; post that, click on **Start streaming**:

5. If your streaming will start then you will get green message under subscription Lambda (**LogsToElastic_es-aws**):

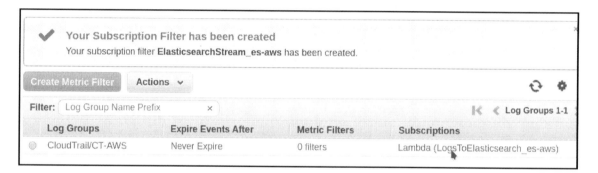

6. Now go to the Lambda console and see the **LogsToElasticsearch_es-aws** function created by itself. Click on that:

7. In the Lambda function, you can see that it has been configured with the endpoint of the cluster **search-es-aws-srui6csde7dp3p77wxdq3wim5q.us-east-1.es.amazonaws.com**:

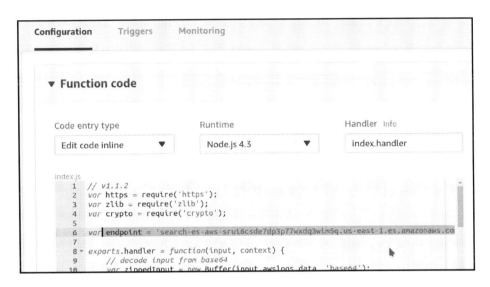

8. If you click on the triggers of this Lambda function, then you will see CloudWatch logs is configured as the source event for this Lambda function:

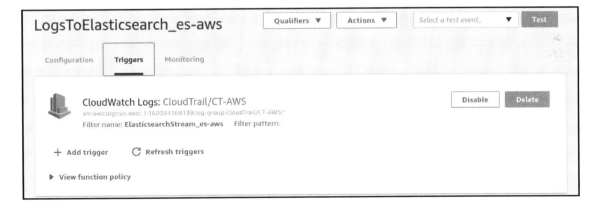

Configuring Kibana to visualize your data

1. Go to Elasticsearch console and click on the cluster that we just created. After that, click on Kibana endpoint (last link):

2. A new Kibana page will open in another tab of your browser, where it will be asking you about the index name to configure it:

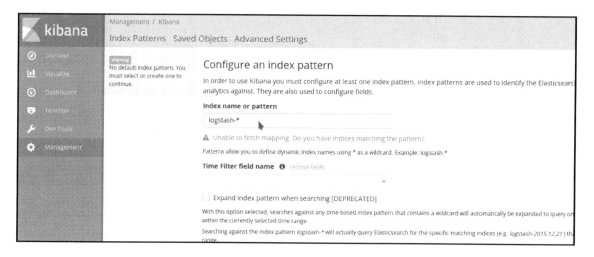

3. Go back to the console and click on the **Indices** tab, copy **cwl-***:

4. Now, paste **cwl-*** in the Kibana index pattern and select @timestamp for the filter. Then, click on **Create**:

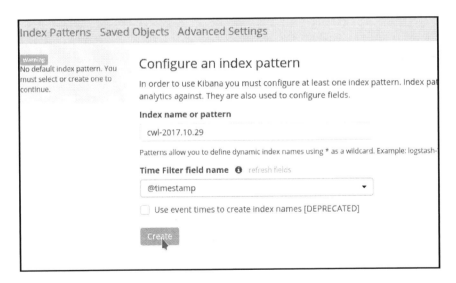

5. After that, in the **Discover** section, you will see a graph and list of all API calls:

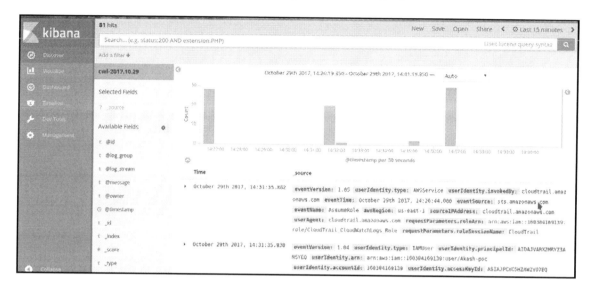

6. There are large volumes of data, bar charts, line and scatter plots, histograms, pie charts, and maps to understand better:

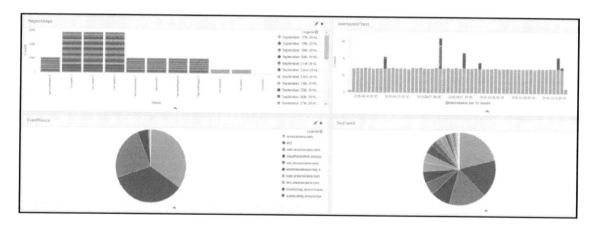

In this book, we haven't covered how to create a dashboard in Kibana, but you can refer to https://www.elastic.co/guide/en/kibana/current/dashboard-getting-started.html.

Leverage the power of Elasticsearch analytics capabilities to analyze your CloudTrail data intelligently, perform mathematical transformations, and slice and dice your data as you see fit.

With this solution in place, you'll now be able to get insights into what is happening in your AWS account across all the regions in real time without breaking a sweat!

9

Microservice Applications in Kubernetes Using Jenkins Pipeline 2.0

Now that we are done with the previous chapters, we are good to start with an alternative Enterprise Grade Container Orchestration platform, Kubernetes, which is booming in the IT industry due to its tremendous features like Automatic binpacking, self healing, automated rollback and etc... So in this chapter, the following recipes related to Kubernetes will be covered:

- Deploying multinode clusters on AWS using the Ansible playbook
- Deploying a multinode production-ready cluster on AWS using Kops
- Deploying a sample application on Kubernetes
- Working with Kubernetes on AWS using AWS resources
- Jenkins pipeline 2.0 (Pipeline as Code) using Jenkinsfile
- Application deployment using Jenkinsfile
- Deploying microservices applications in Kubernetes using Jenkinsfile

Before moving ahead with the recipes, here is a short introduction to Kubernetes and its architecture.

Introduction

In the previous chapter, we saw how ECS works. In a similar way, Kubernetes also enforces its work on containerized applications. When we have to deploy and manage a containerized application, we think of these technologies:

- Openshift
- Kubernetes
- ECS
- Mesosphere
- Docker Swarm

Kubernetes, also knows as K8s, is an open source platform, which is designed to automate deploying, scaling, and operating application containers. This project was started by Google Inc in 2014 and it has marked its place very firmly in IT industry. Kubernetes has the following features:

- **Portable**: It supports public, private, hybrid, multi-cloud
- **Extensible**: It is modular, pluggable, hookable, and composable
- **Self-healing**: It can perform auto-placement, auto-restart, and auto-replication, auto-scaling

With K8s, we can achieve the following very quickly and efficiently:

- Deploying our applications quickly and predictably
- Scaling our applications on the fly
- Rolling out new features seamlessly
- Limiting hardware usage to the required resources only

Kubernetes have master and node architecture patterns. Let's take a look at the architecture and components of Kubernetes.

K8s architecture

A Kubernetes cluster has master components (api server, scheduler, and controller) and Node agents (kubelet) either on a single server or multiple servers. The following diagram gives a clear picture:

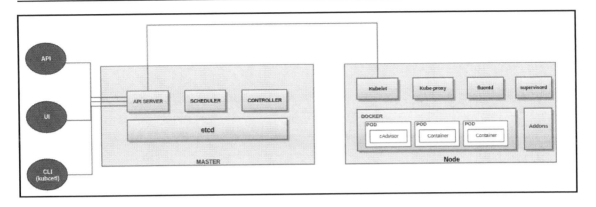

Master components

Master components are responsible for providing the control planes. It makes overall decision about the cluster such as scheduling, detecting, and responding to cluster events. For example, master will start a new container whenever the CPU load will become high and need another resource. It has the following components:

- **API server**: It provides frontend or you can call it a gatekeeper. It exposes the K8's API. We can access the Kubernetes cluster in three ways:
  - API call
  - UI (Kubernetes dashboard)
  - CLI (kubectl)
- **Scheduler**: Responsible for physically scheduling the pods to nodes and taking care of scheduling based on the resources available on hosts.
- **Controller**: It checks the health of the entire cluster. It is a coordinator that ensures nodes are running properly.
- **etcd**: It is a key-value database developed by CoreOS. It's a central database to store the cluster state.

Node components

Node components run on every node, maintaining running pods and providing the Kubernetes runtime environment. The following are the components of Node:

- **Kubelet**: It is the agent, responsible to talk to the API server. It returns health metrics and the current state of the node via `api-server` to etcd as well as Kube-master.
- **Pod**: It is a basic building block of K8s where you can run application container. A pod can run a single container or multiple container. Containers in the same pod have the same hostname.
- **Docker**: It is nothing but runtime engine for containers. Alternative for Docker in Kubernetes is rkt and cri-0.
- **Kube-proxy**: It is responsible for maintaining the entire network configuration. It ensures that one node should communicate with another node and one pod should communicate with another pod. It maintains a distributed network, expose services. It's basically a load balancer for the services.
- **Supervisord**: Both Docker and Kubelet is packaged into supervisord. It's a process manager where multiple child processes can run under a master process.
- **Fluentd**: It is responsible for managing the logs.
- **Addons**: It is responsible for extra package for Kubernetes such as UI and DNS.

 To get deep understanding of the Kubernetes Architecture you can refer to Janakiram MSV YouTube videos for Kubernetes Webinar Series. It will be very helpful.

Once you have a better understanding of the Kubernetes architecture, let's deploy a Kubernetes cluster on AWS.

Deploying multinode clusters on AWS using the Ansible playbook

To deploy a Kubernetes we will need two servers. In the first server, all components of Master will be installed, whereas in second server, all the component of node will be installed.

This setup is not for production purpose, because it won't provide a node-level auto-scaling feature. This can be used for Devlopment or QA purpose. The Ansible playbook is well tested and got LGTM by Kubernetes Maintainers.

Getting ready

Before running a playbook on your local machine to setup Kubernetes cluster, you should have the pre-requisites ready:

- Install Ansible on the machine from where ever you are comfortable to run the Ansible playbook.
- Create an IAM user and attach EC2FullAccess to that user. Then, download the access key and secret key, and configure the keys on your machine from where you will run the Ansible playbook. The alternative to this is you can attach an IAM role to the server, which should have EC2FullAccess Persmission (this applies only when you are running the Ansible playbook from and EC2 servers)
- Launch an EC2 server (CentOS 7) and update the system. Generate a public key of your machine, and paste the key into the authorized_keys file under the SSH folder of the root user of the EC2 server.
- Create the AMI of EC2 server and note the AMI ID and terminate the server.
- Now, create a **Role** as K8s-role (you can keep any name) and attach the EC2FullAccess and EC2ContainerServiceFullAccess policy with that role.

Attaching role to the instance is necessary because Kubernetes API will talk to AWS resources using role only. So if the server has an attached role, then Kubernetes can do the operation on AWS using API.

- Launch two servers (Master t2.large and Node t2.xlarge) with the same AMI ID that you have noted, in the same subnet. It should be public and attach the K8s-role. The Security Group should allow all traffic to self-sg-id.
- Verify whether you are able to login to the server using the root user with the private key that you have generated. If you are able to login to the server, then you are good to go ahead run the Ansible playbook from your machine.

How to do it...

Once we have the preceding prerequisites, we have to perform some simple steps:

1. Clone the Ansible Playbook from my GitHub page and change the directory to see the files present in the cloned directory:

```
# git clone https://github.com/nikitsrj/Kubernetes-Cluster-
Ansible.git
# cd Kubernetes-Cluster-Ansible
# ls
ansible-playbook.yml hosts K8SCONFIG LICENSE mkcrt README.md roles
```

2. Now, edit the `hosts` file and replace the public IP of Master in place of `xx.xx.xx.xx` under [kubemaster]. Similarly, replace the public IP of Node in place of `xx.xx.xx.xx` under [kubenode]. Also, rename your private key (you generated in the beginning) as `kubernetes-cluster.pem` and move it to `~/.ssh` folder if its not there. Make sure the key file permission is `600`:

```
# vi hosts
[kubemaster]
54.252.150.143 ansible_ssh_extra_args='-o StrictHostKeyChecking=no'
ansible_connection=ssh ansible_ssh_user=root
ansible_ssh_private_key_file=~/.ssh/kubernetes-cluster.pem
[kubenode]
54.252.218.247 ansible_ssh_extra_args='-o StrictHostKeyChecking=no'
ansible_connection=ssh ansible_ssh_user=root
ansible_ssh_private_key_file=~/.ssh/kubernetes-cluster.pem
```

Here, we are assuming `54.252.150.143` is IP of Kubernetes Master and `54.252.218.247` is IP of Kubernetes Node.

3. Now, edit the `ansible-playbook.yml` file and enter private IP of Master:

```
# vi ansible-playbook.yaml

---
- hosts: kubemaster
  roles:
  - kube-master

- hosts: kubenode
  vars:
  MASTERPRIVATEIP: 172.31.6.76
  roles:
  - kube-node
```

That's all, and we are ready to go. Now, we have to run the Ansible playbook and wait for around 4-5 minutes. The Ansible playbook will do its magic and setup Kubernetes cluster with a master and a node:

```
# ansible-playbook ansible-playbook -i hosts -vvv
```

Let's discuss, what this Ansible playbook is doing on behalf of us. It runs two tasks. One is for *Master* and another is for *Node*. Let's check it out one by one.

The first task of thee Ansible playbook is performing the following operation on Master:

- Updating the system and installing required packages such as flanneld, etcd, Kubernetes, and Docker.
- Then, generate a secure certificate, which will be used by the API server.
- Modify the configuration file of Kubernetes components by placing the Master's private IP.
- Followed by that, it is downloading the definition manifest file of the Kubernetes dashboard, Kube-DNS and Monitoring.
- It deploys the manifest file on the Kubernetes cluster.
- At the end, it restarts all Kubernetes components services.

Once Ansible will be done performing tasks on Kubernetes master, it will start running a second task on Node:

- On Node as well, it will first update the system and install the required packages.
- Post that, it will modify the configuration file of Kubernetes and register the node with Kubernetes master by mentioning the K8s master's private IP in kubelet configuration file and that too in the `api-server` directive.
- Then, it will restart all the services of Kubernetes nodes.

Once Ansible is done deploying the Kubernetes cluster on those two servers, try to hit the Public IP of master server followed by port 8080 and give the path, UI, that is `http://master_public_ip:8080/ui`:

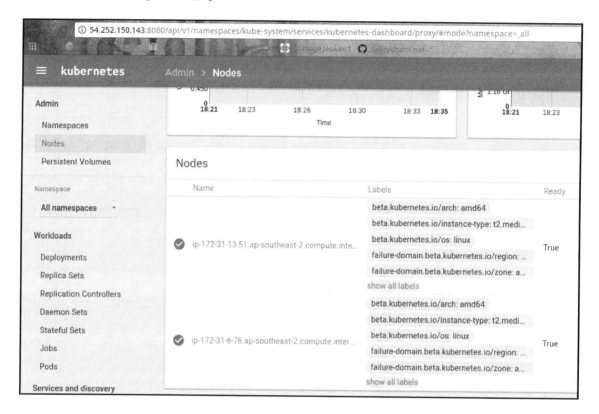

In the preceding image, we can see that we have two nodes right now, in which one is master itself and another is Node. Now, your Kubernetes is ready to deploy any application.

Deploying a multinode production-ready cluster on AWS using Kops

Kops stands for **Kubernetes Operations**. It is a set of tools that is used for installing, operating, and deleting Kubernetes cluster on AWS Cloud. It is considered as the production grade setup for the Kubernetes cluster.

It supports additional functionality, which is mentioned as follows:

- Deploying HA of K8s master
- Supporting easy version upgrade
- Ability to generate configuration files for AWS CloudFormation and Terraform configuration
- Supporting custom Kubernetes add-ons

When the Kubernetes cluster is up and running, we will have to use the `kubectl` command to remotely connect to the master server and manage all the resources.

Getting ready

To use Kops, first of all, your system should have `kubectl` installed. `kubectl` is basically a command-line client tool, which is used to communicate to with the master and perform some operations. So, basically here, we need two things:

- Setting up AWS CLI on your machine and configure the access keys and secret keys of that IAM user, which should have the following policy attached:
    - AmazonEC2FullAccess
    - AmazonRoute53FullAccess
    - AmazonS3FullAccess
    - IAMFullAccess
    - AmazonVPCFullAccess
- Installing the `kubectl` command on your machine (Linux users):

```
# curl -LO https://storage.googleapis.com/kubernetes-
release/release/v1.8.0/bin/linux/amd64/kubectl
# chmod +x kubectl
# mv kubectl /usr/local/bin/kubectl
```

How to do it...

Once we have the `kubectl` command in our local machine, we need to install the `kops` binaries:

```
# wget
https://github.com/kubernetes/kops/releases/download/1.7.1/kops-linux-amd64
# chmod +x kops-linux-amd64
# mv kops-linux-amd64 /usr/local/bin/kops
```

Creating bucket

Now we have to create a S3 bucket to store the Kubernetes state. Kops needs a `state store` to store configuration information of the cluster. For example, how many nodes, instance type of each node and Kubernetes version. The state is stored during the initial cluster creation. Any further changes to the cluster are also persisted to this store as well. In this case, Amazon S3 is the only supported storage mechanism.

Here, we are using the bucket name `kops-bkt` (you should choose a unique name):

```
# aws s3 mb s3://kops-bkt
```

It is recommended to enable versioning on bucket, because it will help to revert or restore to previous versions:

```
# aws s3api put-bucket-versioning --bucket kops-bkt --versioning-
configuration Status=Enabled
```

Once the versioning is enabled on the bucket, define an environment variable pointing to S3 bucket:

```
export KOPS_STATE_STORE=s3://kops-bkt
```

DNS configuration

If you are using Kops 1.6.2 or above, then you can create a general purpose Kubernetes cluster using cluster name end with `.k8s.local`. But for production, it is recommended to use a top-level domain to create a cluster. We need the domain because it will allow the nodes to discover the master and the master to discover all the etcd servers.

The domain may be registered with AWS Route53 or third-party. If it is registered with the third-party, then we have to create a hosted zone in Route53. While creating a hosted zone, it will provide name servers. Using name servers, create NS records for the domain with your registrar.

Here I am using the domain `aiq.io` registered at a third-party registrar:

```
# yum install jq
# ID=$(uuidgen) && aws route53 create-hosted-zone --name k8s.aiq.io --
caller-reference $ID | jq .DelegationSet.NameServers

[
"ns-934.awsdns-32.com",
"ns-192.awsdns-535.co.uk",
"ns-88.awsdns-403.net",
"ns-107.awsdns-110.org"
]
```

Creating a cluster

Now, we can create the Kubernetes cluster. Some of the tasks will happen at the backend during cluster creation are as follows:

- Provisioning EC2 instances
- Setting up AWS resources such as AutoScaling Groups, IAM users, networking components, and Security Groups.
- Installing Kubernetes

Create the cluster by running the following command:

```
# kops create cluster --name k8s.aiq.io --zones ap-southeast-2a --state
s3://kops-bkt --yes
```

 By default, KOPS uses debian as base AMI to deploy Master and Worker Node. You can edit the image and mention custom AMI using `ami-id`. Refer to this link to do the same: `https://github.com/kubernetes/kops/blob/master/docs/images.md`.

It will take some time to spin up the infrastructure and deploy Kubernetes on top of that. This command will create following things:

- One Kubernetes Master in an AutoScaling Group with m3.medium instance type
- Two Kubernetes worker Node in an Auto Scaling Group with a t2.medium instance type
- It will create all the networking components such as VPC, SG, and subnets
- It will create a couple of record set of hosted zone aiq.io

So after giving some time to kops to setup a cluster, let's validate it by running the following command:

```
# kops validate cluster --state=s3://kops-bkt
Using cluster from kubectl context: k8s.aiq.io
Validating cluster k8s.aiq.io
INSTANCE GROUPS
NAME                       ROLE      MACHINETYPE MIN MAX SUBNETS
master-ap-southeast-2a Master    m3.medium   1   1   ap-southeast-2a
nodes                      Node      t2.medium   2   2   ap-southeast-2a

NODE STATUS
NAME                                                      ROLE      READY
ip-172-20-34-168.ap-southeast-2.compute.internal node      True
ip-172-20-46-3.ap-southeast-2.compute.internal   node      True
ip-172-20-61-97.ap-southeast-2.compute.internal  master    True
Your cluster k8s.aiq.io is ready
```

The preceding output shows that our cluster is up and running. Now, we can use our kubectl command to access the Kubernetes information:

```
# kubectl cluster-info
Kubernetes master is running at https://api.k8s.aiq.io
KubeDNS is running at
https://api.k8s.aiq.io/api/v1/proxy/namespaces/kube-system/services/kube-dn
s
```

We can do all the Kubernetes operation of master from our local machine using the kubectl command, but if you want then you can SSH to master server and do the concerned operation using the kubectl command. Now, the question is how you can access the master, because the master server, which gets created by kops, has not given us any key.

While creating the cluster, kops generated one SSH key-pair and put it into the .ssh folder of your current user. So, the private key of that key-pair will be used to ssh to master server.The username to ssh will be `admin`:

```
# ssh -i ~/.ssh/id_rsa admin@52.63.194.198
The programs included with the Debian GNU/Linux system are free software;
the exact distribution terms for each program are described in the
individual files in /usr/share/doc/*/copyright.

Debian GNU/Linux comes with ABSOLUTELY NO WARRANTY, to the extent
permitted by applicable law.
admin@ip-172-20-61-97:~$ sudo su
root@ip-172-20-61-97:/home/admin# cd
root@ip-172-20-61-97:~# kubectl cluster-info
Kubernetes master is running at http://localhost:8080
KubeDNS is running at
http://localhost:8080/api/v1/namespaces/kube-system/services/kube-dns/proxy
```

 The preceding output of `kubectl cluster-info` showing `localhost` as domain instead of `k8s.aiq.io` because we are getting the information from master server only not from remote machine.

Let's get the information regarding nodes:

```
root@ip-172-20-61-97:~# kubectl get nodes -o wide
NAME                                          STATUS   AGE   VERSION   EXTERNAL-IP      OS-IMAGE
ip-172-20-34-168.ap-southeast-2.compute.internal   Ready    7h    v1.7.4    54.153.237.30    Debian GNU/Linux 8
ip-172-20-46-3.ap-southeast-2.compute.internal     Ready    7h    v1.7.4    13.210.138.195   Debian GNU/Linux 8
ip-172-20-61-97.ap-southeast-2.compute.internal    Ready    7h    v1.7.4    52.63.194.198    Debian GNU/Linux 8
```

At this stage, our Kubernetes cluster is ready to use and we can deploy add-ons now.

Kubernetes dashboard (UI)

Here in Kubernetes, the community has provided lots of add-ons, in which we have Kubernetes dashboard, which is a web user interface. This dashboard is helpful for UI administration such as deploying application, resource usage, and monitoring the health of cluster.

On the master server it is as follows:

```
$ kubectl create -f
https://raw.githubusercontent.com/kubernetes/kops/master/addons/kubernetes-
dashboard/v1.6.3.yaml
```

Then navigate to `https://api.<clustername>/ui`, which is **https://api.k8s.aiq.io/ui**

(`/ui` is an alias to
`https://<clustername>/api/v1/proxy/namespaces/kube-system/services/kube`
`rnetes-dashboard`).

The login credentials are:

Username: `admin`
Password: Get by running `kops get secrets kube --type secret -oplaintext` or
`kubectl config view --minify` or `cat ~/.kube/config`:

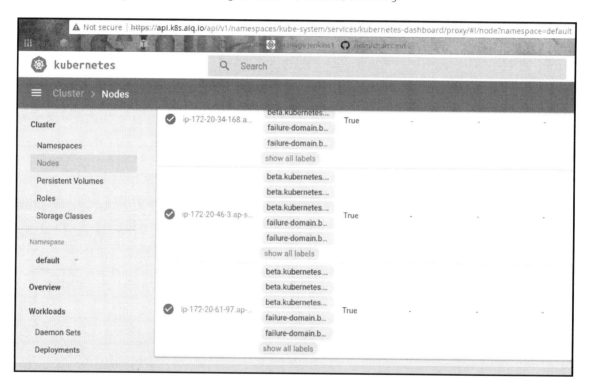

Clean up

To delete a Kubernetes cluster setup by kops, we need to run the following command:

```
# kops delete cluster --state=s3://kops-bkt --yes
```

Deploying a sample application on Kubernetes

Once we have a running K8s cluster, we can run our containerized application. To do so, we can either use a command-line option or we have to create deployment configuration file, where we mention all the details to create the application instance or how to update the instance. First, we will deploy the application using the command line; later, we will use the deployment configuration file to deploy the application.

Getting ready

Basically, there are two things that concern us, one is deployment of application on the K8s cluster and another is accessing the application. To deploy and expose the application, we will be using the `kubectl` command.

How to do it...

To deploy a containerized application in the command line, run the following command:

Syntax: `kubectl run <deployment name> --image=<repo/image> --replicas=<No of replicas> --port=<container port>`

```
$ kubectl run webapp --image=nginx --replicas=2 --port=80
deployment "webapp" created
```

This command is basically running an nginx image, whose deployment name is webapp with two replicas, means two pods will be created. The container is running itself on port 80.

To see running pods in a cluster, run the following command:

```
$ kubectl get deploy,pods
NAME            DESIRED CURRENT UP-TO-DATE AVAILABLE AGE
deploy/webapp 2       2       2          2         34s

NAME                        READY STATUS  RESTARTS AGE
po/webapp-4079742498-ggxq6 1/1   Running 0        33s
po/webapp-4079742498-hl329 1/1   Running 0        33s
```

Now to access the application, we should first get aware of the concept of services in Kubernetes. Each pod, running the application inside it, has its own unique IP, but it is not accessible outside the cluster without service. Services allow our applications to receive traffic. They can be exposed in different ways by specifying a type in `ServiceSpec`:

- `ClusterIP` (default): This will expose the service on an internal IP in the cluster, which will make the service only reachable from within the cluster.
- `NodePort`: This will expose the service on the same port of each selected Node in the cluster using NAT. This will make a service accessible from outside the cluster using : `Superset` of `ClusterIP`.
- `LoadBalancer`: It will create an external load balancer in the current cloud and assigns a fixed, external IP to the service. `Superset` of `NodePort`.

Here, we will expose the application using `NodePort`, because we have to access the application from outside of cluster (LoadBalancer type will be covered in next section).

Run the following command to expose the application:

Syntax: `kubectl expose deployment <deployment name> --port=<containerPort> --type=NodePort`

```
$ kubectl expose deployment webapp --port=80 --type=NodePort
service "webapp" exposed
```

Now, let's see what port has been assigned to the service `webapp`:

```
$ kubectl get svc
NAME           CLUSTER-IP    EXTERNAL-IP   PORT(S)  AGE
kubernetes 100.64.0.1    <none>        443/TCP 2d
webapp         100.71.48.5 <nodes>       80:32078/TCP 1m
```

In the output of preceding command, the service `webapp` got port no `32078`, which can be accessed from outside of the cluster. But before that, let's try to access the service withing the cluster; for that, we have to perform curl Cluster-IP:

```
$ curl 100.71.48.5
<!DOCTYPE html>
<html>
<head>
<title>Welcome to nginx!</title>
<style>
 body {
 width: 35em;
 margin: 0 auto;
 font-family: Tahoma, Verdana, Arial, sans-serif;
```

```
     }
</style>
</head>
<body>
<h1>Welcome to nginx!</h1>
<p>If you see this page, the nginx web server is successfully installed and
working. Further configuration is required.</p>
<p>For online documentation and support please refer to
<a href="http://nginx.org/">nginx.org</a>.<br/>
Commercial support is available at
<a href="http://nginx.com/">nginx.com</a>.</p>
<p><em>Thank you for using nginx.</em></p>
</body>
</html>
```

Now, we are able to access the service within the cluster, to access it outside the cluster. We have to the hit kops endpoint (`api.k8s.aiq.io`) with nodeport assigned by Kubernetes in the `webapp` service, which is `32078`:

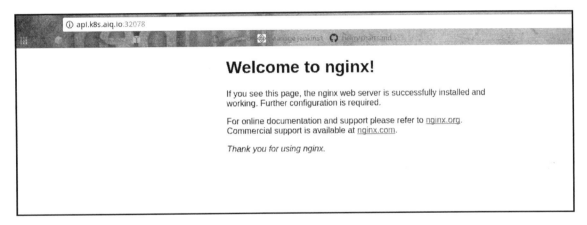

To remove the application from the cluster, first we have to delete the service then deployment as follows:

```
$ kubectl delete svc webapp
service "webapp" deleted
$ kubectl delete deployment webapp
deployment "webapp" deleted
```

Configuration file

The preceding example of the deployment of application was through command line, but in production, we should use the deployment configuration file, to deploy an application because we can update the configuration file and apply the running application as well as provide more options. We will be deploying the same preceding example using a configuration file.

Since we had two commands, one for deployment and another for service, we will have two configuration files. One for deployment and another for service (you can merge both in a single file as well).

Deployment configuration file

```
$ vi nginx-deployment.yaml

apiVersion: extensions/v1beta1
kind: Deployment
metadata:
  name: webapp
spec:
  replicas: 2
  selector:
    matchLabels:
      app: nginx
  minReadySeconds: 5
  template:
    metadata:
      labels:
        app: nginx
    spec:
      containers:
      - name: webapp
        image: nginx
        imagePullPolicy: IfNotPresent
        ports:
        - containerPort: 80
```

The previous configuration is mentioning the following things:

- The kind of file is deployed, and the name is `webapp`.
- The number of replicas will be two, and the name of application is nginx.

- The name of the container is webapp and the image nginx is used.
- `ImagePullPolicy` is `IfNotPresent`, meaning that the image is not present in the cluster or pulled from registry. If its there, then use that image.
- Container port is using 80.

Service configuration file

```
$ vi nginx-service

apiVersion: v1
kind: Service
metadata:
  name: webapp
  labels:
    app: nginx
spec:
  type: NodePort
  ports:
  - port: 80
  selector:
    app: nginx
```

The previous configuration file is mentioning the following things.

- The kind of file is service, and the name of service is webapp.
- Access of service will be done by NodePort, and the service will be assigned to the application nginx.

Now, we have two files in place in the K8s cluster Master server. To deploy the application and its service, we have to run the following commands and check the pods and service:

```
$ kubectl create -f nginx-deployment.yaml
deployment "webapp" created
$ kubectl get deploy,pods
NAME            DESIRED CURRENT UP-TO-DATE AVAILABLE AGE
deploy/webapp 2       2       2          2         34s

NAME                        READY STATUS RESTARTS AGE
po/webapp-4079742498-ggxq6 1/1    Running 0        33s
po/webapp-4079742498-h1329 1/1    Running 0        33s
$ kubectl create -f nginx-service.yaml
service "webapp" created
$ kubectl get svc
NAME         CLUSTER-IP   EXTERNAL-IP   PORT(S)      AGE
```

```
kubernetes 100.64.0.1  <none>      443/TCP      2d
webapp     100.71.48.5 <nodes>     80:32561/TCP 1m
```

We can access the application on node port 32561:

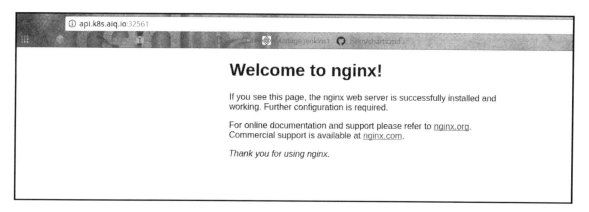

Working with Kubernetes on AWS using AWS resources

We provisioned the Kubernetes cluster on AWS, therefore, we will try to integrate with AWS services wherever possible.

For storing docker images, we will use ECR; for LoadBalancer, we will use ELB; and for persistence storage, we will be using EBS. There are a couple of important points that needs to be taken care before implementing.

1. Each and every master and worker node should be attached with the IAM role that has the permission of AWS resources such as S3, EC2, VPC, Route53, and so on. But that's not enough, we also have to run the `aws configure` command, but we don't need to fill AccessKey and SecretKey but region name, because the key is for global purpose and to provision a resource we have to mention region name.

2. If a Kubernetes cluster is setup by kops or given an argument of `--cloud-provider=aws` in configuration file of Kubernetes, then pulling an image from ECR is not a big deal, Kubernetes will pull the image from ECR without any problem. But if a cluster is setup normally, without any cloud provider, then a secret token needs to be created, which should have authorization token of ECR registries as follows:

- First login to AWS ECR so that `.docker/config.json` will get updated with ECR registry authentication data. `~/.docker/config.json` that is generated from aws ecr `get-login` only lasts 12 hours. It has to be regenerated after 12 hours. Post that, create a file of type secret and run `kubectl` create on that file.

```
$ ECR_LOGIN=$(/root/bin/aws ecr get-login --no-include-email)
$ ${ECR_LOGIN}
$ vi image-pull-secret.yaml

apiVersion: v1
kind: Secret
metadata:
  name: myregistrykey
data:
  .dockerconfigjson: $(cat ~/.docker/config.json | base64 -w 0)
type: kubernetes.io/dockerconfigjson

$ kubectl create -f image-pull-secret.yaml
$ kubectl get secrets
NAME                 TYPE                                DATA AGE
myregistrykey        kubernetes.io/imagepullsecret       3    5d
```

- Once the secret gets created, then the name of that secret token will be passed in the deployment configuration file as follows:

```
apiVersion: v1
kind: Pod
metadata:
    name: private-reg
spec:
   containers:
   - name: private-reg-container
     image: <ECR-repository/Image-Version>
   imagePullSecrets:
   - name: myregistrykey
```

And if we will create deployment using this deployment file, then Kubernetes will pull the image from ECR without any problem.

- Some of our pods need to persist data across pod restart, for example, redis or databases related pod. In order to facilitate this, we can mount folders into our pods that are backed by EBS volumes on AWS.

Getting ready

In this recipe, we will be deploying an application which will cover all our use-cases of using AWS resources:

- Deployment configuration file contains the image whose source will be ECR.
- Service will be exposed using LoadBalancer ELB.
- For persistent storage, EBS will be used and mounted on container.

To achieve the preceding points, we have to perform the operation in the following manner:

1. Create PersistentVolumeClaim of some size of EBS volume
2. Create a deployment configuration and mention the image name, which is present in ECR.
3. In the deployment configuration file, we also need to mention which path will be mounted with that PersistentVolume.
4. Create a service configuration file, where the access of service will be done by ELB.

Let's see the previous points in action.

How to do it...

The following are the methods which we use to deploy an application:

Creating a persistent volume claim

PersistentVolumeClaim is an abstraction over the actual storage system in our cluster. With a claim, we define that we need some amount of storage at some path inside our container. Based on our needs, the cluster management system will provision us some storage out of its available storage pool. In case of AWS, we usually get an EBS volume attached to the node and mounted into our container.

Now, let's create a persistent volume claim template `k8s-pvc.yaml` to create volume using the EBS storage. Post that, let's check the status of volume:

```
$ vi k8s-pvc.yaml

kind: PersistentVolumeClaim
apiVersion: v1
metadata:
  name: k8s-pvc
  labels:
    type: amazonEBS
spec:
  accessModes:
    - ReadWriteOnce
  resources:
    requests:
      storage: 5Gi
```

In the preceding configuration, the following things are mentioned:

- The configuration file is of type `PersistentVolumeClaim` and the name is `k8s-pvc`
- It has been labelled with type `amazonEBS`, which is resposible for provisioning the EBS volume
- Access mode is `ReadWriteonce` means this volume will be attached with one node only
- The storage size of the volume of is 5 GB:

```
$ kubectl create -f k8s-pvc.yaml
persistentvolumeclaim "k8s-pvc" created
$ kubectl get pvc
NAME      STATUS VOLUME                       CAPACITY  ACCESSMODES STORAGECLASS
AGE
     k8s-pvc Bound   pvc-4026924a-b643-11e7-8b7e-02d835446858 5Gi RWO gp2
9h
```

At the same moment, if we see the EBS section of the AWS console, then we will be able to see that a volume has been created and its in an available state:

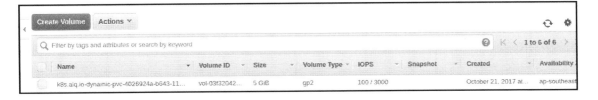

Now, we will use this PVC inside the deployment configuration file.

Deployment configuration file (includes ECR image and PVC)

We have an image in ECR as shown here, which we will be mentioning in our deployment file:

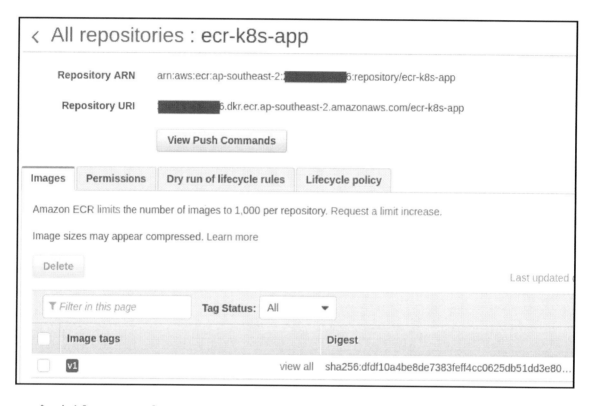

```
$ vi k8s-app.yaml

apiVersion: extensions/v1beta1
kind: Deployment
metadata:
  name: k8s-app
spec:
  replicas: 1
  selector:
    matchLabels:
      app: k8s-app
```

```
  minReadySeconds: 5
  template:
    metadata:
      labels:
        app: k8s-app
    spec:
      containers:
      - name: k8s-app
        image: 2xxxxxxxx6.dkr.ecr.ap-southeast-2.amazonaws.com/ecr-k8s-
app:v1
        imagePullPolicy: IfNotPresent
        ports:
        - containerPort: 8080
        volumeMounts:
        - name: k8s-pvc
          mountPath: "/App/Data"
      volumes:
      - name: k8s-pvc
        persistentVolumeClaim:
          claimName: k8s-pvc
```

The preceding deployment file mentions the following things:

- The kind of file is deployment, and the name of deployment is k8s-app
- There will be only one replica of the deployment
- The name of application as well as the container is k8s-app
- The image used is 2xxxxxxxx6.dkr.ecr.ap-southeast-2.amazonaws.com/ecr-k8s-app:v1
- The container is running on port 8080 and path is /App/Data, which is mounted with the volume k8s-pvc

Now, let's create the deployment using the preceding file. Since this file is deploying on the k8s cluster which was setup by kops, the image pulling issue will not occur:

```
$ kubectl create -f k8s-app.yaml
deployment "k8s-app" created
$ kubectl get pods
NAME                      READY STATUS    RESTARTS AGE
k8s-app-3152459664-v9t8n 1/1   Running  0        3s
```

Once this pod gets created, at that moment of time, we can check from the AWS console, that the status of the volume will be changed to `in-use` from `available`.

Service configuration file (type Loadbalancer)

Once the application is deployed, it's time to expose the application using service. So, we must have the following service configuration file:

```
$ vi k8s-app-svc.yaml

apiVersion: v1
kind: Service
metadata:
  name: k8s-app-svc
  labels:
    app: k8s-app
spec:
  type: LoadBalancer
  ports:
  - port: 80
    targetPort: 8080
  selector:
    app: k8s-app
```

The preceding file is mentioning the following things:

- The file is of service type and the name is `k8s-app-svc`
- This service is assigned to an application labelled with `k8s-app`
- The service is using port `80` on `LoadBalancer`

Let's create the service and go to the AWS LoadBalancing console, and see what's happening over there:

```
$ kubectl create -f k8s-app-svc.yaml
$ kubectl get svc
NAME            CLUSTER-IP EXTERNAL-IP    PORT(S)          AGE
k8s-app-svc 100.71.184.81 a731acf73b647... 80:31876/TCP   10s
```

In the ELB console, we can see that we one LoadBalancer created automatically and both the nodes of k8s is registered automatically with this ELB. Now, let's hit the ELB DNS and access the application:

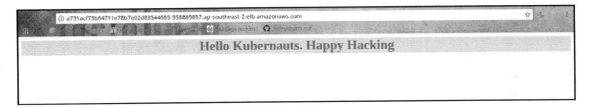

Let's go inside the container and check whether the persistent storage got mounted in the specified path. To get the shell of container from the K8s cluster, run the following command:

syntax: `kubectl exec -it <podname> -- <shell>`

```
$ kubectl exec -it k8s-app-3152459664-v9t8n -- /bin/bash
root@k8s-app-3152459664-v9t8n:/App# df -hT
Filesystem Type Size Used Avail Use% Mounted on
overlay overlay 120G 5.2G 110G 5% /
tmpfs tmpfs 2.0G 0 2.0G 0% /dev
tmpfs tmpfs 2.0G 0 2.0G 0% /sys/fs/cgroup
/dev/xvdce ext4 4.8G 10M 4.6G 1% /App/Data
/dev/xvda1 ext4 120G 5.2G 110G 5% /etc/hosts
```

```
shm tmpfs 64M 0 64M 0% /dev/shm
tmpfs tmpfs 2.0G 12K 2.0G 1% /run/secrets/kubernetes.io/serviceaccount
```

Once we get inside the container and checked the disk size then we found 5 GB disk is mounted in /App/Data.

AWS EBS has an access mode of RWO, which means Read Write Once, that is, volume will be attached and can be read and written by one node only. In Production, you can use EFS for the storage option. EFS have RWX access modes, means Read Write Many, that is, volume will be attached and can be read and get written by multiple nodes. To implement EFS with K8s, refer to `https://github.com/awsstar/EFS-K8S-Doc.git`. Don't clean up the resources and deployment, because we will be using this in the last section of the chapter *Deploying Microservices Application in Kubernetes.*

It is advisable to use ingress controller for all the traffic. You can use Application LoadBalancer for that. Follow this link and try to implement it: `https://aws.amazon.com/blogs/apn/coreos-and-ticketmaster-collaborate-to-bring-aws-application-load-balancer-support-to-kubernetes/`.

Jenkins pipeline 2.0 (Pipeline as Code) using Jenkinsfile

In the world of software development, Jenkins has become an undisputed leader among **continuous integration** (CI) and **delivery and deployment** (CD) tools. Jenkins holds 50-70% of the CI/CD market because of its dedication to open source principles and providing large number of plugins for the integration with another technologies, whether it's related to cloud or monitoring. One of the major contributor in Jenkins is Cloudbees. They are redefining not only the way Jenkins behaves but also the CI/CD practices in a much broader sense. One of those new features is the Jenkins pipeline plugin. But before diving into the Jenkins pipeline, let's take a step back and checkout the reason of the evolving Jenkins Pipeline.

Over time, Jenkins, like most other self-hosted CI/CD tools, have the capacity to handle and store a vast number of jobs. A large number of jobs cause quite an increase in the maintenance cost. The maintenance of ten jobs is easy, but it's difficult to manage when the number increases to hundred. It becomes very tedious and time consuming when we have a large no of jobs in hundreds and thousands.

If you are not an expert with Jenkins or you haven't worked for a big project, you might think that hundreds of jobs is way too much. But the reality is such number usually reaches in a very short time, when team are practicing CD. For example, an average CD flow has following set of tasks that usually runs on each commit:

- Building
- Pre-deployment testing
- Deployment to staging environment
- Post deployment testing
- Deployment to production

These five sets of task will create five separate Jenkins jobs. This is the optimistic one, but many companies use more than five jobs for a single CD flow. Let's say if we have 20 CD flow, then we are already reach a three digit number.

Now, let's talk about another pain point. If we need to change all these jobs from Maven to Gradle, then we will start with modifying them through Jenkins UI, which will take hell lot of time. We can also apply the changes directly to Jenkins XML files, but that is error prone and too complicated. There are a couple of plugins which we can use, but none of them are truly successful.

Basically, the major pain points Jenkins had until recently are as follows:

- Capability to create a vast number of jobs
- Relatively hard and costly maintenance
- Lack of powerful and easy ways to specify deployment flow through code

The solution to all of the preceding problems is the Jenkins pipeline plugin.

Jenkins pipeline is a plugin suit that allows us to mention the job configuration in a single file called **Jenkinsfile** in code style. Basically, it's transition from Freestyle chained jobs to a single pipeline expressed as code, means we can write a single CD flow (which usually consists of five sets of jobs) in a single Jenkinsfile and create a single job. Jenkinsfile can be written in DSL or Groovy.

The additional reason of using Jenkins Pipeline is mentioned as follows:

- **Code**: With the introduction of pipeline plugin, we can mention all the Job stages and action in the Jenkinsfile. The Jenkinsfile will be checked in along with source code in the root directory. It give teams, the ability to edit, review, and iterate the delivery pipeline. It looks something as follows:

```
pipeline {
    agent any
    stages {
        stage('Example') {
            steps {
                echo "Running ${env.BUILD_ID} on ${env.JENKINS_URL}"
            }
        }
    }
}
```

- **Error validation and reporting**: Validation of semantics, syntax, and argument types.
  Check all the syntax and report all the error in one go. (eliminate the issue of fix one typo, re-run build, get to the next typo, rinse, repeat). Errors out if a tool or tool version isn't installed.
- **Durable**: Pipeline can survive both planned and unplanned restarts of Jenkins master.
- **Extensible:** Integration with other plugins.
- **Versatile:** Pipeline has the ability to work in parallel execution, fork/join, and loop. The Jenkinsfile will look like the following, where parallel steps has been mentioned:

```
parallel linux: {
    node('linux') {
        checkout scm
        try {
            unstash 'app'
            sh 'make check'
        }
        finally {
            junit '**/target/*.xml'
        }
    }
},
windows: {
    node('windows') {
        checkout scm
```

```
            /* .. snip .. */
        }
    }
```

- **Blue Ocean:** Blue Ocean is another UI of Jenkins, which mainly deals with job which are having Jenkinsfile. It is designed from the ground up for Jenkins Pipeline. Blue Ocean has a inbuilt Pipeline Editor. It looks like the following:

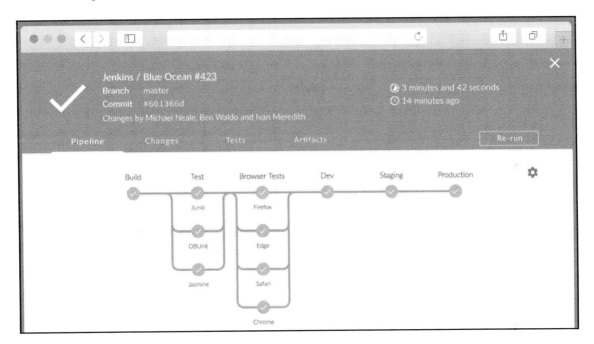

How to do it...

Jenkins pipeline supports two syntaxes, one is declarative and another is scripted. In this chapter, we will be following declarative syntax, because it's easy to understand. The following is the sample of Jenkinsfile, which covers basic stages such as `Build`, `Test`, and `Deploy`:

```
pipeline {
        // agent indicates that Jenkins should allocate an executor and
workspace for this part of the Pipeline
        agent any
        stages {
                //describing stage of the Pipeline
                stage('Build') {
```

```
                                //describes the steps to be run in this stage.
                                steps {
                                        //executes the given shell command
                                        sh 'make'
                                        }
                                }
                stage('Test')   {
                                  steps {
                                        sh 'make check'
                                        junit 'reports/**/*.xml'
                                        }
                                }
                stage('Deploy') {
                                  steps {
                                        echo 'Deploying....'
                                        }
                                }

                }
        }
```

Declarative pipeline

- It's the starting block of the Jenkinsfile. All declarative pipelines must be enclosed within a pipeline block, for example:

```
pipeline {
 /* insert Declarative Pipeline here */
}
```

- pipeline { } block must only consist of sections, Directives, steps, or assignment steps.

Sections

- **agent**: The agent section specifies where the entire pipeline, or a specific stage, will execute in the Jenkins environment depending on where the agent section is placed:

```
pipeline {
   agent {
        // The pipeline will run on Node which is labelled as
master.
        label 'master'
      }
}
```

- **stages**: It contains sequence of one or more stage directives. The `stages` section is the place where all the work described by the pipeline is located. At least one *stage* directive should be there in the `stages` section. A `stage` directive includes the `steps` section. This section defines a series of one or more steps to be executed in a given `stage` directive:

```
pipeline {
  agent any
     stages {
         stage('Example') {
                steps {
                    echo 'Hello World'
                }
            }
         }
     }
```

This was all about writing Jenkinsfile. Now, let's try to deploy an application using Jenkinsfile and visualize it through Blue Ocean.

The syntax and structure of Jenkinsfile covered in this book is very basic to get you all started. It is advisable to refer to the link `https://jenkins.io/doc/book/pipeline/syntax/` for more information. You can also generate the pipeline snippet using the pipeline snippet generator. In this generator, you can get the pipeline snippet of UI job. You can access the snippet generator by going to `http://jenkins-url:8080/pipeline-syntax`.

Application deployment using Jenkinsfile

In this recipe, we will deploy an application using Jenkinsfile. It will be checked in along with the source code. The Jenkins pipeline plugin will automatically detect the Jenkinsfile present in the application and start running the Jenkinsfile and perform all the operation or steps that are mentioned inside Jenkinsfile.

Getting ready

To deploy the application we need to perform the following setup first:

- Jenkins 2.0 installed on a server and make sure that it is running on port 80, cause the application that we will deploy is running on port `8080`. We are not using a third server to deploy the application. We will going to deploy the application on Jenkins server only.

> The previous mentioned setup is for this application deployment only.

- Install Blue Ocean plugin by navigating to **Manage Jenkins** | **Manage Plugins** | **Available** | Search **BlueOcean** | **Install without Restart**.

- Clone this repository (`https://github.com/awsstar/App-Jenkinsfile.git`) and migrate it to your GitHub account so that you can use this application to build and deploy via Jenkins pipeline using your own GitHub account. This needs your GitHub account, because Jenkins will ask for an authorization token of the GitHub account where the application lies and the communication between Jenkins and GitHub can establish.

If we have the preceding setup in place, then we are good to go.

How to do it...

In Jenkins pipeline, we have two scenarios:

1. Write a Jenkinsfile and check in with the source code. Then while creating job, Jenkins Pipeline will detect the Jenkinsfile and run the job.
2. Create a pipeline in the BlueOcean for the application and mention the steps that you want to perform on the source code. Jenkins pipeline will automatically create a Jenkinsfile and push it to the branch you will give.

Either we write the Jenkinsfile and then run the job or create a pipeline which will generate the Jenkinsfile for you and then run the job.

We will see both the scenarios here. First of all, we will see the second scenario, which will generate Jenkinsfile for you.

Create a pipeline in the BlueOcean

1. Go to your Jenkins UI, and click on **Open Blue Ocean**:

2. After that, you will get a page as follows. Then, click on **Create New Pipeline**:

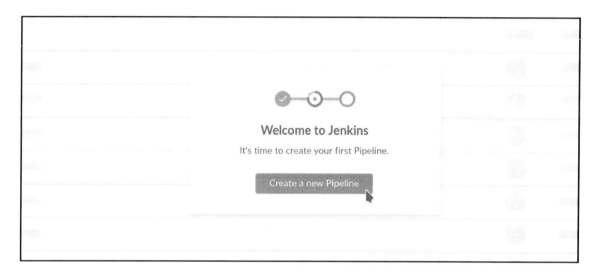

3. Post that, you will land to a new page where you have to select our SCM. In our case, we are using GitHub. Click on **GitHub:**

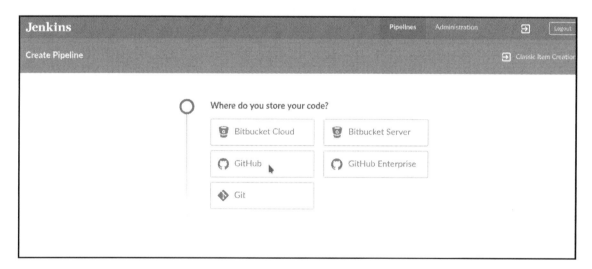

4. After that, Jenkins will ask for an authentication token, because Jenkins needs an access key to authorize itself with GitHub. To get the access key of your GitHub account, open new tab and login to your GitHub account. Then come back to the Jenkins page, and click on **Create an access key here,** mentioned in blue color:

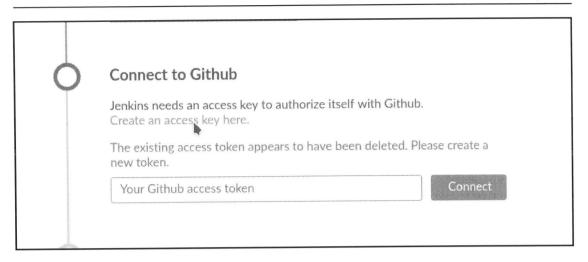

5. When we click on **Create an access key here**, it will redirect you to a new page where you will give the **token description**. Here, I am giving the token description as **Token for Jenkins pipeline**:

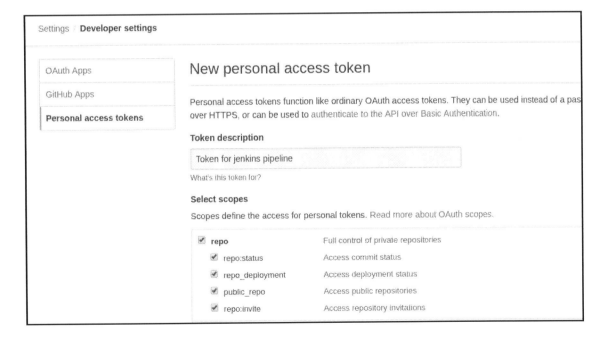

6. Post that, scroll down the page and click on **Generate token**. Then, you will get your personal access token:

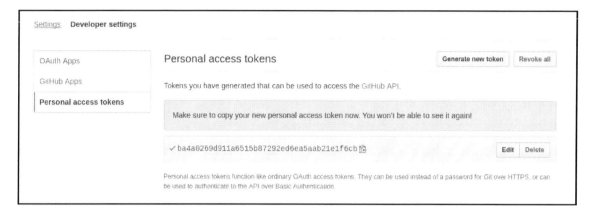

7. Copy the token and paste it in Jenkins where it was asking for access token to connect to GitHub, and then click on **Connect**:

8. Now, it will ask **Which organization does the repository belong to ?** Select the organization (in my case, **awsstar**):

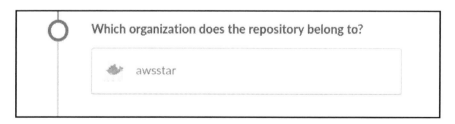

9. Then it will ask for whether to create a new pipeline from the repository or Auto-discover Jenkinsfile from the repository. In this scenario, we will click on **New Pipeline**:

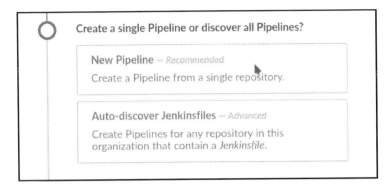

10. After that, it will ask to select the repository (in my case its **App-Jenkinsfile**). Then click on **Create Pipeline**:

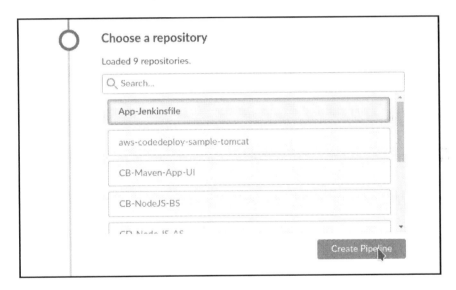

11. We will get a pipeline editor where we will create a pipeline:

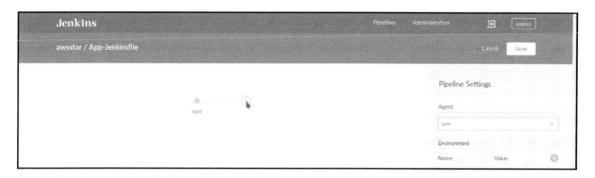

Now before moving ahead, let me tell you couple of things. The application deployment should have the following manual steps:

- `mvn clean compile`: To compile the application
- `mvn package -DskipTests`: To package the application
- `java -jar target/my-first-app-1.0-SNAPSHOT-fat.jar`: To deploy the application

We will enforce the preceding commands in Jenkinsfile using Jenkins pipeline:

1. Select **Agent** any, and then click on the plus sign. After that, give the name of the stage as **Compile**. Then, click on **+ Add Step** and select **shell script**. Post that, enter **mvn clean compile** and then click on back arrow key:

2. Similarly, click on + sign right to **Compile** stage and then give the stage name as **Package** and add the step, shell script **mvn package -DskipTests.** Post that, click on the + sign right to **Package** stage and then give the stage name **Deploy** and add the step, shell script **nohup java -jar target/my-first-app-1.0-SNAPSHOT-fat.jar &.** So at the end, the pipeline will look like this. Now, click on **Save:**

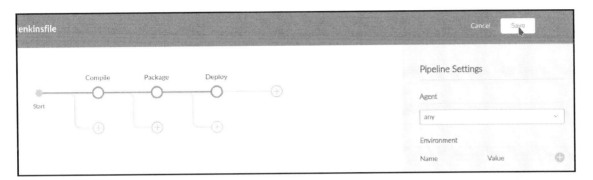

3. Once we click on **Save**, it will ask the commit description and the branch of the repository, where Jenkinsfile will be created:

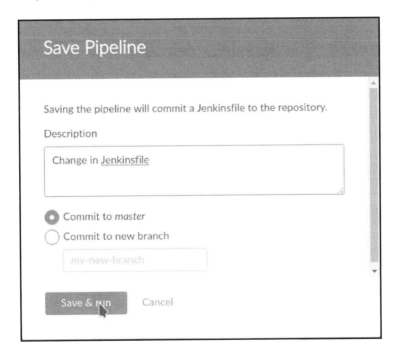

4. Once you click on **Save & run**, then first Jenkins pipeline will generate the Jenkinsfile and push it into the repository and using that Jenkinsfile, the pipeline will start running:

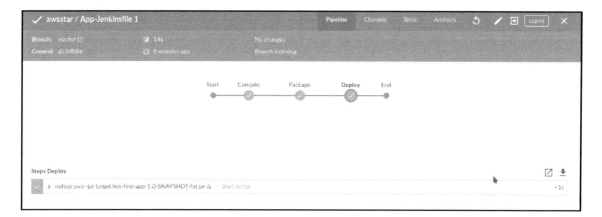

5. We can also see that new file **Jenkinsfile** got uploaded into the GitHub repository. Let's checkout what is their inside the file:

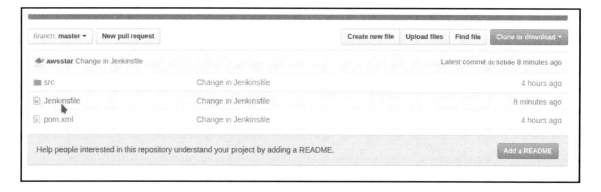

```
pipeline {
  agent any
     stages {
        stage('Compile') {
            steps {
                sh 'mvn clean compile'
                }
               }
        stage('Package') {
            steps {
                sh 'mvn package -DskipTests'
```

```
                    }
                  }
        stage('Deploy') {
              steps {
                    sh 'nohup java -jar target/my-first-app-1.0-
SNAPSHOT-fat.jar &'
                  }
                }
            }
      }
```

6. Now if you will hit the Jenkins URL with port 8080, you will get webpage as follows:

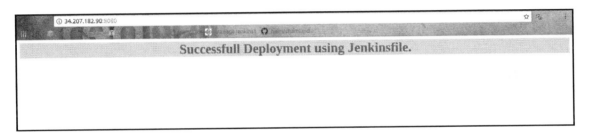

Clean Up

Go to classic UI of Jenkins and search for the Organization name (In my case awsstar), click on that and select **Delete Organization:**

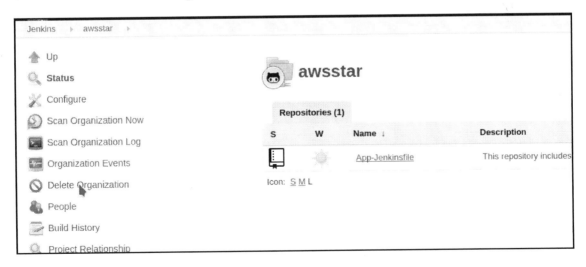

Before moving ahead, clean up the preceding job, because we will be using the same example with different scenario.

Creating a Pipeline using existing Jenkinsfile

In this scenario, we will have a Jenkinsfile already checked in with source code. We are using same example, but in this case, we have Jenkinsfile with us. The following is a snippet of Jenkinsfile:

```
pipeline {
  agent any
    stages {
        stage('Compile') {
            steps {
                sh 'mvn clean compile'
                }
                }
        stage('Package') {
            steps {
                sh 'mvn package -DskipTests'
            }
            }
        stage('Deploy') {
            steps {
                sh 'nohup java -jar target/my-first-app-1.0-SNAPSHOT-
fat.jar &'
            }
                }
        }
    }
```

Now perform step 1 to step 8 of the preceding section. In step 9, instead of selecting **New Pipeline**, we have to select **Auto-discover Jenkinsfile**. After that, it will give another information, that when this option (Auto-discover Jenkinsfile) is selected, Jenkins will actively search for new repositories in awsstar that contain Jenkinsfiles and create Pipelines for them. Then, click on **Create Pipelines**.

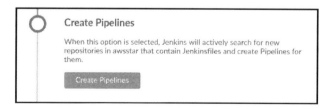

It will discover a repository with Jenkinfile and it will create a pipeline for that and start running it:

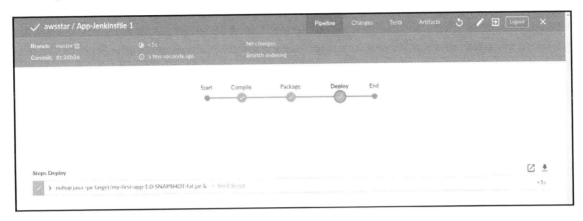

If the Job runs successfully, then hit the Jenkins URL with port 8080:

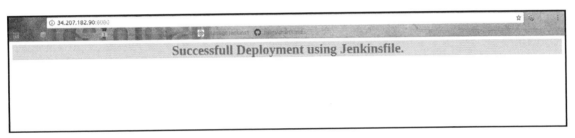

So we saw how we can create a job using Pipeline as a code. Using this methodology, we will either be deploying or updating the microservice application in Kubernetes using Jenkinsfile.

Deploying microservices applications in Kubernetes using Jenkinsfile

This is one of the most important section of the chapter. In this section, we will see how to update the deployment of microservice application in Kubernetes cluster. We will be using the resources that has been created in the recipe *Kubernetes on AWS using AWS resources,* meaning the ECR repository, EBS volume, deployment of application, and load balancer are already in place.

Scenario: Whenever there is change in the code, a new image should get created. The new image should also get updated in the Kubernetes cluster so that Kubernetes should serve the latest application.

To automate the preceding scenario, we will be using Jenkins, and all the steps and configuration will be written in Jenkinsfile.

Getting ready

As I mentioned that we already have couple of resources in place, for example:

- ECR Repository: ecr-k8s-app
- EBS Storage: k8s-pvc (5GB)
- Deployed Application: k8s-app
- Load Balancer through Service: k8s-app-svc
- Jenkins: Your Jenkins URL along with Blue Ocean.

Now the Jenkins server should also need AWS CLI, because image will get built on Jenkins server and get pushed to ECR through Jenkins server only, so to push the image to ECR, Jenkins server need AWS CLI. Also ECR credential helper (`https://github.com/awslabs/amazon-ecr-credential-helper`) should be configured on the Jenkins server, so that every time there shouldn't be any need to authenticate your Jenkins server with ECR. Also, the Jenkins server should communicate to Kubernetes cluster so that Jenkins perform some deployment action on a Kubernetes cluster via SSH. So, the action step as prerequisite is as follows:

- Install `awscli` on the Jenkins server
- Setup ECR-Credentials helper (`https://github.com/awslabs/amazon-ecr-credential-helper`)
- Open the 22 port between the Jenkins server and Kubernetes cluster
- Setup your own application repository by mirroring the URL (`https://github.com/awsstar/K8S-App-Jenkinsfile.git`)

How to do it...

If we have the preceding pre-requisites, then let's discuss the flow of CD. We will try to implement those steps in Jenkinsfile.

Workflow

Whenever the latest code pushed in master branch, Jenkins will get triggered and it will pick up the Jenkinsfile. In the Jenkinsfile, the following things will be mentioned:

- Pull the repository in the Jenkins server
- Then it will build the image of the application
- It will upload the image to ECR
- The next step depends upon the value on parameter, that whether we want to deploy the latest image in Kubernetes cluster or simply want to push the image to ECR
- Then, it will ssh to the Kubernetes cluster and update the latest image in the deployment

Now, we have to implement the workflow in Jenkinsfile:

1. Let's start with the agent section. Agent will be the Jenkins master only:

```
pipeline {
  agent any
}
```

2. Let's talk about the parameter. The name of the parameter is env and the default value of parameter is Deploy. If the parameter is Deploy, then Jenkins will deploy the latest image in K8s cluster, else it will simply upload the image to ECR:

```
pipeline {
    agent any
      parameters {
        string(name: 'env', defaultValue: 'Deploy', description:
'Development Environment')
      }
}
```

3. It's time to build the image. This step will be mentioned in the `stages` section. The tag of the image is equivalent to the build number of Jenkins:

```
pipeline {
  agent any
        parameters {
          string(name: 'env', defaultValue: 'Deploy', description:
'Development Environment')
                }
    stages {
        stage('Building_Image') {
              steps {
                  sh '''
                    cd ${WORKSPACE}
                    REPO="ecr-k8s-app"
                    #Build container images using Dockerfile
                    docker build --no-cache -t
${REPO}:${BUILD_NUMBER} .
                  '''
              }
      }
    }
```

4. Once the image got built then, it will get uploaded to ECR:

```
pipeline {
  agent any
      parameters {
        string(name: 'env', defaultValue: 'Deploy', description:
'Development Environment')
      }
    stages {
        stage('Building_Image') {
              steps {
                  sh '''
                    cd ${WORKSPACE}
                    REPO="ecr-k8s-app"
                    #Build container images using Dockerfile
                    docker build --no-cache -t ${REPO}:${BUILD_NUMBER} .
                  '''
              }
          }
    stage('Pushing_Image_To_ECR') {
              steps {
                  sh '''
                    REG_ADDRESS="2xxxxxxxxx6.dkr.ecr.ap-southeast-
2.amazonaws.com"
                    REPO="ecr-k8s-app"
```

```
                  #Tag the build with BUILD_NUMBER version
                  docker tag ${REPO}:${BUILD_NUMBER}
${REG_ADDRESS}/${REPO}:${BUILD_NUMBER}
                  #Publish image
                  docker push ${REG_ADDRESS}/${REPO}:${BUILD_NUMBER}
      '''
            }
        }
      }
```

5. After that, if the value of parameter is `Deploy`, then Jenkins will deploy the latest image to the Kubernetes cluster, else it won't deploy:

```
   pipeline {
    agent any
        parameters {
          string(name: 'env', defaultValue: 'Deploy', description:
'Development Environment')
          }
    stages {
        stage('Building_Image') {
            steps {
                sh '''
                    cd ${WORKSPACE}
                    REPO="ecr-k8s-app"
                    #Build container images using Dockerfile
                    docker build --no-cache -t ${REPO}:${BUILD_NUMBER} .
                    '''
                }
            }
    stage('Pushing_Image_To_ECR') {
                steps {
                    sh '''
                    REG_ADDRESS="2xxxxxxxx6.dkr.ecr.ap-southeast-
2.amazonaws.com"
                    REPO="ecr-k8s-app"
                    #Tag the build with BUILD_NUMBER version
                    docker tag ${REPO}:${BUILD_NUMBER}
${REG_ADDRESS}/${REPO}:${BUILD_NUMBER}
                    #Publish image
                    docker push ${REG_ADDRESS}/${REPO}:${BUILD_NUMBER}
      '''
            }
        }
    stage('Deploy_In_Kubernetes') {
                steps {
                    sshagent ( credentials: []) {
        sh '''
```

```
     echo "Tag=${BUILD_NUMBER}" > sshenv
     echo "target=${env}" >> sshenv
     scp sshenv admin@52.63.194.198:~/.ssh/environment
     ssh -T -o StrictHostKeyChecking=no -l admin 52.63.194.198 <<'EOF'
     DEPLOYMENT_NAME="k8s-app"
     CONTAINER_NAME="k8s-app"
     NEW_DOCKER_IMAGE="2xxxxxxx6.dkr.ecr.ap-southeast-
2.amazonaws.com/ecr-k8s-app:${Tag}"
     if [ "${target}" = "NoDeploy" ]
     then
        echo "No deployment to K8s"
     else
     kubectl set image deployment/$DEPLOYMENT_NAME
$CONTAINER_NAME=$NEW_DOCKER_IMAGE
     kubectl rollout status deployment $DEPLOYMENT_NAME
     fi
     EOF'''
                                          }
                                    }
                              }
                        }
                  }
```

The preceding Jenkinsfile is the final one and will be checked in to repository along with Source code. Now, go to Blue Ocean console of Jenkins and then create the pipeline using the repository (in my case, **K8S-App-Jenkinsfile**). The Jenkins will start performing all the activity:

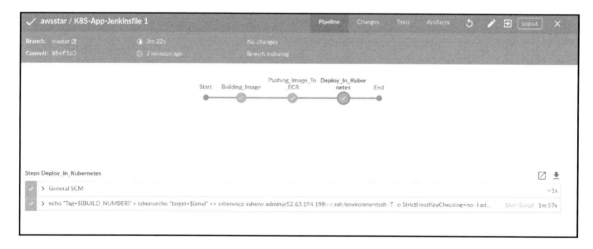

We can see the new image with the tag of build number 1 in ECR.

This time, if you will hit the load balancer, you will get a different web page:

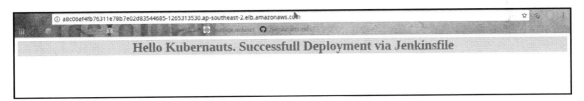

Whenever you update the code in the branch after some time the deployed application on Kubernetes cluster will also get updated with the latest changes.

10
Best Practices and Troubleshooting Tips

In this chapter, we present an overview of the best practices with AWS CodeCommit and Troubleshooting with CodeCommit and CodeBuild. We also provide possible solutions to overcome your problems.

Best practices with AWS CodeCommit

It's very important for an enterprise to always keep some standard procedure while implementing anything new. So, at that moment, we look into the best practices related to that resource and how we can really use it in production.

Here are some concise best practices related to AWS CodeCommit:

- **Region selection**: It's always good to have the repository in the region where you are building or deploying the application; it means if you have the repository in `us-east-1`, but your build service states that CodeBuild is setup in a different region, you need to migrate the repository to the region where CodeBuild exists. Developer tools of AWS mostly integrate with the services of the same region.
- **Access permission reference**: We should use the IAM service to create a separate IAM user for different developers, and based on that, we can assign the action permission on specific repositories. For example, if there are five developers working on repository A and another five on repository B, the first developer or team lead working on repository A should have all the action permission, but the other four should have some limited permission on repository A only. We can do the same for repository B. This will implement the security concern.

- **Cross region replication**: Different enterprise plans are based on their Disaster recovery policy, so they use to replicate the code across regions. In this way, cross-region CI/CD pipelines can also be planned. AWS Lambda can be used to achieve that.

- **Enforce Git commit message policy:** I saw many enterprises using some special kind of message within commit. These commit messages are generally related to the task no or the feature no that the developers are working on. This policy makes it easy to track the record of commit on the feature. This policy is generally applied on the Git repository for maintaining the code quality. For example, a company uses JIRA (issue tracking tool developed by Atlassian) for tracking tasks and features in a situation, a team lead creates a task, let's say " Creating sample calculator" and assigns it to EMP-A and tags the task as DEV-82. If EMP-A created the code of the sample calculator and tried to commit that code into repository then, EMP-A must give DEV-82 in commit message, other wise EMP-A won't be able to push the code. So, it will be something as follows:

```
# git commit -m " DEV-82 change in calculator-addition function"
```

  Here, DEV-82 will match as the tag of the task and allow the EMP-A to commit its code in the repository.

- **Integrate AWS CloudWatch**: Whenever there is a change in the state of the repository such as pushing latest code to the repositories, this kind of event can be integrated with AWS Cloudwatch, and based on that, it will trigger the AWS SNS Topic or AWS Lambda function to again trigger workflows.

Troubleshooting with CodeCommit

In this recipe, we will try to figure out the possible solutions of some common errors:

1. **Access error: Public key denied when connecting to an AWS CodeCommit repository**

Problem: The moment you try to access the repository using the SSH Git URL of AWS CodeCommit repository, an error will appear **Error: public key denied**.

Possible solutions: This error may appear because of no proper set up of the SSH public key. You have to generate the SSH public and private key and upload the public key to the associated IAM user.

Sometimes, we used to upload the public key of the X user and try to access the repository by being the Y user.

1. **Git error: RPC failed; result=56, HTTP code = 200 fatal: The remote end hung up unexpectedly**

   Problem: When pushing a large change, a large number of changes or a large repository, and long-running HTTPS connections are often terminated prematurely due to networking issues or firewall settings.

   Possible solutions: Push with SSH instead. Also, make sure you are not exceeding the size limits for individual files.

2. **Access Error: Encryption key access denied for an AWS CodeCommit repository from the console or the AWS CLI**

   Problem: The moment you try to browse the CodeCommit service either from the AWS Console or CLI, an error message will appear **EncryptionKeyAccessDeniedException** or the user is not authorized for the KMS default master key for CodeCommit `aws/codecommit` in your account.

   Possible solutions: This issue can be solved by easily subscribing to the AWS key management service with the AWS account. For that, you can go to the AWS IAM console, choose encryption keys, and start follow the instructions.

3. **Console Error: Cannot browse the code in an AWS CodeCommit repository from the console**

   Problem: When you try to browse the contents of a repository from the console, an error message appears denying access.

   Possible solutions: The possible reason of this error is that the IAM policy applied to your AWS account that does not have the permission to access the code from the AWS CodeCommit console.

Troubleshooting with CodeBuild

Few of the possible issues are discussed over here:

1. Problem: "Failed to upload artifacts: Invalid arn" When Running a Build

When you run a build, the UPLOAD_ARTIFACTS build phase fails with the error **Failed to upload artifacts: Invalid arn**.

Possibilities: Your Amazon S3 output bucket is in a different AWS region than the AWS CodeBuild build project.

Solutions: You can edit the project and point the proper s3 bucket which is in your region.

2. Problem: Runtime error (did not find expected alphabetic or numeric character at line XX)

After the provisioning phase of build, when the DOWNLOAD_SOURCE phase is encountered, it will try to check the BuildSpec.yml and fail at that moment.

Possibilities: The syntax and expected output of the BuildSpec.yml parameter will not be correct.

Solutions: You can edit the BuildSpec.yml properly and mention the correct value of the parameter.

3. Problem: "AWS CodeBuild is experiencing an issue" When Running a Build

When you try to run a build project, you receive the following error during the build's provisioning phase: **AWS CodeBuild is experiencing an issue**.

Possibilities: Your build is using environment variables that are too large for AWS CodeBuild. AWS CodeBuild can prompt errors once the length of all environment variables (all names and values added together) reach a combined maximum of around 5,500 characters.

>**Solution**: Use the Amazon EC2 Systems Manager Parameter Store to store large environment variables. Use the AWS CLI in your build commands to work with these stored environment variables.

Index

A

Amazon EC2 Container Registry (Amazon ECR)
  about 176
  components 176
  Docker Image, tagging with repository details
   180
  image, pushing 176, 181
  repository, creating 177
  setting up 176
  used, for authenticating Docker client 179
  working with 176
Amazon EC2 Container Service (ECS)
  about 182
  containers, verifying inside Container instance
   197
  core components 183
  services, writing 182
  steps, for deploying static application in ECS
   cluster 186, 190, 192, 197
  task definitions, writing 182
AMI
  creating, of EC2 Instance with AWS Lambda
   266, 274
  creating, of EC2 Instance with CloudWatch 266,
   274
Ansible EC2 dynamic inventory
  used, for creating AWS infrastructure 259, 261
Ansible playbook
  used, for deploying multinode clusters 312, 316
Ansible
  about 254
  automation 255
  features 255
  file structure 257
  installation 256
  syntax 257
  used, for deploying web server 258

  workflow 256
application
  configuration file 326
  deploying, on kubernetes 323
  deploying, with Jenkinsfile 342
  deployment configuration file 326
  service configuration file 327
  writing 86, 87, 88
Auto Scaling
  creating 133, 137, 140
  used, for creating AWS CodeDeploy application
   140
automated deployment
  benefits 80
AWS CLI
  used, for setting up AWS CodeCommit 27, 31
AWS CloudFormation
  about 235
  CloudFormation template, writing 235
  concepts 236
AWS CloudTrail logs, with Kibana
  CloudWatch logs, streaming in Elasticsearch
   300, 303
  CloudWatch, configuring 294
  Elasticsearch, creating 296, 299
  enabling 292
  Kibana, configuring to visualize data 304, 307
  Lambda, used for streaming 290
  Lambda, used for visualizing 290
  workflow 291
AWS CodeBuild console
  used, for building Maven application 56, 57, 66
AWS CodeBuild
  implementing 43, 44
  pricing 45
  used, for building NodeJS application via
   Buildspec.yml 66, 69, 70, 71, 76

AWS CodeCommit
  about 16, 18
  benefits 17
  best practices 361
  Git repository, migrating 36, 37, 38
  setting up 127, 130
  setting up, for SSH users with AWS CLI 27, 31
  troubleshooting with 362
  URL 19
  using, for HTTP users 19
AWS CodeDeploy
  about 80
  benefits 81
  components 81, 82
  creating, with Auto Scaling 140
  deployment strategy 83, 84, 85, 86
  used, for deploying static application in EC2
    instance 89, 92, 94, 98, 102, 105
AWS CodePipeline
  about 105, 107
  used, for Continuous Deployment of static
    application 107, 110, 114, 118, 120
  working 107
AWS Config
  about 276
  configuring, for AWS resources 283, 285
  used, for sending notifications through SNS 276
AWS developers tools
  Jenkins, integrating 145, 148, 157, 159
AWS IAM
  URL 21
AWS infrastructure
  creating, with Ansible EC2 dynamic inventory
    259, 261
AWS Lambda
  about 265
  function, creating 285
  trigger, creating 287
  used, for creating AMI of EC2 Instance 266, 276
  used, for sending notifications through SNS 276
AWS resources
  AWS Config service, configuring 283, 285
  deployment configuration file 332
  persistent volume claim, creating 330
  service configuration file 334

using, in Kubernetes 328

B

BitKeeper 9
blue-green deployment 84
BlueOcean
  pipeline, creating 343, 348
build spec 67
Build Specification 45
Buildspec.yml
  about 67
  sample NodeJS application, building with AWS
    CodeBuild 66, 69, 70, 71, 76
  syntax 67, 68, 69

C

CC-AWSSTAR-APP
  URL 145
CI/CD pipeline
  about 121
  benefits 122
  benefits, achieving 122
  challenges 123
  scenario 122
  workflow 123
CloudFormation repository
  URL 250
CloudFormation template
  about 236
  URL 245
  used, for creating stack 245, 249
  writing 238, 241, 244
  writing, for JSON 237
  writing, for YAML 237
CloudFormation
  production-ready web application infrastructure,
    creating 249
  used, for creating production-ready web
    application infrastructure 251
CloudWatch
  logs streaming 300
  logs streaming, in Elasticsearch 303
  used, for creating AMI of EC2 Instance 266, 274
cluster 183
CodeBuild

creating, for build stage 216, 218
   troubleshooting with 364
CodeCommit
   setting up, for application source 214
CodePipeline
   creating, with CloudFormation 224, 229, 231
   creating, with CodeBuild 224, 229, 231
   creating, with CodeCommit 224, 229, 231
components, AWS ECR
   authorization token 176
   image 176
   registry 176
   repository 176
   repository policy 176
components, AWS ECS
   cluster 183
   container instance 183
   service 185
   task definitions 184
containers 164
Continuous Deployment
   of static application, with AWS CodePipeline
      107, 110, 114, 118, 120
continuous integration (CI) 336

D

declarative pipeline
   URL 341
delivery and deployment (CD) 336
deployment 79
deployment strategy, in AWS CodeDeploy
   blue-green deployment 84
   in-place deployment 83
Distributed version control system (DVCS) 9
Docker client
   authenticating, with ECR 179
Docker containers
   about 165
   container, executing 168
   containers 165
   customer details, obtaining 172
   daemonized containers, creating 170
   data volume, adding 172
   Docker engine, installing 166
   Dockerfile, used for containerizing application

173
   executing, as non-root user 167
   images 165
   images, pushing to Dockerhub 175
   name, assigning to container 170
   persistent storage, managing 172
   ports, exposing 171
   registry 165
   stopped container, starting 169
   working 167
Docker Image
   tagging, with repository details 180
DownloadBundle 88

E

ECR credential helper
   URL 180, 354
Elasticsearch
   CloudWatch logs streaming 300, 303
   creating 296, 299
   URL 300

F

features, K8s
   extensible 310
   portable 310
   self-healing 310

G

Git repository
   migrating, to AWS CodeCommit 36, 37, 38
Git
   about 9
   benefits 9
   features 11
   implementation, with GitHub 12, 16
   installation 12, 16
   reference 16

H

helper files
   contents 219, 221, 224

I

IAM role
  URL 89
images 165
in-place deployment 83
Infrastructure as Code (IaC) 233
inventory file 257

J

Java application
  Apache Maven, installing 46
  Apache Maven, verifying 46
  building, with Maven 46, 48, 49, 50
  Java, installing 46
  Java, verifying 46
Jenkins pipeline 2.0
  Jenkinsfile, using 336
Jenkins Pipeline
  about 337
  advantages 338
Jenkins Server
  setting up 142, 145
Jenkins
  integrating, with developer tools 145, 148, 157, 159
Jenkinsfile
  about 337
  agent 341
  cleaning up 351
  declarative pipeline 340
  pipeline, creating in BlueOcean 343, 348
  stages 341
  URL 342
  used, for creating pipeline 352
  used, for deploying application 342
  used, for deploying microservices application 353
  using, in Jenkins pipeline 2.0 336
  workflow 355, 358

K

Kibana
  configuring, to visualize data 304, 307
  URL 307

Kubernetes (K8s)
  about 310
  architecture 310
  AWS resources, using 328
  features 310
  master components 311
  microservices application, deploying with Jenkinsfile 353
  node components 312
  sample application, deploying 323
Kubernetes Operations (Kops)
  about 316
  bucket, creating 318
  cleaning up 322
  cluster, creating 319, 321
  DNS configuration 318
  Kubernetes dashboard (UI) 321
  used, for deploying multinode production-ready cluster on AWS 316

L

launch configuration
  creating 133, 137, 140

M

master components, K8s
  about 311
  API server 311
  controller 311
  etcd 311
  scheduler 311
Maven application
  building, with AWS CodeBuild console 56, 57, 66
  used, for building Java application 46, 48, 49, 50
microservice-based applications
  characteristics 162
  deploying, in kubernetes with Jenkinsfile 353
microservices
  about 161, 162
  deployment 164
  designing 163
  designing guidelines 163
monolithic architecture 161
multinode clusters

deploying, on AWS with Ansible playbook 312,
   316
multinode production-ready cluster
   deploying, on AWS with Kops 317

N

node components
   about 312
   addons 312
   docker 312
   fluentd 312
   kube-proxy 312
   kubelet 312
   pod 312
   supervisord 312
NodeJS application
   building, with AWS CodeBuild via Buildspec.yml
      66, 69, 70, 71, 76
   building, with yarn 51, 53, 56
   dependencies, installing 55
   NodeJS, installing 52
   NodeJS, verifying 52
   Yarn, installing 52
   Yarn, verifying 52
notifications
   sending, through SNS with Config 276
   sending, through SNS with Lambda 276

P

PersistentVolumeClaim 330
pipeline
   creating, with Jenkinsfile 352
playbook 257
plugins
   installing 142, 145
Postfix Relay
   URL 145
pricing 45
production-ready web application infrastructure
   creating, with CloudFormation 249, 251
Project Object Model (POM) 48

R

Remote Method Invocation (RMI) 162
restrictions

applying 31, 32, 33, 34
Revision control system (RCS) 8

S

S3 Bucket
   creating 131, 132
   static application, deploying in EC2 instance with
      AWS CodeDeploy 89, 92, 94, 98, 102, 105
   versioning 131, 132
security
   applying 31, 32, 33, 34
service 185
service-oriented architecture (SOA) 162
SSH users
   AWS CodeCommit, setting up with AWS CLI 27,
      31
static application
   Continuous Deployment, to AWS S3 with AWS
      CodePipeline 107, 110, 114, 118, 120
   deploying, from S3 Bucket with AWS
      CodeDeploy 89, 92, 94, 98, 102, 105
Subversion (SVN) 9

T

Terraform 234

V

version control system (VCS)
   about 8
   benefits 8
   centralized version control system 9
   distributed version control system 9
   local version control system 8
   types 8

W

web server infrastructure
   Amazon ECR, creating 213
   architecture 202
   Auto Scaling, registering with load balancer 212
   ECS cluster, creating 206, 208
   load balancer, creating 209, 212
   setting up, to host application 205
   workflow 202, 204

Y

yarn

installing 52
used, for building NodeJS application 51, 53, 56
verifying 52

39421260R00214

Made in the USA
Lexington, KY
18 May 2019